MW00808655

MINNESOTA CAMPING

JAKE KULJU

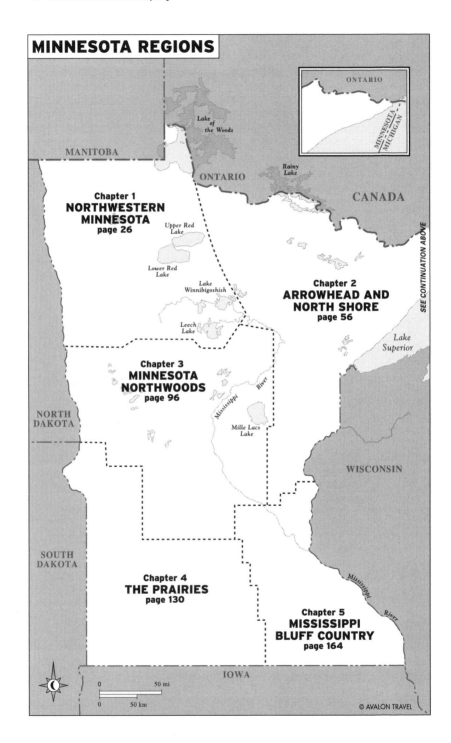

MINNESOTA REGIONS

Chapter 1
NORTHWESTERN MINNESOTA
page 26

Chapter 2
ARROWHEAD AND NORTH SHORE
page 56

Chapter 3
MINNESOTA NORTHWOODS
page 96

Chapter 4
THE PRAIRIES
page 130

Chapter 5
MISSISSIPPI BLUFF COUNTRY
page 164

MANITOBA

ONTARIO

CANADA

Lake of the Woods

Rainy Lake

Upper Red Lake

Lower Red Lake

Lake Winnibigoshish

Leech Lake

Lake Superior

Mississippi River

Mille Lacs Lake

NORTH DAKOTA

SOUTH DAKOTA

WISCONSIN

Mississippi River

IOWA

ONTARIO

MINNESOTA

MICHIGAN

SEE CONTINUATION ABOVE

0   50 mi
0   50 km

© AVALON TRAVEL

Contents

How to Use This Book

ABOUT THE CAMPGROUND PROFILES

The campgrounds are listed in a consistent, easy-to-read format to help you choose the ideal camping spot. If you already know the name of the specific campground you want to visit, or the name of the surrounding geological area or nearby feature (town, national or state park, forest, mountain, lake, river, etc.), look it up in the index and turn to the corresponding page. Here is a sample profile:

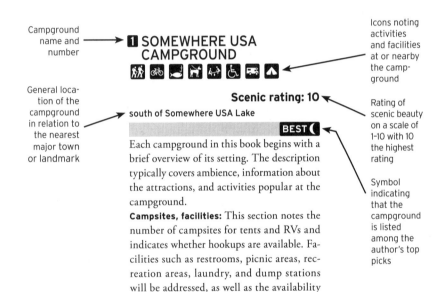

Campground name and number

Icons noting activities and facilities at or nearby the campground

General location of the campground in relation to the nearest major town or landmark

1 SOMEWHERE USA CAMPGROUND

Scenic rating: 10

south of Somewhere USA Lake

Rating of scenic beauty on a scale of 1-10 with 10 the highest rating

BEST (

Symbol indicating that the campground is listed among the author's top picks

Each campground in this book begins with a brief overview of its setting. The description typically covers ambience, information about the attractions, and activities popular at the campground.

Campsites, facilities: This section notes the number of campsites for tents and RVs and indicates whether hookups are available. Facilities such as restrooms, picnic areas, recreation areas, laundry, and dump stations will be addressed, as well as the availability of piped water, showers, playgrounds, stores, and other amenities. The campground's pet policy and wheelchair accessibility is also mentioned here.

Reservations, fees: This section notes whether reservations are accepted, and provides rates for tent sites and RV sites. If there are additional fees for parking or pets, or discounted weekly or seasonal rates, they will also be noted here.

Directions: This section provides mile-by-mile driving directions to the campground from the nearest major town or highway.

Contact: This section provides an address, phone number, and website, if available, for the campground.

ABOUT THE ICONS

The icons in this book are designed to provide at-a-glance information on activities, facilities, and services available on-site or within walking distance of each campground.

- Hiking trails
- Biking trails
- Swimming
- Fishing
- Boating
- Canoeing and/or kayaking
- Winter sports

- Hot springs
- Pets permitted
- Playground
- Wheelchair accessible
- RV sites
- Tent sites

ABOUT THE SCENIC RATING

Each campground profile employs a scenic rating on a scale of 1 to 10, with 1 being the least scenic and 10 being the most scenic. A scenic rating measures only the overall beauty of the campground and environs; it does not take into account noise level, facilities, maintenance, recreation options, or campground management. The setting of a campground with a lower scenic rating may simply not be as picturesque that of as a higher rated campground, however other factors that can influence a trip, such as noise or recreation access, can still affect or enhance your camping trip. Consider both the scenic rating and the profile description before deciding which campground is perfect for you.

MAP SYMBOLS

▦▦▦▦▦	Expressway	(80)	Interstate Freeway	✗	Airfield
▫▫▫▫▫	Primary Road	(101)	U.S. Highway	✗	Airport
▫▫▫▫	Secondary Road	(21)	State Highway	○	City/Town
□□□□□	Unpaved Road	66	County Highway	▲	Mountain
··········	Ferry	◯	Lake	▲	Park
—·—·—	National Border	◯	Dry Lake	)(	Pass
—··—	State Border	◯	Seasonal Lake	◉	State Capital

INTRODUCTION

© JAKE KULJU

Author's Note

I am from north-central Minnesota, the heart of the forest and lake country, where people can still get lost in the woods, catch 10-pound walleye, and disappear into the oxbows of the winding Upper Mississippi River. Striding through majestic pine forests, swinging from gnarly oak branches, and swimming in north country rivers are what I do best.

Minnesota is the land of the northwoods; the land of 10,000 lakes; the land of Lake Superior, of voyageurs, and of Paul Bunyan. It is one of the few states left in our country that still tug at our sense of awe, evoking a kind of mystery, a wonder at the dark wilderness hiding in the deep pine forests and among the sky-blue lakes that fill its landscape. Minnesota is the northernmost of the contiguous 48 states, extending its northwest angle like a proud flag into the Canadian Shield.

There is more here than water and woods, however. Minnesota's diverse landscapes and habitats include the sweeping prairies that enter from the west, ushered in by the grassy Dakotas. The Red River Valley in the northwest is home to some of the richest farmland and largest specimens of remnant prairie left on the continent. Lake Superior's mythic north shore is perhaps Minnesota's most well-known camping destination, enveloped by the Superior National Forest, the fabled Boundary Waters Canoe Area Wilderness, and dozens of state parks huddled around the waterfalls, cliffs, and rivers that enter mighty Gitchi Gumi, the world's largest freshwater lake.

The St. Croix River Valley and the Mississippi River Gorge form the eastern border of the state, and campgrounds here take advantage of the awesome power of these mighty rivers. The St. Croix is rife with unexplainable potholes dug deep into the stone riverbed, towering cliffs that rock climbers adore, and blufftops that rise high above the water. Farther downstream, the St. Croix empties into the Mississippi and continues south to the real bluff country—where King's and Queen's Bluffs rise hundreds of feet above the river valley, giving campers views that stretch for miles into the distance.

The dense woodlands of Central Minnesota are where the myriad rivers follow their courses through shady cedar groves, cathedral-like pines, and prime hunting land.

Even though Minnesota's most well-known outdoor destinations are in the internationally renowned Boundary Waters Canoe Area Wilderness and along Lake Superior and its rugged north shore, you can find a wealth of nature and wild spaces all over the state. Vast tallgrass prairies rife with blooming wildflowers, craggy cliffsides along rushing river ravines, and high blufftop overlooks with expansive vistas of the mighty Mississippi River fill the pages of this book. From the rolling prairie lands of southwestern Minnesota to the major bird migratory corridor along the sloughs of the Minnesota River Valley, the state will reveal more peaceful natural spaces than you can shake a walking stick at. Try climbing the wooden steps up the ravine walls along the Whitewater River, catching trout on peaceful Loon Lake in the Savanna Portage State Forest, or cliff diving into Lake Superior along the Baptism River.

Far from being just "flyover" country, Minnesota's parks and campgrounds are full of natural wonders. The best way to experience the state is by strapping yourself into a pair of hiking boots and experiencing those wonders firsthand.

See you out there.

Best Campgrounds

Can't decide where to camp this weekend? Check out these picks for the best campgrounds in the state, listed in a range of categories.

【 Best Canoe-In Campgrounds
Upper Mississippi River Canoe Campsites, Northwestern Minnesota, page 42.
Big Fork River Canoe Campsites, Arrowhead and North Shore, page 59.
Boundary Waters Canoe Area Wilderness (BWCAW), Arrowhead and North Shore, page 62.
Hinsdale Island Campground, Arrowhead and North Shore, page 78.
Crow Wing River Canoe Campsites, Minnesota Northwoods, page 101.
Mississippi River Canoe Campsites, Minnesota Northwoods, page 107.
St. Croix River Canoe Campsites, Mississippi Bluff Country, page 165.

【 Best for Families
Old Mill State Park, Northwestern Minnesota, page 28.
Itasca State Park, Northwestern Minnesota, page 42.
Long Lake Campground, Northwestern Minnesota, page 49.
Fall Lake Campground, Arrowhead and North Shore, page 63.
McKinley Park Campground, Arrowhead and North Shore, page 79.
Moose Lake State Park, Minnesota Northwoods, page 113.
Lake Shetek State Park, The Prairies, page 141.
Forestville/Mystery Cave State Park, Mississippi Bluff Country, page 184.

【 Best for Fishing
Mantrap Lake Campground, Northwestern Minnesota, page 44.
Boundary Waters Canoe Area Wilderness (BWCAW), Arrowhead and North Shore, page 62.
Glendalough State Park, Minnesota Northwoods, page 98.
Libby Dam Recreation Area, Minnesota Northwoods, page 109.
Lake Shetek State Park, The Prairies, page 141.
Camp Lacupolis, Mississippi Bluff Country, page 179.
Whitewater State Park, Mississippi Bluff Country, page 185.

【 Best Lakeshore Campgrounds
Zippel Bay State Park, Northwestern Minnesota, page 32.
Boundary Waters Canoe Area Wilderness (BWCAW), Arrowhead and North Shore, page 62.
Temperance River State Park, Arrowhead and North Shore, page 82.
Split Rock Lighthouse State Park, Arrowhead and North Shore, page 89.
Lake Lida Campground, Minnesota Northwoods, page 97.
Lake Shetek State Park, The Prairies, page 141.
Myre Big Island State Park, Mississippi Bluff Country, page 188.

◖ Best for Tent Camping

Star Island Campground, Northwestern Minnesota, page 39.

Boundary Waters Canoe Area Wilderness (BWCAW), Arrowhead and North Shore, page 62.

Temperance River State Park, Arrowhead and North Shore, page 82.

Tettegouche Lake Superior Cart-In, Arrowhead and North Shore, page 86.

Split Rock Lighthouse State Park, Arrowhead and North Shore, page 89.

Sakatah Lake State Park, The Prairies, page 152.

Afton State Park, Mississippi Bluff Country, page 175.

Vinegar Ridge Campsites, Mississippi Bluff Country, page 191.

◖ Best for Views

Zippel Bay State Park, Northwestern Minnesota, page 32.

Boundary Waters Canoe Area Wilderness (BWCAW), Arrowhead and North Shore, page 62.

Savanna Portage Campground, Minnesota Northwoods, page 108.

Father Hennepin State Park, Minnesota Northwoods, page 113.

Glacial Lakes State Park, The Prairies, page 133.

Sibley State Park, The Prairies, page 135.

Lac qui Parle State Park, The Prairies, page 135.

Blue Mounds State Park, The Prairies, page 155.

Frontenac State Park, Mississippi Bluff Country, page 178.

John A. Latsch State Park, Mississippi Bluff Country, page 186.

Great River Bluffs State Park, Mississippi Bluff Country, page 187.

Camping Tips

GEAR SELECTION AND MAINTENANCE

Tents

A good tent is the foundation of a successful camping experience. Maslow's hierarchy of needs lists shelter as a main component for humans to not just survive, but thrive. Camping is best when you are dry, warm, and safe. A sturdy, weatherproof tent can make the difference between a soggy weekend in the rain and a dry, cozy camping trip. I always choose tents that have bathtub-style floors made of waterproofed, rip-stop nylon. Choosing a tent with one or more vestibules is also wise, because a vestibule gives you a place to store your gear without it taking up precious sleeping space. A properly vented tent will keep you feeling fresh and will prevent daytime heat from building up. Keep these things in mind when purchasing a tent, but, most importantly, find one that fits you and will let you sleep well. Having a good night's rest makes all the difference.

Sleeping Bags and Pads

If a good tent is a camper's first priority, then quality sleeping gear is a close second. Comfortable sleeping bags and pads come in all varieties, from mummy bags to bivy sacks. I tend to opt for sleeping bags rated at temperatures 10–20 degrees colder than the temperature where I plan to camp. Today's sleeping bags can be stuffed with down or synthetic insulating fibers that can keep you comfortable on summer nights and cozy in subzero temperatures while winter camping.

BOB RACE

With the world going high-tech, **tents** of today vary greatly in complexity, size, price, and put-up time. And they wouldn't be fit for this new millennium without offering options such as moon roofs, rain flies, and tent wings. Be sure to buy the one that's right for your needs.

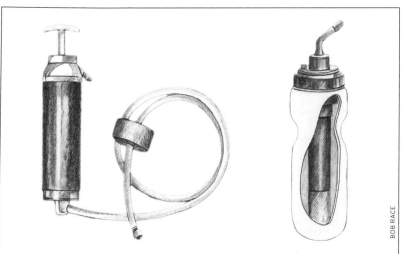

BOB RACE

Water filters are a wise investment since all wilderness water should be considered con-taminated. Make sure the filter can be easily cleaned or has a replaceable cartridge. The filter pores must be 0.4 micron or less to remove bacteria.

I also recommend inflatable sleeping pads: They pack up to the size of a football, weigh less than a pound, and take only five minutes to inflate. It is also wise to have waterproof stuff sacks for your sleeping bag and pad to prevent them from getting wet in rainy, snowy, or rough water conditions.

Food and Cooking Gear

Camp food has come a long way from roasted hot dogs and canned beans, largely due to more sophisticated cooking equipment. Campers can now carry an entire kitchen in their pack. Compact camping stoves, titanium pots and pans, dehydrated and freeze-dried food technology, and lightweight cooking utensils pioneered by companies like MSR, REI, Optimus, and JetBoil have made cooking lightweight, easy, and less messy. My camp cook set includes a set of lightweight shallow stainless steel bowls, durable plastic camp utensils, a small spice kit, a lightweight stove, and an aluminum pot and pan. The entire getup weighs a little more than two pounds, boils water in less than 10 minutes, and can easily handle cooking a meal for four people. I highly recommend investing in quality cooking equipment. A well-fed camper is a happy camper.

Water Treatment

If you decide not to carry your own water, make sure you have some kind of water filtration system with you. I would never recommend drinking from any kind of untreated urban water source, whether you filter it or not. Out in the field, the threat of *Giardia lamblia* is a serious one, and giardiasis can cause you great discomfort. Simple water filtration systems are available at outdoor outfitting stores for reasonable prices and will ensure that your drinking water is safe.

First-Aid Kit

You don't need to tote a first responder kit with you, but you should have the basics, including Band-Aids, a flashlight, moleskin for blisters, aspirin, and a small bandage or two. I also carry a pocketknife, a pack of waterproof matches, and a small flashlight, just in case.

When you are camping, especially in unfamiliar territory, it is important to be prepared for mishaps. If you are planning on hiking or exploring in more remote areas, carry a lightweight sleeping bag, a blanket, or a small tarp with you on long hikes to keep you dry and safe should you need to spend the night on the trail. A whistle can help draw attention if you are hurt or lost, and having a compass along is never a bad idea.

CLOTHING

The reason Minnesotans talk about the weather so much is because there is a lot of it here in the Upper Midwest. Blue sky in the morning doesn't necessarily mean sunshine in the afternoon. Campers need to be prepared for changing weather, especially on backcountry or canoe camping trips. Your regular summer clothes might be fine when RV camping on the lake in southern Minnesota, but paddling along the Upper Mississippi in a sudden spring rainstorm requires a more robust wardrobe. Remember that the seasons should determine your clothing selections. Don't go overboard, but make sure you have the basics to keep you warm and dry, especially during the colder months.

What to Wear

You can start by examining the type of fabric your clothing is made of. Cotton absorbs and holds moisture, whereas polyester and polyester-blend fabrics dry faster. More advanced fabrics are designed to wick moisture away from your skin and release it through evaporation. If you plan on spending a lot of time outdoors, it is a good idea to spend some money on a few items of good clothing that will keep you comfortable.

I also always recommend wearing a hat and having a good set of rain gear, including rain pants. On weekend camping trips with the family to a nearby park this may not always be necessary, but if rain strikes or the bugs get bad in the middle of the woods, having a head covering and a rain jacket can make the difference between a memorable storm encounter and a miserable and dangerous night spent shivering in your tent.

A hat can also be useful for protecting your eyes from the sun and/or keeping your head warm during cold weather. In the late fall and winter always wear waterproof boots and carry gloves and a warm jacket. Long underwear can also be your best friend when the temperature drops while you are out camping.

Keeping Dry

No one likes getting sweaty. It can even be dangerous during the cold seasons, leading to chills and hypothermia. The clothes that keep you dry and warm at home aren't necessarily the same clothes you want to take into the wilds of Minnesota. Polyester and polyester-blend fabrics dry fast, while cotton holds moisture once it gets wet. Several brands of specialized outdoor clothing employ high-tech fabrics that wick moisture from the skin. Having waterproof clothing can also save your butt when a spring storm emerges over the tree line without notice, or when the snow starts flying. Wool is always a safe bet for staying warm. Even if it gets wet, wool holds body heat. Weaving technology is very advanced today and provides several non-itchy wool items, including socks, shirts, and pants. Gore-Tex is my favorite waterproof fabric. It lasts long and is quite durable.

FLORA AND FAUNA

It is a virtual guarantee that you will encounter all manner of animals and insects at any given Minnesota campsite during every season of the year. Knowing about what is out there can help prepare you for these encounters and even enjoy the wide variety of flora and fauna Minnesota is home to.

Bears

The thick forests, wide open grasslands, and sweeping wetlands that cover the state are rife with wildlife. Most animals that you will encounter are small and nonthreatening. The ubiquitous whitetail deer, for example, lives all over

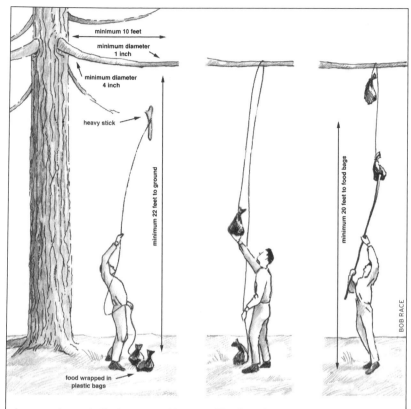

minimum 10 feet

minimum diameter
1 inch

minimum diameter
4 inch

heavy stick

minimum 22 feet to ground

food wrapped in
plastic bags

minimum 20 feet to food bags

BOB RACE

In an area frequented by bears, a good **bear-proof food hang** is a must. Food should be stored in a plastic bag 10 feet from the trunk of the tree and at least 20 feet from the ground.

the state in all types of habitat and would rather run into a lake than come close to a human. Minnesota's northernmost camping areas are in black bear territory, however. Although bear encounters are extremely rare, it is important to know what to do and what not to do in the unlikely event that you come across a bear.

Here are some tips to prevent bear encounters:

• Avoid carrying odorous foods.

• Make noise; bears hate to be surprised, so let them know you are coming by singing, whistling, or talking loudly.

• Travel with someone else or in a group.

• Bears are most active during dawn and dusk, so plan your hikes during the day and stay on marked trails.

If you *do* encounter a bear on a hike, here are some tips to help you survive your bear encounter:

• Remain calm and avoid sudden movements.

• Do not approach the bear; give it plenty of space.

• Let the bear know that you are human— talk to it and wave your arms. Bears have bad eyesight, and if one is unable to identify you it may come closer for a better look.

• Never run from a bear. Running can elicit a chase.

• If the bear approaches you, distract it by throwing something on the ground near it. If it draws the bear's attention, walk away while it is distracted.

• If you carry pepper spray, make sure you are trained in its use and can trust it if a bear attacks you.

• Never feed a bear.

Birds

The migration seasons are always very exciting in Minnesota. Hundreds of thousands of birds move through one of the continent's major bird migration corridors on their way to their spring and winter feeding grounds. Flocks of pelicans take over the wetlands surrounding Green Lake, belted kingfishers and black-billed magpies rest in the forests and wetlands of Paul Bunyan State Forest, and herons from the great blue to green and white hunt and nest in the sloughs and marshes of the Minnesota River Valley National Wildlife Refuge. The U.S. Fish and Wildlife Service Migratory Birds website (www.fws.gov/Midwest/MidwestBird) has a complete list of birds that call Minnesota home on their way through during the spring and fall.

I strongly encourage you to plan your camping trips during the spring and fall migration seasons. Not only will the beauty of the birds astound you, but you will get a deeper understanding of why nature conservation efforts in our state are so important. Thousands of birds

MINNESOTA'S NATIVE AMERICANS

Minnesota has a rich Native American history. The abundant wild game, vegetation, and fresh water have provided nourishment, shelter, and meaning to several Native American tribes through the centuries. Much of their culture still persists in Minnesota, manifested in the wild-rice harvesting, protected fishing waters, and historic village sites throughout the state.

Red Lake, Lake Ogechie, and Big Island (to name just a few) were the sites of early Native American settlements and gathering places. The Boundary Waters Canoe Area Wilderness has many examples of Native American art on its stone cliffs. In Mille Lacs Kathio State Park, evidence of Native American villages dates back more than 9,000 years – first by the Dakota, and then the Ojibwe, who both recognized the land for its abundant natural wealth. The ancient village walls, shoreline rice pits, and tool artifacts found here have drawn national attention. Several areas in the state, including the Mille Lacs Kathio site, have been recognized as national historical sites by the federal government.

While members of several tribes have lived in Minnesota at various times throughout history, the most notable groups are the Ojibwe and Dakota. When European settlers came to Minnesota, these were the people they encountered and the communities that they both clashed and cooperated with. Although Native American culture no longer exists as it did then, many of the trails in this book pay tribute to the sacred lands, memorials, and villages that were once inhabited by these people. Take some time to educate yourself about the historical significance of these areas – you may find that knowing about the villages, survival tactics, rituals, and myths that came from the state's original inhabitants will enrich your Minnesota camping experience. The Minnesota Historical Society (www.mnhs.org) is a wonderful resource for Native American history and information.

and animal species are dependent on Minnesota's critical habitat areas for food, nesting, and shelter. Without places like the lush Minnesota River Valley, the dense forests north of the metro, and the numerous freshwater lakes and rivers that blanket our landscape, these animals would quickly become endangered.

Insects

Insects are an unavoidable part of the Minnesota outdoors. Whether it is the mosquitoes of the woods, the flies of the fields, the ticks in the grass, or all three, you will probably emerge from your camping trip with an itchy bite or two. The best insect repellent is covered skin. Wearing a broad-rimmed hat, covering your neck and arms, and wearing high socks or pants will keep most mosquitoes and flies away, but ticks are another story.

Minnesota has more than a dozen varieties of ticks, including the black-legged tick, which carries Lyme disease. Ticks can show up on even the most prepared camper. If you notice a tick on you, remove it immediately with a pair of sharp tweezers, making certain to isolate the mouth area, and then pull it out. Be sure to identify it when you get home, and watch for symptoms. Most Lyme disease symptoms occur one to three weeks after a tick bite and can include flu-like symptoms such as nausea, headaches, muscle soreness, fever, neck stiffness, and rash. Make sure to thoroughly check your skin for ticks or bites during and after camping trips. See a doctor immediately if you suspect that you might have Lyme disease.

Edible Plants

One of the greatest joys of camping and hiking in Minnesota is coming across patches of ripe raspberries or wild blueberries, seeing wild plums dangling from trees, and smelling the crab apples that ripen in autumn. But before you start chomping on handfuls of wild berries, make sure you know how to identify them. There are some clever imposters out there that can give you a stomachache,

or worse. If you are unsure about a berry or wild fruit, do not eat it. Either take a sample home or to someone who knows how to identify it, or just leave it be. It isn't worth the gut ache.

CAMPING ETHICS
Camping with Pets

Dogs are sensational companions, and they are always enthusiastic about being outside. Having a four-legged friend along for a camping trip can turn regular dog walking into a truly enjoyable outdoors experience. They are nosy little buggers, though, and if they aren't chasing or barking at wildlife, they are getting into animal droppings or leaving their own. Make sure you keep your dog on a leash and carry the proper waste disposal equipment to keep trails clean and safe.

Most of the parks and campgrounds in this book allow dogs, but many do not. Please contact the park or campground you plan on camping in if you wish to bring your dog. All Minnesota state parks allow dogs, as does the Minnesota Valley National Wildlife Refuge, but several county parks and some city parks do not. And when they do, they always require a dog to be kept on a leash no longer than six feet.

Just because your dog is an animal, it doesn't mean that it will get along with the wildlife. Keep your dog away from porcupines, raccoons, and skunks, and always check for ticks when you return home.

Preventing Wildfires

One of the best parts about camping is lying around the fire at night—talking with your fellow campers, roasting marshmallows, and just taking in the quiet nature that surrounds you. To ensure a safe campfire experience, it is important to follow fire safety regulations and to pay attention to fire hazard levels in the places you camp. The Minnesota Department of Natural Resources (www.dnr.state.mn.us) issues fire hazard levels weekly; check the website for updates before heading out on a trip.

At your campsite, follow these basic steps to prevent wildfires:

• Never leave a fire unattended. Always be within sight of the flames.

• Have water, sand, or a fire blanket with you whenever a fire is burning.

• Before going to sleep or leaving your campsite, completely extinguish your fire with water and/or sand. Stir the coals and make sure all the hot spots have been doused.

Wilderness Ethics

The land of 10,000 lakes is world-famous for its pristine wilderness, its towering trees, and its beautiful sky blue waters. You can help keep it that way by practicing a little respect each time you use the outdoors—simply leave no trace on the trails and in the parks that you visit. Don't leave your mark with knife, pen, or paint on any rocks, cliffsides, or trees. Other people want to enjoy nature without having to see "John + Marsha = True Love 4 Ever" scrawled on a towering red pine or chipped into a sandstone cliff face. You can also do your part by picking up rubbish you see along the trail or around fire rings and tent pads. Carrying a small trash bag and hauling out a few items you may find can make a world of difference.

Many state lands in the south and western parts of Minnesota are taking part in prairie restoration projects. Tallgrass prairie once covered more than one-third of the state. Today many of the wildflowers, native grasses, prairie shrubs, and grassland wildlife that once thrived here are endangered. Respect these restoration efforts by remaining on established trails and campsites and leaving wildflowers in the field. Their natural bouquets will look better under the open sky than on your kitchen counter.

LEAVE NO TRACE

Natural spaces are an increasingly valuable commodity in today's overdeveloped world. By practicing Leave No Trace (www.lnt.org) guidelines, we can help to preserve the integrity and beauty of our local natural settings. Use the following list to get an idea of what it means to leave no trace. The more time you spend in nature, the better you will become at minimizing your impact.

• Preserve the past: Examine, but do not touch, cultural or historic structures and artifacts.

• Leave rocks, plants, and other natural objects as you find them.

• Avoid introducing or transporting nonnative species.

• Do not build structures or furniture, or dig trenches.

• Pack it in, pack it out. Inspect your campsite and rest areas for trash or spilled foods. Pack out all trash, leftover food, and litter.

• Observe wildlife from a distance. Do not follow or approach animals.

• Never feed animals. Feeding wildlife damages their health, alters natural behaviors, and exposes them to predators and other dangers.

• Control pets at all times, or leave them at home.

CAMPING GEAR CHECKLIST

Make your list and check it twice. It has always been helpful for me to have a backpack designated for camping trips that is always ready to rock with these items. That way, if the chance to get outside comes up spontaneously, you can just grab your bag and head out the door. It is important to carry with you what you need, both for comfort and for safety. Here is what I always have on hand:

• Camp stove and aluminum pot for boiling water and cooking
• Compass
• Fire-starting material, such as dryer lint or birch bark
• First-aid kit
• Flashlight
• Flint and steel
• Food and cooking gear
• Gloves and long underwear (for cold weather)
• Hat with brim (or a warm hat for cold weather)
• Insect repellent
• Pocketknife
• Rain jacket and pants
• Sleeping bag and pad
• Sunglasses
• Tent
• Trail map
• Water and a water filtration system
• Waterproof matches
• Whistle

NORTHWESTERN MINNESOTA

© KERSTIN HANSEN

BEST CAMPGROUNDS

Minnesota's northwest is best known for the
headwaters of the Mississippi River in Lake Itasca State Park. The region
is also home to rich Native American culture, some of the largest lakes in
the state, and the western prairies that carry the powerful, sweeping winds
across the Red River Valley from the Rockies and across the Dakotas.

The Red River State Recreation Area, created just over a decade ago, is
a prime camping area along the Red and Red Lake Rivers that is perhaps
one of the best ways to experience camping in the northwest. The Red
River Valley is a famous historical and cultural Minnesota landmark, and
this 1,200-acre greenway lies along the banks of the Red's waters. Prairie
parklands, deciduous forest, and coniferous forest all meet here, making
it one of the most diverse habitat regions in the state.

The region lends itself to wildlife-watching and nature sightseeing.
Northwestern Minnesota has several official sightseeing routes, the most
popular being the Minnesota Wildflower Route and the Pine to Prairie
Birding Trail. The transitional zones that exist here between prairie and

forest, combined with the large lakes, reedy wetlands, and wild-rice-laden waterways, make this a stop along one of the nation's busiest bird migratory corridors. You will also have access to the Central Lakes State Trail, with its 55 miles of hiking and biking through the heart of the region.

The iconic landmark of the northwest is Red Lake. Covering more than 440 square miles, Red Lake is the largest natural freshwater lake within the state. A long peninsula slices through the lake, dividing it into upper and lower regions. The huge lake is sparsely populated, with few people residing along it and in the surrounding area.

The summers are short, the winters are long, and the camping is uncommonly peaceful, private, and quiet. While most tourists are cruising the north shore, parking their RVs in the crowded parks around the metro, or flocking to the southeast to watch the leaves change color, the northwest enjoys vast expanses of prairie, shady forests full of wildlife, and massive freshwater lakes full of fish that are visited by only a fraction of the people traveling around the rest of the state.

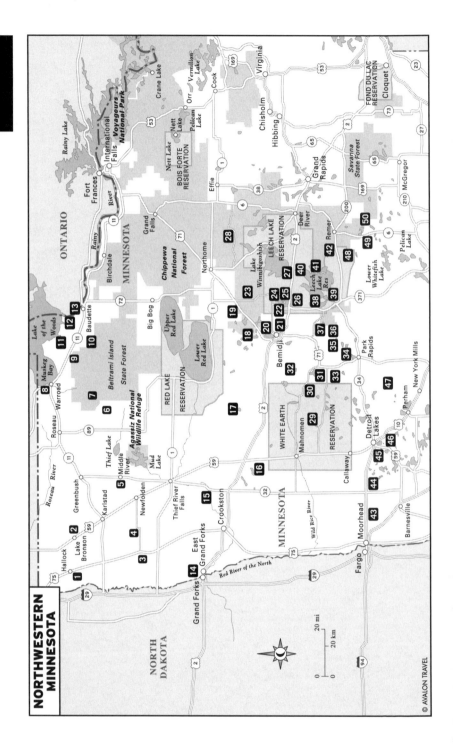

1 HORSESHOE CAMPGROUND

Scenic rating: 4

in Hallock

This city campground sits on the south end of Hallock, located on a dramatic horseshoe bend in the Two Rivers waterway. Hallock has barely a 1,000-person population, so the small grove of trees that separates the campground from the city provides sufficient shelter from the light traffic on its city streets. The camping area and park are one of the largest chunks of real estate in town and are right on the water.

The campsites, contained in two small loops, lie in an open clearing with few trees for shade or privacy. The small town is a few miles west of Lake Bronson State Park, which is a local attraction. If you'd rather be closer to town and spend the day in the park, Horseshoe Campground is the spot for you.

Campsites, facilities: There are 24 sites for tents and RVs. Picnic tables, fire rings, toilets, showers, and a dump station are provided. A playground, pool, and ball field are available. Some facilities are wheelchair accessible. Leashed pets are permitted.

Reservations, fees: Reservations are accepted at 218/843-2737. Sites are $10 per night. Open from mid-May to October.

Directions: From Broadway Street and N. Atlantic Avenue in Hallock, drive east on Broadway Street for 0.25 mile to N. Cedar Avenue. Turn left and drive 200 feet into Tourist Park to the campground driveway on the right side of the road. Turn right into the camping area 300 feet straight ahead.

Contact: Horseshoe Campground, 218/843-2737.

2 LAKE BRONSON CAMPGROUND

Scenic rating: 8

in Lake Bronson State Park

From high atop the observation tower in Lake Bronson State Park, you can see the interchange of prairie, oak savanna, and aspen forest saddling the gentle hills near Lake Bronson.

Most of the campsites are clustered in tree cover that presses on the north shore of Lake Bronson. Farther east in the park, stamped on a transitional zone between prairie and forest, another three-loop campground offers campers a quieter, more private spot. The eastern campground also offers a prairie camping experience along a corridor of tallgrass that sweeps through the park.

Lake Bronson is one of the few sizable lakes in the area and is heavily used in the summer for recreation. A large sandy beach is less than 0.25 mile from the campground, connected by a footpath. The park's hiking trails, wildlife, and water sports make it a valuable area resource.

Campsites, facilities: There are 157 sites for tents and RVs up to 50 feet; 35 sites have electrical hookups. There are also three backpacking sites, two canoe-in sites on Moose Island, and one group campsite for up to 200 people. Picnic tables, fire rings, drinking water, toilets, showers, and a dump station are provided. Hiking trails, paved and unpaved biking trails, cross-country ski trails, a fishing pier, swimming beach, playground, and volleyball court are available. There is one wheelchair-accessible site; some facilities are also wheelchair accessible. Leashed pets are permitted.

Reservations, fees: Reservations are accepted from April 2 to October 31 866/857-2757 or online at www.stayatmnparks.com ($8.50 non-refundable reservation fee) and can be made up to one year in advance. Reservations are not required the rest of the year. Sites are $12–24 per night. Open year-round, with limited facilities in winter.

Directions: From Lake Bronson, drive east on County Road 28 for approximately 2 miles. Keep straight at the park entrance and follow the road to the park office.

Contact: Lake Bronson State Park, 218/754-2200, www.dnr.state.mn.us/state_parks.

3 ISLAND PARK MUNICIPAL CAMPGROUND

Scenic rating: 5

in Argyle

The Middle River is strung with charming small towns like pearls, and Argyle is one of the more charming ones. With just a few hundred residents, the town has a diner, a pub, and a happy little downtown area. The area is dominated by farmland, except for the ribbon of trees that follows the Middle River across the landscape.

The campground has just four campsites in a little city park on the east side of town. They are well shaded and private, within walking distance of town and right on the meandering Middle River. With sites under $10 for tents and RVs, this tree-lined river campground is a real oasis.

Campsites, facilities: There are four sites for tents and RVs; some sites have hookups. Picnic tables, fire rings, toilets, showers, and a dump station are provided. A playground and horseshoe pits are available. Leashed pets are permitted.

Reservations, fees: Reservations are accepted at 218/437-6621. Sites are $8–9 per night. Open from May to the end of October.

Directions: In Argyle, drive east on 5th Street across River Street to the city park. The campground is straight ahead along the looped driveway.

Contact: City of Argyle, 218/437-6621.

4 OLD MILL STATE PARK

Scenic rating: 7

in Old Mill State Park

BEST (

Lining the banks of the meandering Middle River of northern Minnesota, Old Mill State Park is a rare patch of original landscape amidst the developed farmland spreading from the Red River Valley. The park lies on a transitional zone between forest and prairie, blanketed in wildflowers and absolutely full of wildlife. Bring your binoculars if you plan on camping here—you will see dozens of beaver, deer, hawks, and owls.

The single-loop campground is about 20 feet from the Middle River; a swinging bridge crosses the water just south of the campsites. The sites closer to the river enjoy more tree cover and shade. Each site has its own gravel driveway, leaving plenty of space and privacy.

An old mill from the late 19th century is located in the park near the original 1882 homestead site of the Larson family. The park fires up the old grist mill once a year to grind flour and put on a demonstration at the historical homestead site—great fun for families. The park is also used in the winter for cross-country skiing and sledding. A warming house with a wood stove is available during the winter for sliders and skiers.

Campsites, facilities: There are 26 sites for tents and RVs up to 67 feet; 10 sites have electrical hookups. There is also one tent-only group campsite for up to 150 people. Picnic tables, fire rings, flush and vault toilets, drinking water, and showers are provided. A playground, swimming beach, hiking and cross-country skiing trails, a sliding hill, a warming house, and a volleyball court are available. Leashed pets are permitted.

Reservations, fees: Reservations are accepted from April 2 to October 31 866/857-2757 or online at www.stayatmnparks.com ($8.50 non-refundable reservation fee) and can be made up to one year in advance. Reservations are not required the rest of the year. Sites are $12–24 per night. Open year-round.

Directions: From Thief River Falls, drive north on Highway 59 for 17.4 miles. Turn left on E. Minnesota Avenue, which becomes 330th Street NW. In 10.3 miles, turn right onto 240th Avenue NW. The park entrance is on the left in 0.3 mile.

Contact: Old Mill State Park, 218/437-8174, www.dnr.state.mn.us/state_parks.

⑤ MIDDLE RIVER COMMUNITY CAMPGROUND

Scenic rating: 5

in Middle River

There are small towns, and then there is Middle River. This tiny community of about 300 people is in one of the rare areas of northwest Minnesota that isn't surrounded by lakes. The lazy Middle River runs through the small town, established on the edge of forest and farmland in one of Minnesota's most rural areas.

A small park with 12 campsites is wedged between the west part of town and the river. The campground is on a small clearing by the water with a shower facility and covered picnic area that puts a shine on an otherwise unimpressive little city park. This campground is a convenient stopover for campers on their way farther north or to some of the big fishing lakes who can't make the drive all in one day.

Campsites, facilities: There are 12 campsites for tents or RVs. Picnic tables, fire rings, toilets, showers, and a dump station are provided. A picnic area, restaurant, and snowmobile trail are available. Leashed pets are permitted.

Reservations, fees: Reservations are not accepted. Sites are $10 per night. Open from April to late November.

Directions: From the intersection of Highway 32 and Hill Avenue in Middle River, drive west on Hill Avenue directly into the campground.

Contact: Middle River Community Campground, 218/222-3608.

⑥ HAYES LAKE CAMPGROUND

Scenic rating: 8

in Hayes Lake State Park

One of the more robust state parks in Minnesota, Hayes Lake State Park really has something for almost anyone. Hiking, biking, skiing, bird-watching, fishing, and sledding are a few of the activities the park offers. Two campground loops lie on the north shore of the lake in heavy woods that surround its shores. Each site has a short gravel driveway, plenty of tree cover, and lots of privacy.

The park is notable for the many orchids that grow in the forests around the lake and along the Rosseau River. Blueberry picking is excellent here in the late summer.

Campsites, facilities: There are 35 sites for tents and RVs up to 40 feet; 18 sites have electrical hookups. There are also two backpacking sites and one group campsite for up to 60 people. Picnic tables, fire rings, flush and vault toilets, showers, and a dump station are provided. A hiking trail, cross-country ski trail, mountain-biking trail, boardwalk, playground, picnic shelter, skating rink, sliding hill, fishing pier, swimming beach, and boat access are available.

Reservations, fees: Reservations are accepted from April 2 to October 31 866/857-2757 or online at www.stayatmnparks.com ($8.50 non-refundable reservation fee) and can be made up to one year in advance. Reservations are not required the rest of the year. Sites are $12–24 per night. Open year-round, with limited facilities in winter.

Directions: From Roseau, drive south on Highway 89 for 15 miles. Turn left onto County Road 4. The park entrance is 9 miles dead ahead.

Contact: Hayes Lake State Park, 218/425-7504, www.dnr.state.mn.us/state_parks.

7504, www.dnr.state.mn.us/state_forests/facilities/cmp00001/index.html.

◢ BEMIS HILL CAMPGROUND
🚶 ❄ 🐎 🚐 ⛺

Scenic rating: 7

in Beltrami Island State Forest

Bemis Hill is a popular horse riding area in the Beltrami Island State Forest. The camping area is managed by Hayes Lake State Park, just a little over three miles down the road.

The campground holds four equestrian sites and two primitive sites. Sites are first come, first served, but rarely are all occupied by overnight visitors. Birch and aspen dominate the forest in this area, providing shade and privacy between sites; enjoy the soft rustle of their leaves during breezy summer evenings.

Bemis Hill is one of the highlights of the Beltrami Island State Forest. A winter sledding rope and ski shelter are popular during the winter, and berry-picking is good here in the late summer, especially blueberries and raspberries. Hunters often camp here in the fall, so make sure to wear blaze orange clothing when camping and hiking here late in the season. And keep in mind that the hiking trails here are shared with horses.

Campsites, facilities: There are two sites for tents and RVs and four equestrian sites with hitching posts and mounting areas. Picnic tables, fire rings, drinking water, vault toilets, and garbage cans are provided. Hiking trails and a sledding hill are available. Leashed pets are permitted.

Reservations, fees: Reservations are not accepted. Sites are $12–16 per night. Self-registration is required at the campground. Open from April to mid-November.

Directions: From Wannaska, drive south on Highway 89 for 1 mile to County Road 4. Turn left and drive 8.6 miles.

Contact: Hayes Lake State Park, 218/425-

◣ WARROAD CITY CAMPGROUND
🚴 🏊 🎣 🚐 🐎 🚣 ♿ 🚐 ⛺

Scenic rating: 7

in Warroad

Stowed on the southern shore of Lake of the Woods, Warroad is a Minnesota city with an august reputation as being one of the coldest, hardiest places to live in the country. Radio stations all over the state broadcast the temperature in Warroad every day to remind the rest of us that no matter how cold it might feel in our town, it is colder in Warroad.

The city park campground packs the almost 200 sites in like sardines. Most people come in RVs, but there are always a few tent campers. The weather on the lake can be volatile, so having a sturdy camping structure is a must. The campground is just across the street from the more spacious Lakeview Park, which offers open areas, a swimming pool, beach, and paved biking trail.

Campsites, facilities: There are 182 sites for tents and RVs; 32 sites are tent-only, and some sites have hookups. Picnic tables, fire grills, toilets, showers, and a dump station are provided. A fishing pier and dock, boat launch, fishing charters, playground, and bike trail are available. A swimming beach, outdoor pool, restaurant, camp store, and laundry facilities are nearby. Some facilities are wheelchair accessible. Leashed pets are permitted.

Reservations, fees: Reservations are accepted at 218/386-1004. Sites are $20 per night for tents and $30 per night for RVs. Open from May to October.

Directions: From the intersection of Highway 11 and Lake Street NE, drive east on Lake Street 0.5 mile to 4th Avenue. Turn left and drive 4 blocks to the Lakeview Park entrance sign. Turn right and drive 200 feet to the city park campground entrance on the right side of the road.

Contact: City of Warroad, 218/386-1004 or 218/386-1454, www.warroad.org.

9 BLUEBERRY HILL CAMPGROUND

🏃 ❄ 🐕 ⛺

Scenic rating: 6

in Beltrami Island State Forest

Aptly named, this campground lies on a hill full of blueberry bushes in Beltrami Island State Forest. A small gravel parking area is carved out of the heavy tree cover that characterizes this entire area. The hill itself is more of a small incline, but it is full of blueberries, especially in late summer.

The eight primitive, walk-in sites are within 200 yards of the parking area and are easily located along footpaths. This campground is a relatively quiet one, and you will often be the only camper here, unless the berries are ripe. Locals and others who know of the berry patch here camp in late July and August or come during the day just to gather blueberries.

While extremely rare, bear encounters can happen here, especially during berry-picking season. Practice caution when walking in the woods.

Campsites, facilities: There are eight walk-in sites for tents. Picnic tables, fire rings, vault toilets, garbage cans, and drinking water are provided. Hiking and snowmobile trails are available. Leashed pets are permitted.

Reservations, fees: Reservations are not accepted. Sites are $12 per night. Self-registration is required at the campground. Open from April to mid-November.

Directions: From Williams, drive west on Highway 11 for 4 miles. The campground is on the left side of the road just past 86th Avenue NW.

Contact: Zippel Bay State Park, 218/783-

6252, www.dnr.state.mn.us/state_forests/facilities/cmp00002/index.html.

10 FAUNCE CAMPGROUND

🏃 🐕 🚐 ⛺

Scenic rating: 7

south of Williams

Beltrami Island State Forest is one of Minnesota's more untouched wilderness areas, and the Faunce Campground is right in character. The small campground is 12 miles from the nearest town and sits surrounded by an ocean of state forest in all directions.

Each campsite has a private, short driveway under heavy tree cover. The sites are very primitive, with little more than a table and a clearing for your car and tent; you will often be the only camper here. The campground has a well, but it can be frozen or unprimed. Make sure to bring your own drinking water. A hiking trail tours the campground and links to a footpath that leads deeper into the state forest. Be prepared to encounter wildlife, including bears.

Campsites, facilities: There are six sites for tents or RVs up to 50 feet. Picnic tables, fire rings, a vault toilet, and garbage can are provided. Leashed pets are permitted.

Reservations, fees: Reservations are not accepted. Sites are $12 per night. Open from April to mid-November.

Directions: From Williams, drive south on County Road 2 for 11.5 miles. The road becomes Faunce Forest Road. A gravel driveway on the left side of the road leads to the campground. If you reach Santa Ana Road you've gone a mile too far.

Contact: Zippel Bay State Park, 218/783-6252, www.dnr.state.mn.us/state_forests/facilities/cmp00003/index.html.

11 ZIPPEL BAY STATE PARK

Scenic rating: 9

in Zippel Bay State Park

BEST (

The south shore of Lake of the Woods is dressed in miles and miles of white sandy beaches. Some of the finest are near Zippel Bay, where a state park both preserves them and makes them available to the public. Gorgeous lakeside views and bird-watching opportunities abound here.

The park has three campgrounds on its eastern end: Lady's Slipper, Birch, and Ridge. The three loops accommodate just 50 campsites, which makes camping here very quiet and peaceful. The sites are totally buried in the thick northwoods forests that surround Lake of the Woods. Hiking trails wind through the pines and birch, leading to the sandy beaches along the lake.

Because there are so few sites, call or use the state park's website well ahead of the date you intend to camp in order to secure a reservation.

Campsites, facilities: There are 57 sites for tents and RVs up to 50 feet and one group campsite for up to 45 people. Picnic tables, fire rings, vault toilets, showers, and a dump station are provided. A fishing pier, swimming beach, hiking and skiing trails, and volleyball court are available. Leashed pets are permitted.

Reservations, fees: Reservations are accepted from April 2 to October 31 866/857-2757 or online at www.stayatmnparks.com ($8.50 non-refundable reservation fee) and can be made up to one year in advance. Reservations are not required the rest of the year. Sites are $12–24 per night. Open year-round, with limited facilities in winter.

Directions: From Baudette, drive north on Highway 172 for 10 miles. Turn left onto County Road 8. The road leads directly to the park 6 miles ahead.

Contact: Zippel Bay State Park, 218/783-6252, www.dnr.state.mn.us/state_parks.

12 LAKE OF THE WOODS CAMPGROUND

Scenic rating: 7

northwest of Baudette

Lake of the Woods Campground is on the mighty Rainy River just inland from Lake of the Woods. Within shouting distance of the Canadian border, the campground provides direct access to the river and dock space for your boat.

The sites are stacked into open areas between lines of oak trees about 200 feet from the riverbank. The campground is popular with anglers who want access to the river and the lake. Form follows function, and this campground has few frills. Other than a water access point and a place to sleep, there isn't much else here.

Campsites, facilities: There are 87 sites for tents and RVs. Picnic tables, fire rings, toilets, showers, and a dump station are provided. A boat ramp, playground, fishing charters, dock space, outdoor pool, laundry facilities, Internet access, and a camp store are available. Some facilities are wheelchair accessible. Leashed pets are permitted.

Reservations, fees: Reservations are accepted at 218/634-1694. Sites are $23 per night for tents and $38 per night for RVs. Open from mid-May to October.

Directions: From Baudette, drive northwest on Highway 172 for 9.5 miles. Turn right onto County Road 32. The campground is less than 1 mile ahead on the right side of the road.

Contact: Lake of the Woods Campground, 218/634-1694.

13 TIMBER MILL COMMUNITY PARK

Scenic rating: 7

in Baudette

As far as city campgrounds go, Baudette has one of the classiest. Timber Mill's campground underwent a renovation to reopen in 2008 with updated facilities and campsites. The modest campground now has 18 sites, modern showers and restrooms, and a beautiful view right on the Rainy River.

The sites are located on the Rainy River, right off Highway 11 on the Canadian border. As part of the renovation, new trees were planted and roads made, so the shade and privacy have yet to come to fruition. But the river view, boat ramp, skate park, and ball fields are first class.

Campsites, facilities: There are 18 sites for tents and RVs; some sites have hookups. Picnic tables, grills, toilets, showers, and a dump station are provided. A biking and hiking trail, boat ramp, and playground are available. Some facilities are wheelchair accessible. Leashed pets are permitted.

Reservations, fees: Reservations are accepted at 218/634-1850. Sites are $5 per night. Open from mid-May to October.

Directions: From Baudette, drive east on Main Street for 1 mile to Tourist Park Avenue. Turn left. The park and campground are the first right just a few hundred feet ahead.

Contact: City of Baudette, 218/634-1850, http://ci.baudette.mn.us.

14 SHERLOCK PARK CAMPGROUND

Scenic rating: 7

in Red River State Recreation Area

Created after the 1997 flood that devastated much of the East Grand Forks area, the Red River State Recreation Area lies along the river of the same name. The floodplain was redrawn by the U.S. Army Corps of Engineers, and a large greenway, Sherlock Park, was placed along the river's banks as it flows through town.

The park does its best to deliver the natural beauty of the Red River and the floodplain wildlife and vegetation native to the valley. The campground sits adjacent to downtown East Grand Forks, nestled along a bend in the river. There are nearly 100 sites here in two tight loops set on the river floodplain. There are few trees, and the proximity to downtown makes the campground feel more like a city park than a state recreation area.

A swimming beach, playground, and fishing pier are nearby. A paved trail links the campground to the river walkway and bike path, leading up- and downstream along the 1,200-acre greenway.

Campsites, facilities: There are 98 sites for tents and RVs up to 50 feet; 64 sites are pull-through, and 70 sites have full hookups. There are also four backpacking sites and one group campsite for up to 40 people. Picnic tables, fire rings, flush and vault toilets, showers, and a dump station are provided. A paved biking and hiking trail, playground, fishing pier, swimming beach, and canoe access are provided. There are five wheelchair-accessible campsites. Leashed pets are permitted.

Reservations, fees: Reservations are accepted from April 2 to October 31 866/857-2757 or online at www.stayatmnparks.com ($8.50 non-refundable reservation fee) and can be made up to one year in advance. Reservations are not required the rest of the year. Sites are $12–24 per night. Open from mid-May to early November, weather permitting.

Directions: From East Grand Forks, drive west on 4th Street NE for 0.6 mile into Sherlock Park. Turn left on 6th Avenue NW and drive one block to 3rd Street NW. Turn right into the park. The campground is on the left in less than 300 feet.

Contact: Red River State Recreation Area, 218/773-4950, www.dnr.state.mn.us/state_parks.

15 VOYAGEUR'S VIEW CAMPGROUND

Scenic rating: 7

on Red Lake River

Not to be confused with the Red River, the Red Lake River is a side-winding river that flows from Red Lake west to the Red River. Voyageur's View is just north of Red Lake Falls, and takes advantage of the cluster of rapids and meanders that fill the river. The campground is popular for tubing and canoeing during the summer and cross-country skiing during the winter. In summer, the campground provides a shuttle service for tubers and canoeists who head downstream for a day or afternoon on the river.

There are 100 sites in the campground, which has little tree cover; there is little privacy or shade, but plenty of space. A large grove of trees in nearby Sportsmans Park stands between the campground and town, giving the campground a more remote feeling than its proximity to town would suggest.

Campsites, facilities: There are 100 sites for tents and RVs. Picnic tables, fire rings, toilets, showers, and a dump station are provided. River tubing with shuttle service, a playground, hiking/biking/skiing trail, swimming beach and a camp store are available. Some facilities are wheelchair accessible. Leashed pets are permitted.

Reservations, fees: Reservations are accepted at 218/253-4329 (a one night nonrefundable deposit is required). Sites are $23–30 per night for tents and $25–35 per night for RVs. There's a two-night minimum on weekends, a three-night minimum holiday weekends. Open from late May to early September.

Directions: From Thief River Falls, drive south on Highway 32 for 17.5 miles to Red Lake Falls. Turn right on County Road 13 and drive north for 1 mile. The campground is on the left just before crossing the river.

Contact: Voyageur's View Campground, 218/253-4329, http://voyageursview.com.

16 LAKE SARAH FARMERS UNION PARK

Scenic rating: 7

on Lake Sarah south of Erskine

The campsites on Lake Sarah line a small grassy opening in a wooded strip of land between Lake Sarah and Union Lake. The park is on the western shore of the lake and is just a few dozen feet from the water, providing direct access to the lake and stunning sunrises across the water.

There are 24 shaded and private sites, set in an open field in the middle of a wooded loop. This is an ideal family campground, equipped with a swimming beach, playground, and shady picnic shelters all near the water. Fishing along the shore can be fruitful, especially at dawn and dusk. The campground also hosts a youth camp for two weeks each summer, so make sure to call ahead to schedule around the event.

Campsites, facilities: There are 24 sites for tents and RVs; 18 sites have electrical hookups. Picnic tables, fire rings, toilets, showers, and a dump station are provided. A swimming beach, playground, and picnic shelter are available. Leashed pets are permitted.

Reservations, fees: Reservations are accepted at 218-687-3408. Sites are $15 per night for tents and $20 per night for RVs. Open from mid-May to September.

Directions: From Erskine, drive south on Highway 59 for 2 miles. Turn right onto Highway 41. In 4 miles, turn left on 200th Avenue SE. Drive south 0.5 mile to the entrance on the left.

Contact: Lake Sarah Farmers Union Park, 218/687-3408, www.mfu.org/education/camp.

17 CLEARBROOK CITY PARK

Scenic rating: 5

in Clearbrook

Clearbrook City Park is a little patch of trees and grass in the middle of small-town Clearbrook. Within 20 minutes of three decent fishing lakes, the campground is most notable for its affordable site rate rather than a relaxing atmosphere. The campground's 35 sites fight for space in the tiny park, and the lack of a view makes this an entirely utilitarian camping experience.

The park does feature a municipal pool (required fee), a playground, and shower facilities, but again, don't come here for the view. Clearbrook is only about 15 miles from Red Lake, which you may soon find yourself heading to after camping here.

Campsites, facilities: There are 35 sites for tents and RVs; some sites have hookups. Picnic tables, fire rings, toilets, showers, and a dump station are provided. A playground and outdoor pool are available. Some facilities are wheelchair accessible. Leashed pets are permitted.

Reservations, fees: Reservations are accepted at 218/776-2323. Sites are $7.50 per night for tents and $15 per night for RVs. Open from April to October.

Directions: From the intersection of Main Street and Railroad Avenue in downtown Clearbrook, drive north on Main Street for 100 feet to the campground driveway. Turn right and drive another 100 feet into the park and the camping loop straight ahead.

Contact: Clearbrook City Park, 218/776-2323, www.clearbrookmn.com/Lodging.htm.

18 HAMILTONS FOX LAKE CAMPGROUND

Scenic rating: 5

on Fox Lake north of Bemidji

Hamiltons on Fox Lake is, funnily enough, a great place to camp when fishing on nearby Turtle and Beltrami Lakes. Fox Lake is a tiny body of water in a large lakes area that also includes Three Island Lake, Movil Lake, Turtle River Lake, and big Lake Bemidji.

The campground is a three-loop configuration on the lake's northeast shore. A large reed bed lies between the open water and the camping area with three docks jutting into the lake. The sites are wound together in an open field encircled by a gravel road. It isn't pretty, but it is a good location for northland fishing trips. The campground also rents canoes, fishing boats, and outboard motors.

Campsites, facilities: There are 70 sites for tents and RVs (full hookups). Picnic tables, fire rings, toilets, showers, and a dump station (fee) are provided. A boat ramp, dock space, canoe rental, fishing boat and motor rental, a swimming beach, bicycle rental, playground, laundry facilities, wireless Internet, and cable TV (fee) are available. Some facilities are wheelchair accessible. Leashed pets are permitted.

Reservations, fees: Reservations are accepted at 218/586-2231. Sites are $35 per night. Open from early May to mid-September.

Directions: From Bemidji, drive north on Highway 71 for 10 miles. Turn left on County Road 22. The campground is 4 miles ahead on the left just after Dandelion Lane.

Contact: Hamiltons Fox Lake Campground, 218/586-2231, www.CampOnFoxLake.com.

19 PINE TREE PARK

Scenic rating: 6

near Blackduck

Pine Tree Park is on Blackduck Lake just west of the golf course. The area is a patchwork of farmland and forest. Blackduck Lake is surrounded by a ring of large pine trees; the ones at the campground are the best specimens.

The campground is set in a thick patch of red and white pines on the lake's eastern shore. Two campground loops hold about 15 sites each, and they are well spaced among the pines. Sites in the northern loop are closer to the restroom and the lake lookout spot, which gives a view of the large, tree-covered island in the middle of the lake.

The occasional stray ball from the golf course finds its way into the park, but otherwise this is one of the most peaceful places in the county to spend the night.

Campsites, facilities: There are 29 sites for tents and RVs. Picnic tables, fire rings, toilets, showers, and a dump station are provided. A hiking and biking trail, cross-country ski trail, golf course, and boat ramp are available.

Reservations, fees: Reservations are accepted at 218/835-4803 (a $5 reservation fee and a one-night deposit are required). Sites are $15 per night for tents and $17 per night for RVs. Open from May to late September.

Directions: In Blackduck, drive west on Summit Avenue W for 1.5 miles. Turn right at the Blackduck Golfcourse (marked by a sign). The campground is on the left in 0.25 mile.

Contact: Pine Tree Park, 218/835-4803, www.blackduckmn.com.

20 LAKE BEMIDJI CAMPGROUND

Scenic rating: 9

in Lake Bemidji State Park

The Lake Bemidji State Park campground is popular for its white sandy beach, excellent hiking trails, and rare bog flora. The park has almost 100 sites but separates them into four loops, which makes each loop feel like a small campground. The trees that cover the north side of the lake where the park is located also shade and shelter the campsites, filling the air with the sweet scent of pine and making for some wonderful autumn leaf-watching when the hardwoods begin to change color.

One of the best ways to experience the park is by hiking on the wheelchair-accessible bog boardwalk. The large tamarack bog in Lake Bemidji State Park houses rare plants such as the lady's slipper, dragon's mouth, pitcher plant, and sundew, which only grow in bog environments. The park's white sandy beach is also a popular attraction.

Campsites, facilities: There are 95 sites for tents and RVs up to 50 feet; four sites are pull-through and 43 sites have hookups (30-amp). There are also two tent-only group campsites for up to 30 and 50 people each. Picnic tables, fire rings, flush and vault toilets, showers, and a dump station are provided. A bog boardwalk, hiking, biking, and wheelchair-accessible trails, skiing and skate-skiing trails, playground, canoe access, swimming beach, fishing pier and warming house are available. There are four wheelchair-accessible sites. Leashed pets are permitted.

Reservations, fees: Reservations are accepted from April 2 to October 31 866/857-2757 or online at www.stayatmnparks.com ($8.50 non-refundable reservation fee) and can be made up to one year in advance. Reservations are not required the rest of the year. Sites are $12–24 per night. Open year-round, with limited facilities in winter.

Directions: From Bemidji, drive north on Paul Bunyan Drive for 1 mile to Old Highway 2. Turn left and drive for 0.3 mile to Irvine Avenue NW. Turn right and drive for 3 miles to Lakewood Drive NW. Turn right and drive for 0.5 mile. Turn left at Bemidji Road NE. In 1 mile, turn right onto County Road 20. The park entrance is 1.5 miles ahead on the right. Turn onto State Park Road NE and drive for 0.6 mile to the campground.

Contact: Lake Bemidji State Park, 218) 308-2300, www.dnr.state.mn.us/state_parks.

21 ROYAL OAKS RV PARK

Scenic rating: 5

south of Bemidji

Before you tent campers flip past this entry, note that there are three tent sites at this otherwise RV-only park. Sure, the campground is about 100 feet from the Highway 2 exit for Bemidji, and sure, it isn't on a lake or river, though they run rampant throughout this entire region of Minnesota. But this little park a somehow manages to scrap together enough charm to make it a cozy, worthwhile place to park your RV or pitch your tent. The thick grove of oak, pine, and aspen shields a surprising amount of traffic noise from the campground, and the sites enjoy plenty of shade and privacy in the wooded grove. A hiking and biking trail explores the patch of woods, and a playground keeps the children happy. Bemidji and its big lake and state park are just a 10-minute drive to the north, so camping here for much less is a real deal, in my book.

Campsites, facilities: There are 63 sites for RVs and three sites for tents; pull-through sites are available. Picnic tables, fire rings, toilets, showers, and a dump station are provided. A hiking and biking trail, playground, Internet access, and laundry facilities are available. Some facilities are wheelchair accessible. Leashed pets are permitted.

Reservations, fees: Reservations are accepted at 218/751-8357. Sites are $19 per night for tents and $25 per night for RVs. Open from May to mid-October.

Directions: From Bemidji, drive south on Paul Bunyan Drive for 0.6 mile. Turn left onto Midway Drive S. In 0.6 mile the road merges back up with Paul Bunyan Drive. Follow it for 0.3 mile until it becomes Highway 187. The campground will be on your left in just over 1.5 miles, right before Highway 2. If you cross Highway 2 you have gone too far.

Contact: Royal Oaks RV Park, 218/751-8357.

22 OAK HAVEN RESORT

Scenic rating: 6

east of Bemidji

Oak Haven is ideal for families who like to fish and enjoy the luxuries of home while camping in the northwoods. Oak Haven is a resort first and a campground second, but the facilities are just as top-notch for campers as they are for cabin dwellers. Decked out with a sauna, playground, fishing boats, two pools, and canoes, Oak Haven has plenty of activities to fill your time.

The campground is harbored along the Mississippi headwaters as they flow toward Cass Lake. The dozen sites are in a single loop with heavy tree cover that fills the oxbow the river makes here between Wolf and Andrusia Lakes. Anglers and boaters have access to nine lakes from the campground.

Campsites, facilities: There are 12 sites for tents and RVs up to 40 feet; some sites have hookups. Picnic tables, fire rings, toilets, showers, and a dump station are provided. A playground, sauna, dock space, fishing boat rental, boat ramp, indoor and outdoor pool, and canoe rental are available. Some facilities are wheelchair accessible.

Reservations, fees: Reservations are accepted

at 877/860-9948 (50 percent deposit required). Sites are $35 per night for tents and $39–44 per night for RVs. There's a three-night minimum on holiday weekends. Open year-round.

Directions: From Bemidji, drive east on County Road 8 for 8 miles. The entrance to the campground is on the left side of the road marked by a large Oak Haven Resort sign.

Contact: Oak Haven Resort, 218/335-2092, www.bemidjiresort.com.

23 WEBSTER LAKE CAMPGROUND

Scenic rating: 7

in the Blackduck Area of Chippewa National Forest

Webster Lake is in the heart of the Chippewa National Forest in northern Minnesota. Nearly 10 miles from the nearest town, tucked away on gravel roads amid dozens of lakes scattered across the densely wooded landscape, this remote campground will give you a real taste of the Minnesota wilderness.

The sunsets here are amazing and are alone worth the labyrinthine drive it takes to get to the campground. Nights are pitch black and make for wonderful stargazing and watching the northern lights. Campsites are nestled in a snug little loop on Webster Lake's eastern shore. The campground has a boat ramp and hiking trails for exploring the forest. Be cautious while walking through the woods, as bears are sometimes encountered in this remote area.

Campsites, facilities: There are 15 sites for tents or RVs; some sites have hookups. Picnic tables, fire rings, toilets, and a dump station are provided. A boat ramp, hiking trail, and picnic area are available. Leashed pets are permitted.

Reservations, fees: Reservations are accepted at 877/444-6777 or www.recreation.gov ($10

nonrefundable fee). Sites are $14 per night for tents and $23 per night for RVs. Open from mid-May to mid-November.

Directions: From Blackduck, drive south on County Road 39 for 7 miles. Turn left onto Rabideau Lake Road NE. In 1.2 miles turn right onto Webster Lake Road NE. Drive for 1.7 miles to the campground sign. Turn right and follow the campground sign, taking the next left into the parking area.

Contact: Chippewa National Forest, Blackduck Area, 218/835-4291, www.fs.fed.us/r9/forests/chippewa/recreation/camping/blackduck.php.

24 KNUTSON DAM CAMPGROUND

Scenic rating: 7

on the northeast shore of Cass Lake

Knutson Dam is mostly used as a river access point to the Mississippi River and as a place to spend an afternoon catching some fish below the dam. The campground here is rather charming, with just 14 sites set in a single loop that hugs Cass Lake just as the Mississippi River leaves it heading toward Lake Winnibigoshish.

The sites are located on the heavily wooded side of the river, tucked into the trees. The campground is managed by Chippewa National Forest and is kept clean and simple. There isn't much here beyond picnic tables, fire rings, and tent space.

Campsites, facilities: There are 14 campsites for tents and RVs. Picnic tables, fire rings, drinking water from a well, toilets, and garbage cans are provided. Dock space and a boat ramp are available. Some facilities are wheelchair accessible. Leashed pets are permitted.

Reservations, fees: Reservations are accepted at 877/444-6777 or www.recreation.gov ($10 nonrefundable fee). Sites are $16 per night. Open from mid-May to mid-September.

Directions: From the town of Cass Lake, drive east for 6 miles on Highway 2. Turn left onto County Road 10 and drive for 5 miles. The campground is on the left side of the road.

Contact: Chippewa National Forest, Cass Lake Ranger District, 218/835-4291, www. fs.fed.us/r9/forests/chippewa/recreation/camping/casslake.php.

25 STAR ISLAND CAMPGROUND
🏃 ≈ 🚣 🎣 🏕 ⛺

Scenic rating: 9

on Cass Lake

BEST (

Star Island is the largest island on Cass Lake. The island is heavily wooded with pine, maple, and aspen trees and can only be reached by canoe.

Star Island has an arcing harbor-like area at its southern end, and this is where you will find the small, three-site campground. There is almost always a cool breeze blowing across the water onto the west side of the island. Luckily, the bulk of the forested isle effectively shelters the camping area from strong winds. The sites are huddled together, well protected from the weather, and are exposed only to gorgeous sunrises and excellent fishing. A hiking trail leads from the camping area to Lake Windigo, a lake within a lake in the center of the island.

Campsites, facilities: There are three sites for tents. Picnic tables, fire rings, vault toilets, showers, and a dump station are provided. There is no drinking water, and garbage must be packed out. Leashed pets are permitted.

Reservations, fees: Reservations are not accepted. There is no fee. Open year-round.

Directions: From the Mississippi River inlet into Cass Lake, paddle across Allens Bay and around the west side of the island to the west side of the narrow peninsula in the center of the lake on the north end of the island.

Contact: Chippewa National Forest, Cass

Lake Ranger District, 218/335-8600, www. fs.fed.us.

26 NORWAY BEACH RECREATION AREA
🏃 🚲 ≈ 🚣 🏕 🐕 ♿ 🚐 ⛺

Scenic rating: 8

on the southern shore of Cass Lake

Cass Lake lies along the Upper Mississippi River and is one of the largest lakes in the state; its southern shore is a prime fishing location.

The campgrounds along Norway Beach Road are classic examples of the Chippewa National Forest. More than 100 campsites are arranged within four loops: Norway Beach, Cass Lake, Chippewa, and Wanaki. Private, well-spaced, primitive sites are set near the water and among plenty of trees. Of the four loops, only the Chippewa loop has electric hookups; the rest of the sites are rustic with limited facilities.

The Norway Beach campground has great recreational facilities; its swimming beach is first-rate, and a 17-mile hiking trail passes right through the campground and follows the lakeshore.

Campsites, facilities: There are 170 sites for tents and RVs. Picnic tables, fire rings, toilets, showers, and a dump station are provided. A swimming beach, two boat ramps, and a hiking and biking trail are available. Some facilities are wheelchair accessible. Leashed pets are permitted.

Reservations, fees: Reservations are accepted at 877/444-6777 or www.recreation.gov ($10 nonrefundable fee). Sites are $21 per night for tents and $23 per night for RVs. Open from mid-May to mid-September.

Directions: From the town of Cass Lake, drive east on Highway 2 for 3.8 miles. Turn left onto Norway Beach Road NW. Follow the road 0.6 mile to the beach and campground.

Contact: Chippewa National Forest, Cass

Lake Ranger District, 218/835-4291, www.
fs.fed.us/r9/forests/chippewa/recreation/camp-
ing/casslake.php.

27 WINNIE CAMPGROUND

Scenic rating: 9

in Lake Winnibigoshish

Winnie Campground lies on the western shore
of Lake Winnibigoshish—or "Big Winnie," as
the locals call it—just north of the Mississippi
River inlet into the lake. Big Winnie is one
of the state's largest lakes and a mythic stop
along the Mississippi River's marathon journey
to the Gulf of Mexico.

The entire stretch of the lake lies at the
feet of this campground, treating campers
to stunning sunrises, bright moonlit nights,
and enchanting cathedral-like pine forest. The
campground is laid out in two loops just about
20 feet from the water, and nearly every site
has a footpath that leads directly to the water.
The sites each have a short gravel driveway
and are buried in the towering red and white
pine trees that line this part of the shore. The
campground has a boat ramp and a small system of hiking trails that tour the area.

Campsites, facilities: There are 35 sites for
tents only. Picnic tables, fire rings, toilets,
showers, and a dump station are provided.
A boat ramp and hiking trails are available.
Leashed pets are permitted.

Reservations, fees: Reservations are not accepted. Sites are $14 per night. Open from
mid-May to late October.

Directions: From Cass Lake, drive east for 6
miles on Highway 2. Turn left onto County
Road 10 and drive 2 miles to Forest Road 2171.
Turn right and drive 6 miles to Forest Road
2168. Take another right and drive 4 miles to the
campground (the road dead-ends at the lake).

Contact: Chippewa National Forest, Cass
Lake Ranger District, 218/835-4291, www.
fs.fed.us/r9.

28 NOMA LAKE CAMPGROUND

Scenic rating: 7

in Chippewa National Forest, north of
Lake Winnibigoshish

Tiny Noma Lake sits in the Chippewa National Forest north of Lake Winnibigoshish.
The campground lies on a narrow isthmus
between Noma and the larger Clear Lake just
a hundred feet to the west across the county
road. The campsites here are strung along an
artery that branches off of County Road 31
east of Northome.

The two small lakes are in an extremely
rural area of the state; the campground is more
than a 20-mile drive from the nearest town.
This solitude ensures there is virtually no light
pollution at the campground, making stargazing and spotting northern lights particularly
enjoyable.

Campsites, facilities: There are 14 sites for
tents and RVs. Picnic tables, fire rings, toilets,
and garbage cans are provided. A fish-cleaning
station, nearby boat ramp, and hiking trail are
available. Leashed pets are permitted.

Reservations, fees: Reservations are not accepted. Self-registration is required at the
campground. Sites are $12 per night. Open
year-round.

Directions: From Northome, drive east on
Highway 1 for 14.4 miles. Turn right onto
County Road 27. In 5 miles the road becomes
County Road 31. Continue for another 4.5
miles to Noma Lake. The campground is on
the left side of the road just after Forest Road
3446.

Contact: Blackduck Ranger District, Chippewa National Forest, 218/835-4291, www.
fs.fed.us/r9/forests/chippewa/recreation/camp-
ing/blackduck.php.

29 ELK HORN RESORT & CAMPGROUND

Scenic rating: 7

on South Twin Lake east of Waubun

You may want to underline the word "resort" in the title of this campground, as indoor lodging is the primary emphasis at Elk Horn. On the south shore of scenic and rather large South Twin Lake, the resort and campground are carved out of a dense pine and hardwood forest that surrounds the water.

The campground consists of a little corral of campsites scattered underneath the trees. The resort occupies a small clearing on the lake's south shore and is within driving distance of 12 state wildlife management areas. Elk Horn offers first-class recreation, with a swimming beach, biking and hiking trail, pontoons, and fishing docks at your disposal.

Campsites, facilities: There are 80 campsites for tents and RVs. Picnic tables, fire rings, toilets, showers, and a dump station (fee) are provided. A swimming beach, biking and hiking trail, camp store, pontoon rentals, a boat ramp, fishing boats, dock space, canoe rental, playground, and camp store are available. Some facilities are wheelchair accessible. Leashed pets are permitted.

Reservations, fees: Reservations are accepted at 218/935-5437 or 888/828-5472 (one night's deposit is required). Sites are $24 per night for tents and $28–35 per night for RVs. A three-night minimum stay is required on holidays. Open from late April to October.

Directions: From Waubun, drive east on Highway 113 for 12 miles. Turn left on County Road 4. The campground is 4 miles ahead on the right side of the road just after Snider Lake.

Contact: Elk Horn Resort, 218//935-5437, www.elkhornresortandcampground.com.

30 LONG LAKE PARK & CAMPGROUND

Scenic rating: 7

northwest of Itasca State Park

Towering pine trees, calm northwoods waters, lively fishing, and beautiful sunsets give the Long Lake Park campground the *je ne sais quoi* that all northwoods campgrounds aspire to.

The campsites are nested into two large loops, each with a short driveway and a private clearing in the trees. There is a surplus of peace and quiet here, even though Highway 200 is only 0.25 mile away. There is little traffic, especially at night, and the beautiful surroundings at each site and the serenity of Long Lake easily make up for any distant highway noise.

The park is bursting with hiking trails, a swimming beach, boat ramp, water skiers, and a nifty playground, giving you plenty to do when you venture out from your little alcove in the woods.

Campsites, facilities: There are 91 sites for tents and RVs; some sites have hookups. There are also two group campsites for up to 30 and 50 people each. Picnic tables, fire rings, toilets, showers, and a dump station are provided. Fishing boats, a boat ramp, playground, hiking trail, swimming beach, laundry facilities, and a camp store are available. Some facilities are wheelchair accessible. Leashed pets are permitted.

Reservations, fees: Reservations are accepted at 218/657-2275 (one night's deposit is required). Sites are $20–23 per night for tents and $25–27 per night for RVs. The group sites are $50–60 per night. There's a two-night minimum on weekends, a three-night minimum on holiday weekends. Open from early May to late September.

Directions: From the intersection of Highway 200 and Highway 92, drive east on 200 for 2 miles. The campground entrance is on the right at Heart Lake Road.

Contact: Long Lake Park & Campground, 218/657-2275, www.longlakepark.com.

31 ITASCA STATE PARK

Scenic rating: 8

in Itasca State Park

BEST (

The headwaters of the mighty Mississippi are just a tiny trickle coming out of Lake Itasca in northern Minnesota. That doesn't stop thousands of people from coming to visit the start of the continent's longest river, though. Containing 32,000 acres and 100 lakes, Itasca is Minnesota's oldest state park and probably its best known.

The campground here is massive, swelling with more than 200 sites, many of which are made for big-rig RVs. For tent campers and backpackers looking to get into the woods, there are 11 backpacking sites and 11 cart-in sites that offer seclusion and respite from the throngs that come to see the headwaters.

There's plenty for families to do here: have your picture taken by the headwaters marker, stand in the enchanting grove of massive red pines, or hike to the centuries-old Indian Cemetery deep within the park. Campers have access to paved hiking and biking trails that tour the headwaters area, as well as groomed cross-country ski trails in the winter.

People come here from all over the world, so you will want to make your reservations well ahead of time—at least six months ahead.

Campsites, facilities: There are 223 sites for tents and RVs up to 60 feet; 100 sites have electrical hookups. There are also 11 backpacking sites, 11 cart-in sites, and one group campsite for up to 50 people. Picnic tables, fire rings, drinking water, flush and vault toilets, showers, and a dump station are provided. Hiking trails, paved biking trails, cross-country skiing trails, a boardwalk, playground, swimming beach, fishing pier, and warming house are available. There are four wheelchair-accessible sites and a wheelchair-accessible trail. Leashed pets are permitted.

Reservations, fees: Reservations are accepted from April 2 to October 31 866/857-2757 or online at www.stayatmnparks.com ($8.50 non-refundable reservation fee) and can be made up to one year in advance. Reservations are not required the rest of the year. Sites are $12–24 per night. Open year-round, with limited facilities in winter.

Directions: From Park Rapids, drive north on Highway 71 for 20.5 miles. Turn left onto Highway 200 W. In 0.2 mile, turn left onto Highway 123 and drive for 1.2 miles. Turn right to stay on the highway and take a left in another 0.2 mile onto Park Drive. In 0.2 mile the road becomes County Road 122. In 2 miles, turn right onto Campground Road. The campground is dead ahead in 1 mile.

Contact: Itasca State Park, 218/266-2100 www.dnr.state.mn.us/state_parks.

32 UPPER MISSISSIPPI RIVER CANOE CAMPSITES

Scenic rating: 9

on the Mississippi River, from the headwaters to Lake Winnibigoshish

BEST (

As the Mississippi River snakes its way out of Itasca State Park and begins its long, slow arc across northern Minnesota to Lake Bemidji, Cass Lake, and Lake Winnibigoshish, it is peppered with small canoe campsites. Each of these dozen or so sites is accessible only by canoe from the river. Marked by small, wooden, numbered signs, many of these sites have a "middle of nowhere" feel to them, far from cities and country roads that can't reach the floodplain that surrounds the narrow river. The sites are very primitive, with just a clearing for a tent or two and a fire ring.

Campsites, facilities: There are approximately 12 sites for tents only. Sites are located along the Mississippi River, from the headwaters to Lake Winnibigoshish. Picnic tables, fire rings, and vault toilets are provided. There is no drinking water; you must bring your own. Leashed pets are permitted.

Reservations, fees: Reservations are not accepted. There is no fee. Open year-round, weather permitting.

Directions: Canoeists can conveniently put-in at Lake Itasca State Park, Cass Lake, and Lake Bemidji. An accurate map of the river and the location of these sites is essential; maps can be ordered from the Minnesota Department of Natural Resources at info@dnr.state.mn.us.

Contact: Minnesota Department of Natural Resources, 218/308-2372, www.dnr.state. mn.us/watertrails/mississippiriver/one.html.

33 HUNGRYMAN LAKE CAMPGROUND

Scenic rating: 8

south of Itasca State Park

Hungryman Lake is just eight miles south of Itasca State Park, one of the state's most popular attractions and the headwaters of the Mississippi River. The area has literally hundreds of lakes for fishing and hiking in Two Inlets State Forest.

The campground lies on a pine-covered ridge above Hungryman Lake. The primitive sites are set in a single loop among the evergreens and have views of the water. There is a boat ramp on Hungryman Lake, below the ridge along the gravel road that passes by the campground. A swimming beach and fishing area are also nearby.

Campsites, facilities: There are 14 sites for tents and RVs. Picnic tables, fire rings, vault toilets, drinking water, and garbage cans are provided. A swimming beach, boat ramp, and fishing area are available. Leashed pets are permitted.

Reservations, fees: Reservations are not accepted. Sites are $12 per night. Self-registration is required at the campground. Open from April to mid-November.

Directions: From Park Rapids, drive north on Highway 71 for 10 miles. Turn left onto

County Road 41 and drive for 1.5 miles to Cedar Lake Road. Turn right and drive for 1 mile to the three-way intersection. Turn left and drive for 0.7 mile to the campground on the right side of the road.

Contact: Itasca State Park, Two Inlets State Forest, 218/266-2100, www.dnr.state.mn.us/ state_forests/facilities/cmp00048/index. html.

34 VAGABOND VILLAGE CAMPGROUND

Scenic rating: 6

north of Park Rapids

The lake-heavy landscape north of Park Rapids just begs to be camped in, and Vagabond Village offers a hearty handout. Located on the east end of Potato Lake, the campground lies within a 10-minute drive of dozens of other nearby lakes. Yes, I said dozens.

Equipped with more than 100 sites, the campground is a mecca for campers of all stripes. Vagabond Village won't exactly turn away tent campers, but they prefer the big rigs. The place is usually soaked through with RVs, packed in like sardines in five tight loops between Green Pines Road and the lake. Most of the sites have at least one tree, but there is no privacy here. A line of seasonal sites lies closer to the water, but even those don't have much shade or privacy, which is somewhat ironic given the fact that the entire lakes area is covered in one of the state's densest forests.

The recreational amenities here are a highlight of the campground. A shuffle board game, tennis courts, canoes, and a wooden playground are fun ways to spend the afternoon.

Campsites, facilities: There are 126 sites for tents and RVs; pull-through sites are available, and some sites have hookups. Picnic tables, fire rings, toilets, showers, and a dump station are provided. A tennis court, playground, dock space, fishing boat rental, canoe rental, wireless Internet, laundry facilities, and a camp stores are available. Leashed pets are permitted.

Reservations, fees: Reservations are accepted at 218/732-5234 ($50 deposit required). Sites are $35.50–$40 per night. Two-night minimum stay on weekends, three-night minimum on holiday weekends. Credit cards are not accepted. Open from early May to late September.

Directions: From Park Rapids, drive east on 1st Street W for 0.5 mile. Turn left onto County Road 99. In 1 mile the road becomes County Road 1. Drive for another 3.2 miles to County Road 18. Turn right and drive for just 0.3 mile to Green Pines Road. Turn left and drive for 2.1 miles directly into the campground.

Contact: Vagabond Village Campground, 218/732-5234, www.vagabondvillage.com.

35 MANTRAP LAKE CAMPGROUND

Scenic rating: 8

in Paul Bunyan State Forest

BEST (

Get your fishing rods ready, because Mantrap Lake is a designated muskie lake. The lake is a big, squiggly, odd-shaped body of water with several oblong islands, peninsulas, and isthmuses dividing its muskie-rich waters.

The day-use area and campground are frequently used water access points for anglers lusting after the elusive muskie. The three-loop campground is about 500 feet away from the boat access and swimming beach; the bulk of the lake lies to the east of the access point at the campground. The primitive sites each have a short gravel driveway and are separated from each other by approximately 50 feet and as many towering pines.

Campsites, facilities: There are 36 sites for tents and RVs. Picnic tables, fire rings, toilets, drinking water, and garbage cans are provided.

A swimming beach, fishing area, hiking trail, boat ramp, and dock are available. Some facilities are wheelchair accessible. Leashed pets are permitted.

Reservations, fees: Reservations are not accepted. Sites are $12 per night. Self-registration is required at the campground. Open from April to mid-November.

Directions: From Park Rapids, drive east on Highway 34 for 2.1 miles. Turn left at County Road 4. In 10.3 miles turn right onto County Road 24. Drive for 1.5 miles and turn left onto Jewel Drive. Take the first right onto Jack Fish Drive in 0.4 mile. The campground is at the end of the road in 0.7 mile.

Contact: Itasca State Park, 218/266-2100, www.dnr.state.mn.us/state_forests/facilities/cmp00036/index.html.

36 WHISPERING PINES RESORT & CAMPGROUND

Scenic rating: 6

north of Nevis

Whispering Pines is on the southern shore of West Crooked Lake, which is connected to Crooked and East Crooked Lakes. The thick woods of nearby Paul Bunyan State Forest vie for space with the hundreds of lakes that spread their fingers across this land.

The campground is about a 10-minute drive to Itasca State Park to the west and Leech Lake to the east. The campground is also part resort, which fortunately doesn't affect the camping fee as much as it does in other resorts. The sites are a little close together, but the pine and oak trees that blanket the resort, as well as the woodsy lakeside feel of the place, give the campground a charming, "up north" feel. Campers have access to three lakes, plus canoe and fishing boat rentals, dock space, and a swimming beach. Fishing is excellent along the Crooked Lakes chain.

Campsites, facilities: There are 21 sites for

tents and RVs. Picnic tables, fire rings, toilets, showers, and a dump station are provided. A playground, canoe rental, dock space, fishing boat rental, swimming beach, and camp store are available. Some facilities are wheelchair accessible. Leashed pets are permitted.

Reservations, fees: Reservations are accepted at 218/652-4362. Sites are $25 per night for tents and $29 per night for RVs. Open from May to October.

Directions: From Nevis, drive north on Highway 2 for 1 mile. Turn right on Highway 40. In 2 miles, turn right on County Road 86. The campground is 3 miles ahead on the left side of the road at the intersection of Highview Drive.

Contact: Whispering Pines Resort & Campground, 218/652-4362.

37 GULCH LAKE CAMPGROUND

Scenic rating: 7

in Paul Bunyan State Forest

Ironically, Gulch Lake Campground isn't on Gulch Lake; it's actually closer to Nelson Lake, Bass Lake, and Lake 21. This nonmotorized area of the forest allows access to the Gulch chain of lakes as well as the Lake 21 day-use area about 0.25 mile away, where you will find a swimming beach, boat ramp, and fishing area.

The woodsy Gulch Lake campground has a single loop of only eight sites, about 10 miles east of Itasca State Park. This campground is hardly ever used, as the more popular Itasca State Park is so close, and the state forest's other nearby campground, Mantrap Lake, provides a better view. This spot actually serves as a nice base camp for exploring the region; it's close to the Mississippi River, within 0.25 mile of three lakes, and is very quiet and secluded. The shaded sites are very private, and you'll probably be the only one camping here. And the stargazing is otherworldly.

Campsites, facilities: There are eight sites for tents and RVs. Picnic tables, fire rings, vault toilets, a hand pump for water, and garbage cans are provided. Hiking trails, a boat ramp, and a swimming beach are all nearby. Leashed pets are permitted.

Reservations, fees: Reservations are not accepted. Sites are $12 per night. Self-registration is required at the campground. Open from April to mid-November.

Directions: From the intersection of Highway 200 and Highway 64, drive south for 4 miles on Highway 64. Turn right onto E. Gulch Trail. In 1.2 miles turn right at the T in the road. Turn left in 0.8 mile at the fork in the road. The campground is 0.2 mile ahead on the right side of the road.

Contact: Itasca State Park, 218/266-2100, www.dnr.state.mn.us/state_forests/facilities/cmp00037/index.html.

38 MOONLIGHT BAY RESORT AND CAMPGROUND

Scenic rating: 6

northwest of Walker

The phrase "small RV campground" isn't encountered often, but Moonlight Bay breaks the mold. A single loop of campsites sits in the middle of a small resort on Leech Lake's western shore. There are cabins and indoor lodging at this resort, but the campground is given ample space on the grounds.

The campsites are all for RVs, with the exception of one small tent site. The sites are fairly close together, but large oak trees grow in each, giving as much shade and privacy as they can. Leech Lake's Welsh's Bay is just yards away from the camping area and will send you off to sleep with the sounds of gentle waves.

The resort provides canoes, kayaks, fishing boats, and dock space, emphasizing its proximity to one of the state's largest lakes.

Campsites, facilities: There are 13 sites for

RVs (full hookups) and one site for tents. Picnic tables, fire rings, toilets, showers, and a dump station are provided. Canoes and kayaks (free), dock space, fishing boat rentals, a playground, bike trail, wireless Internet, and a heated outdoor pool are available. Leashed pets are permitted in campsites only; some breed restrictions apply.

Reservations, fees: Reservations are accepted at 888/973-7078. Sites are $30 per night for tents and $32 per night for RVs. There is a fee of $3 per pet per day. Three-night stays are required on holiday weekends. Open from May to October.

Directions: From Walker, drive northwest on Highway 371 for 5.2 miles. Turn right onto Wedgewood Road. The resort and campground are 0.7 mile ahead on the right side of the road.

Contact: Moonlight Bay Resort and Campground, 218/547-1443, www.moonlighton-leech.com.

39 STONY POINT CAMPGROUND

🧍 🏊 ⛵ 🎣 🚣 🐪 ♿ 🚐 ⛺

Scenic rating: 9

on Leech Lake

Stony Point is covered by a patch of rare old-growth forest—one of the few remaining in the state—set on Leech Lake's large southern peninsula. Most of the trees in the grove are more than 200 years old.

The campground consists of a single loop of 44 sites sheltered by the canopy of these huge trees. Stony Point is more developed than most national forest campgrounds in the state, with electricity, showers, a developed boat ramp, and two harbor areas. It is a popular day-use area for both its lake access and its old-growth forest. Sites fill up here quickly every day of the week during the summer. (Sites 1–7 are first come, first served, so you might get lucky without reservations.)

Leech Lake is the third largest lake in Minnesota and is famed for its walleye and muskie fishing. Stony Point gives boaters and anglers access to the southeastern bays and shorelines of the lake. The Stony Point hiking trail tours the old-growth forest, with canopy views of a rare variety in Minnesota. Oak, elm, maple, and ash trees all mingle here, creating a diverse habitat for birds and wildlife.

Campsites, facilities: There are 44 sites for tents and RVs. Picnic tables, fire rings, toilets, showers, and a dump station are provided. A boat ramp, two harbor areas, hiking trail, swimming beach, and picnic area are available. Some facilities are wheelchair accessible. Leashed pets are permitted.

Reservations, fees: Reservations are accepted at 877/444-6777 or www.recreation.gov ($10 nonrefundable fee). Sites are $23 per night. Open from mid-May to late September.

Directions: From Walker, drive east on Highway 200 for 6.5 miles to Onigum Road NW. In 4.2 miles turn right onto Stony Point Camp Road NW. Turn left to stay on Stony Point Camp Road in 3.1 miles. The campground and picnic area are 0.2 mile ahead on the right.

Contact: Chippewa National Forest, Walker Area, 218/547-1044, www.fs.fed.us/r9/forests/chippewa/recreation/camping/walker.php

40 NEW LEECH LAKE CAMPGROUND & RESORT

🧍 🚴 🏊 ⛵ 🚐 ⛷ 🐕 🚐 ⛺

Scenic rating: 6

south of Bena

If you are from Minnesota, you have heard of Leech Lake, and for good reason. It is home to one of the most mythic and elusive fish of the northland: the legendary muskie. Anglers come from all over the state to try to tempt this big game fish into their boats.

The New Leech Lake Campground gives anglers convenient access to the lake while providing an affordable, comfortable camping experience. The campground is on Portage Bay, a popular fishing and ice fishing spot. In the winter, a small village of ice houses cluster on the bay, and many anglers camp at the campground overnight. The campsites lie along the outer edge of the resort in an open grassy area interspersed with oak, maple, and poplar trees. Some of the sites are close to the campground's smaller dock and fishing area. There is indoor lodging here as well, closer to the interior of the resort.

Campsites, facilities: There are 72 sites for tents and RVs; some sites have hookups. Picnic tables, fire rings, toilets, showers, and a dump station are provided. A lodge, swimming beach, boat ramp, dock space, child-care center, hiking and biking trail, and a camp store are available. Leashed pets are permitted.

Reservations, fees: Reservations are accepted at 218/654-3785. Sites are $28 per night for tents and $30 per night for RVs. There is a $5 pet fee per pet per night. Open from May to the end of October.

Directions: From Bena drive south on Highway 2 for 3.2 miles. Turn left onto Portage Road NE. In a little more than 1.5 miles the road becomes Sunset Beach Road. The campground is 4.5 miles ahead on the left at the end of the road.

Contact: New Leech Lake Campground & Resort, 218/654-3785, www.leechlakecampground.com.

41 LEECH LAKE RECREATION AREA

Scenic rating: 7

on Leech Lake

Placed at the outlet of Leech Lake on the Leech Lake River, this recreation campground is managed by the U.S. Army Corps of Engineers (ACOE). While the lake's name may be a bit distasteful, the parasite the lake is named after does not characterize the campground.

The ACOE keeps tidy campgrounds all over the country, and this is one of their finest. The 77 campsites are well spaced, shaded by the oaks, pines, maples, and aspens that fill the recreation area.

The campground has two boat ramps, a hiking trail that plumbs the forest grove south of the camping area, and a marsh that provides excellent bird-watching and fishing opportunities. Fishing below the dam is a nice little hot spot for walleye, pike, and bass.

Campsites, facilities: There are 77 sites for tents and RVs; 29 sites are first come, first served. There is one group campsite. Pull-through sites are available, and some sites have hookups. Picnic tables, fire rings, drinking water, toilets, showers, and a dump station are provided. A hiking trail, playground, dock space, fishing boat rental, two boat ramps, and laundry facilities are available. Some facilities are wheelchair accessible. Leashed pets are permitted.

Reservations, fees: Some sites can be reserved at 877/444-6777 or online at www.recreation.gov ($10 reservation fee). Sites are $10–32 per night. There's a two-night minimum on weekends and a three-night minimum on holiday weekends. Open from May to late October.

Directions: From Bena, drive south on County Road 8 for 7.3 miles. Turn right onto Federal Dam Drive NE. Turn right in 0.1 mile to stay on Federal Dam Drive. The campground is just past the dam on the left side of the road.

Contact: U.S. Army Corps of Engineers, Leech Lake Recreation Area, 218/654-3145, www.mvp.usace.army.mil/recreation/default.asp?pageid=66.

42 MABEL LAKE NATIONAL FOREST CAMPGROUND

Scenic rating: 7

in Chippewa National Forest

Mabel Lake is a small but scenic lake located south of much larger Leech Lake. The

Mabel Lake campground is a cheap, convenient place to stay if you want to spend some time fishing on Leech Lake but don't want to pay top dollar at the lakeside resorts and campgrounds.

The single-loop campground is maintained by Chippewa National Forest. About half of the campsites are set along the lake, and these are definitely the preferred spots. Sites are considered primitive, with only a picnic table, fire ring, and garbage cans. There is a hand pump for water, so make sure to bring your own drinking water to prime the pump and during winter when the pump will be frozen.

This is a small, remote campground, but it is fairly well known. Since the Forest Service doesn't accept reservations, make sure you get here early to secure a site during the summer.

Campsites, facilities: There are 22 sites for tents and RVs. Picnic tables, fire rings, vault toilets, showers, and a hand pump for water are provided. A hiking trail and swimming beach are available. Leashed pets are permitted.

Reservations, fees: Reservations are not accepted. Sites are $14 per night. Self-registration is required at the campground. Open from mid-May to mid-September.

Directions: From Remer, drive west on Highway 200 for 6 miles. Turn right onto Forest Road 2104. The campground is 0.75 mile ahead at the second left.

Contact: Chippewa National Forest, Walker Area, 218/547-1044, www.fs.fed.us.

43 BUFFALO RIVER CAMPGROUND

Scenic rating: 9

in Buffalo River State Park

Buffalo River State Park is a prairie lover's paradise. The park is home to one of Minnesota's largest remnant prairies. The sweeping grassland is full of prairie flowers and the skittish bobolinks, prairie chickens, marbled godwits, and upland sandpipers that cluster in the few remaining prairie-scapes left in the upper Midwest.

The campground holds 44 sites, arranged in a loop amid a small swath of trees between the river and the prairie. The loop is about 0.25-mile long and offers plenty of space between sites. There are just enough trees to afford a decent amount of privacy, and each site is rather large, with space for several tents. Sites on the north end of the loop have a view of the prairie as it sweeps northward for miles and miles. The tree-lined Buffalo River is about 200 feet from the campground. Hiking trails tour the hummocks and hills of this scenic park.

Campsites, facilities: There are 44 sites for tents and RVs up to 50 feet; 35 sites have hookups (20-, 30-, and 50-amp). There is also one group campsite for up to 100 people. Picnic tables, fire rings, drinking water, flush and vault toilets, showers, and a dump station are provided. A swimming beach, fishing area, hiking and cross-country skiing trails, swimming pool, and warming house (in winter) are available. There are two wheelchair-accessible sites. Leashed pets are permitted.

Reservations, fees: Reservations are accepted from April 2 to October 31 866/857-2757 or online at www.stayatmnparks.com ($8.50 non-refundable reservation fee) and can be made up to one year in advance. Reservations are not required the rest of the year. Sites are $12–24 per night. Open year-round, with limited facilities in winter.

Directions: From Moorhead, drive east on Highway 10 for 14 miles. Turn right onto 155th Street. The campground is 0.8 mile ahead on the right.

Contact: Buffalo River State Park, 218/498-2124, www.dnr.state.mn.us/state_parks.

44 LEE LAKE CAMPGROUND

Scenic rating: 5

southeast of Hawley

Lee Lake is on the northwestern edge of a thick cluster of lakes in the Detroit Lakes area. Anglers and campers flock to the Detroit Lakes region every summer looking for good fishing, swimming, and water skiing in the seemingly countless number of lakes that bejewel the land. Lee Lake is in one of the more rural reaches of the state, lost in the mosaic of lakes, rivers, gravel roads, and small towns that make up northwestern Minnesota.

The campground is a small operation of just seven sites set in a single loop near the lake's eastern shore. Plenty of trees cover the campground and park, providing ample shade and a moderate amount of privacy between sites. Lee Lake is a park as well as a campground, and is used during the day by locals for its swimming pool, camp store, and boat ramp.

Campsites, facilities: There are seven sites for tents and RVs. Picnic tables, fire rings, toilets, showers, and a dump station are provided. A playground, outdoor pool, boat access, and laundry facilities are available. Some facilities are wheelchair accessible. Leashed pets are permitted.

Reservations, fees: Reservations are accepted at 218/937-5306. Sites are $20 per night for tents and $25 per night for RVs. Open from May to late September.

Directions: From Hawley, drive east on Highway 10 for 3.8 miles. Turn right onto 270th Street S. Take the second right, 0.8 mile ahead. The campground is just 0.1 mile ahead on the left side of the gravel road.

Contact: Lee Lake Campground, 218/937-5306.

45 LONG LAKE CAMPGROUND

Scenic rating: 5

west of Detroit Lakes

Minnesota has dozens of Long Lakes, but this lake has one of the better campgrounds. Long Lake Campground, west of Detroit Lakes, focuses on recreation; swimming, boating, and water skiing, along with a playground and a game room, are available to campers. Recreation on the lake is superb, as Long Lake is actually quite long, stretching south from the campground for nearly two miles.

The campground has several wooded sites, but about half of them are in an open field with no shade or privacy. The sites close to the water are nestled a grove of trees and enjoy direct access to the lake. There are several docks here, as well as a large boat ramp and parking area.

Campsites, facilities: There are 81 sites for RVs. Picnic tables, fire rings, toilets, showers, and a dump station are provided. A swimming beach, playground, dock, boat ramp, and camp store are available. Leashed pets are permitted.

Reservations, fees: Reservations are accepted at 218/847-8920. Sites are $30 per night. Open from early May to late September.

Directions: From Detroit Lakes, drive west on Highway 10 for 2.5 miles. Turn left onto W. Long Lake Road. The campground is 0.7 mile ahead on the left just before Cherry Hill Road.

Contact: Long Lake Campground, 218/847-8920.

46 COUNTRY CAMPGROUND

Scenic rating: 5

on Glawe Lake south of Detroit Lakes

Country Campground is on the southern shore of Glawe Lake and is best described as the kind of place perfect for a large family reunion. The campground is nestled between a dozen small lakes next to a large, open grassy field. The recreational facilities here are the real prize: An exercise room, paddleboats, game room, croquet, softball field, and ping pong table are all available for campers at no extra charge.

"Family Style Camping" is what you'll find here—a big, white sign declares so at the campground entrance. The campsites are in three loops adjacent to the open field south of Glawe Lake. The grassy, level sites have no trees and little privacy, but if you are having a family reunion here, you don't need it, right?

Campsites, facilities: There are 30 sites for tents and RVs up to 60 feet; 16 sites are pull-through, and some sites have hookups. Picnic tables, fire rings, toilets, showers, and a dump station are provided. A playground, exercise room, wireless Internet, paddleboats, dock, and game room are available.

Reservations, fees: Reservations are accepted at 218/847-9621. Sites are $28 per night. Open from May to October.

Directions: From Detroit Lakes drive west on W. Lake Drive for 2.2 miles along Detroit Lake. Turn left at Long Bridge Road. In 0.2 mile, take the first right onto Nodaway Drive. The campground is just over 1 mile ahead on the left side of the road.

Contact: Country Campground, 218/847-9621, www.countrycampground.org.

47 CITY OF WOLF LAKE CAMPGROUND
🏊 🛶 🚤 🐕 🚶 🚐 ⛺

Scenic rating: 6

on Wolf Lake

The Wolf Lake campground, in Waterfront Park on the eastern shore of Wolf Lake, is just over a mile from town. The park is a clean, modern facility with excellent camping. This isn't a wilderness experience, by any stretch of the imagination, but it is a nice, quiet spot on the shores of a beautiful northwoods lake with excellent facilities and a swimming beach.

The campsites are sprinkled among the trees and grassy areas between the lake and a gravel road that leads into the park. There are only 14 sites, so privacy and general quiet are a given. The lake has decent fishing, and the affordable rate to pitch a tent here results in a great deal.

Campsites, facilities: There are 14 campsites for tents and RVs. Picnic tables, fire rings, toilets, showers, and a dump station are provided. A swimming beach, boat access, and playground are available. Leashed pets are permitted.

Reservations, fees: Reservations are accepted at 218/538-9500. Sites are $10 per night for tents and $20 per night for RVs. Open from May to mid-October.

Directions: From Wolf Lake, drive west on Highway 36 for 0.5 mile. Turn right onto Wolf Pack Road. Waterfront Park and the campground is 0.6 mile ahead at the end of the road.

Contact: City of Wolf Lake, 218/538-9500.

48 AUSTIN'S SWAMP CAMPGROUND
🏊 🛶 🚤 🐕 🚐 ⛺

Scenic rating: 7

on Girl Lake west of Longville

The abundance of lakes in the Longville area is hard to wrap your mind around if you aren't from the area. An aerial view reveals almost as much land as water, giving relevance to the phrase "Land of 10,000 Lakes," which Minnesotans broadcast so proudly to the rest of the country.

This small park is on the eastern shore of Girl Lake, with a single-loop campground on a small inlet leading into Girl Lake. A boat ramp allows access to Girl Lake and Woman Lake.

Longville is near the Mud Lake and Goose Lake trail systems, just a few miles northwest off County Road 5. Campers can follow hiking and mountain biking trails through the thick pine and hardwood forests that fill the spaces between the myriad lakes sprawled across the landscape.

Campsites, facilities: There are 58 sites for tents and RVs. Picnic tables, fire rings, toilets, showers, and a dump station are provided. Pontoon rental, dock, boat ramp, and swimming beach are available. Leashed pets are permitted.

Reservations, fees: Reservations are accepted at 218/363-2610. Sites are $20 per night. Open from mid-May to October.

Directions: From Longville, drive west on County Road 5 for less than 0.25 mile to Girl Lake. The campground is on the left side of the road.

Contact: Longville Campground, 218/363-2610.

49 BIG SPRINGS RESORT & CAMPGROUND

Scenic rating: 6

on Big Thunder Lake

Thunder Lake has one of the more august names among Minnesota's 10,000 lakes. The Big Springs campground sits on the lake's eastern shore not far from a single, large island. The small campground is a single loop of just 12 sites set in the heavily wooded resort area.

RVers usually fill these sites, as with most resort and campground combinations. Campers will find hiking trails through the pines, a swimming beach, and a boat ramp for recreation on the lake. Water-skiing is popular here on sunny summer days, as is fishing in every season.

Campsites, facilities: There are 12 sites for tents and RVs. Picnic tables, fire rings, toilets, showers, and a dump station are provided. A hiking trail, swimming beach, fishing boat rental and boat ramp, camp store, and playground are available.

Reservations, fees: Reservations are accepted

at 218/566-2322. Sites are $25 per night for tents and $35 per night for RVs. Open from early May to late September.

Directions: From Outing, drive north on Highway 6 for 8 miles. Turn left onto S. Thunder Lake Drive NE. The campground is 1 mile ahead on the right side of the road

Contact: Big Springs Resort, 218/566-2322.

50 BAKER AND WHITE OAK LAKE CAMPGROUND

Scenic rating: 6

along the Moose River ATV trail

In the Land O'Lakes State Forest, there is a small, little-known camping area with just two sites. The primitive sites are next to the Moose River ATV trail, primarily used by campers who come here to link up to the trail. During the weekends, there can be a decent amount of ATV traffic, so I wouldn't recommend coming here for peace and quiet in the summer. Winter is a different story. If the road is plowed, there is complete silence in the forest and there is little traffic on the trails, if any.

The campsites are set in clearings amid the heavy pine, birch, and aspen forest near the Moose River. The mosquitoes can be a nightmare in the early summer, so come prepared or plan to camp later in the season.

Campsites, facilities: There are two sites for tents only. Picnic tables, fire rings, pit toilets are provided. An ATV trail is available. Leashed pets are permitted.

Reservations, fees: Reservations are not accepted. Sites are $12 per night. Self-registration at the campground is required. Open year-round.

Directions: From Outing, drive north on Highway 6 for 7 miles. Turn right onto Draper Tower Forest Road. Follow the road and ATV trail for 3.5 miles to the campsites.

Contact: Land O'Lakes State Forest, 218/833-8710, www.dnr.state.mn.us.

ARROWHEAD AND NORTH SHORE

© JAKE KULJU

BEST CAMPGROUNDS

Canoe-In Campgrounds
Big Fork River Canoe Campsites, **page 59.**
Boundary Waters Canoe Area Wilderness
 (BWCAW), **page 62.**
Hinsdale Island Campground, **page 78.**

Families
Fall Lake Campground, **page 63.**
McKinley Park Campground, **page 79.**

Fishing
Boundary Waters Canoe Area Wilderness
 (BWCAW), **page 62.**

Lakeshore Campgrounds
Boundary Waters Canoe Area Wilderness
 (BWCAW), **page 62.**
Temperance River State Park, **page 82.**
Split Rock Lighthouse State Park, **page 89.**

Tent Camping
Boundary Waters Canoe Area Wilderness
 (BWCAW), **page 62.**
Temperance River State Park, **page 82.**
Tettegouche Lake Superior Cart-In, **page 86.**
Split Rock Lighthouse State Park, **page 89.**

Views
Boundary Waters Canoe Area Wilderness
 (BWCAW), **page 62.**

The Arrowhead region is the Minnesota of our

dreams: the landscape we conjure in our minds when we talk about the
land of 10,000 lakes, the mighty Lake Superior, the endless rivers and
wetlands, the great fishing, and the snowy winter wonderlands that make
camping here so challenging and rewarding.

Lake Superior's north shore is a wilderness of state and national forests,
full of robust trout and salmon streams and rivers, isolated north country
lakes, the Sawtooth range, and dozens of pristine camping opportunities.
It enjoys a rare ability to satisfy both the hard-core camper and the family
on a weekend excursion "up north." One of the best places to experience
the shore is at the mouth of the Cascade River. Cascade River State Park
is close to the charming harbor town of Grand Marais, and it has a wonderful view of Lake Superior and the rushing Cascade River – perfect for
families looking to explore the area near Highway 61. For the backcountry
camper, the Cascade is a 17-mile stretch of undeveloped waterway along
the Superior Hiking Trail, flowing from deep within the Superior National
Forest. Follow the famous trail while camping in the forest, or blaze your
own path through the pristine wilderness, camping wherever you like –
just make sure to bring a compass.

The defining characteristic of this landscape is Lake Superior – Gitchi
Gumi itself. Filled with dense pine and hardwood forests, fields of peat
bogs, river lowlands full of wild blueberries and raspberries, black bear,

whitetail deer, mink, otter, and beaver — it's no wonder that the voyageurs made so many trails, canoe routes, and portages through this rich land. Many of their historic routes are still preserved, not only in the Boundary Waters Canoe Area Wilderness, but in Jay Cooke State Park on the St. Louis River and in several of the chains of lakes south in the Superior National Forest.

People from all over the world are drawn to the mystery and pristine natural quality of the Boundary Waters Canoe Area Wilderness (BWCAW). Its thousands of square miles of undisturbed wilderness, countless clear-water lakes, and miles of canoe portage routes make it one of the most rugged and authentic camping experiences you may ever have.

If you plan on spending much time here, you should also plan on honing your canoeing skills. Minnesota is a canoeing destination for paddlers from all over the world, and the Arrowhead region is the best place to do it. Whether you prefer rapids and white-water–laced rivers or glass-smooth lakes full of loon song, you will find them here in places like Tettegouche State Park, the Cloquet Valley State Forest, and on Lake Superior itself. One of my favorite places to camp is along a short stretch of the Superior Hiking Trail that dips south of Highway 61, following the lakeshore for a little more than a mile. This unofficial camping spot is right on the water and, on clear nights, reflects the moon so brightly that you can walk around by its light.

ARROWHEAD AND NORTH SHORE

ONTARIO

Rainy Lake

Baudette

Fort Frances

2

Birchdale

Rainy River

11

International Falls

4

Voyageurs National Park

5

Kabetogama

Ash River

6

1

Big Bog

3

Grand Falls

MINNESOTA

53

Crane Lake

9

7-8

Superior National Forest

Upper Red Lake

Nett Lake

Nett Lake

BOIS FORTE RESERVATION

Pelican Lake

Orr

Vermilion Lake

71

Northome

Chippewa National Forest

Effie

33

Cook

37

38-39

Tower

169

41

Embarrass

1

34

29-30

31-32

35

36

Biwabik

Aurora

Lake Winnibigoshish

6

38

28

Chisholm

Virginia

Eveleth

16

52

LEECH LAKE

27

Hibbing

7

RESERVATION

2

Deer River

Leech Lake Reservoir

65

Sax

53

Remer

200

Grand Rapids

200

Savanna State Forest

2

169

65

FOND DU LAC RESERVATION

Cloquet

58

Lower Whitefish Lake

371

6

73

59

Pelican Lake

210

McGregor

23

Gull Lake

27

Moose Lake

60

Kerrick

210

Baxter

Garrison

Malmo

35

Mille Lacs Lake

McGrath

Sandstone

WI

Vineland

Isle

27

MINNESOTA

169

© AVALON TRAVEL

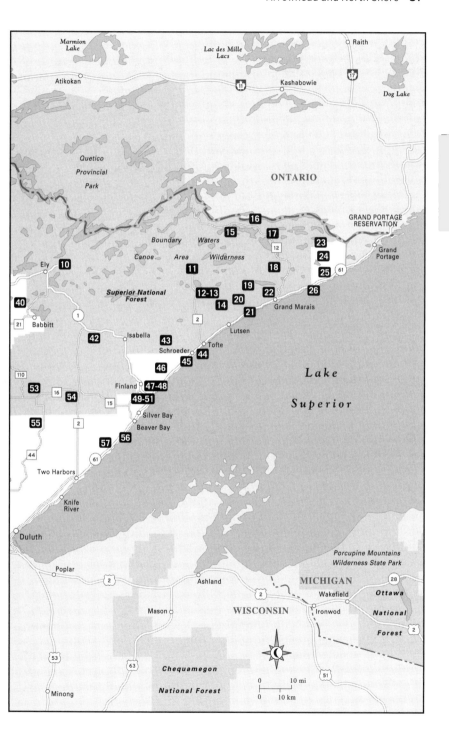

1 BIG BOG CAMPGROUND

Scenic rating: 5

in Big Bog State Recreation Area

The northern interior of Minnesota is full of big, fat, juicy lakes, and Big Bog Campground is right on one. Set on the Tamarac River's west bank near its headwaters on Upper Red Lake's eastern shore, all of the campground's sites are within 100 yards of the water. The campground can also be accessed by boat from the river; mooring docks are available for campers and visitors.

The campground's classic two-loop drive-in design allows for moderate privacy. Lush grassy areas lie in the middle of each loop, while pine and hardwood trees surround the loops and continue throughout the campsites, giving each plenty of shade.

The park is divided into two units: northern and southern. The campground is in the southern unit, but the best recreation is in the northern unit, less than a mile north on Highway 72. There you can visit the largest peat bog in the lower 48 states and hike a mile-long boardwalk through the bog to see the plants and wildlife that live in its interior.

Campsites, facilities: There are 21 tent sites and 26 RV sites with electrical hookups; one pull-through site is available. RV length is restricted to 60 feet. Picnic tables, a boat ramp, drinking water, fish cleaning station, fire rings, showers, and flush and vault toilets are provided. Campsites 6 and 23 and the shower building are wheelchair accessible. Leashed pets are permitted.

Reservations, fees: Reservations are accepted from April 2 to October 31 866/857-2757 or online at www.stayatmnparks.com ($8.50 non-refundable reservation fee) and can be made up to one year in advance. Reservations are not required the rest of the year. Sites are $12–24. Open year-round, with limited facilities in winter.

Directions: From Waskish, take Highway 72 north for approximately 2 miles. Turn right into the campground entrance, marked by a state park sign.

Contact: Big Bog State Recreation Area, 218/647-8592, www.dnr.state.mn.us.

2 FRANZ JEVNE STATE PARK

Scenic rating: 9

in Franz Jevne State Park

Franz Jevne is one of my favorite state parks—its beautiful views of the Rainy River and huge northwoods pine trees are as pristine as Minnesota gets. Despite its name, the Rainy River usually flows beneath blue skies during the summer. Jack pines, birches, and towering white pines deliver a classic northwoods forest complete with whispering breezes and dappled sunlight on cloudless days. A high rock outcropping just south of the campground will interest hikers.

The small, single-loop campground lies between the outcropping and the Rainy River. (Watch for high water in the spring as the shoreline often floods when the river is high.) Sites are spaced several dozen feet apart; the walk-in sites are completely hidden from view from the parking lot.

Hiking and fishing are the key activities along the Rainy River. You can fish from shore or use the boat launch to catch walleye, northern pike, bass, and, if you're lucky, sturgeon. The campground is linked to six miles of hiking trails that follow the river past two sets of rapids and up to the rock outcropping south of the campground.

Campsites, facilities: There are 18 sites for tents and RVs and three walk-in tent-only sites. The RV length limit is 30 feet, and there are only three sites with electrical hookups. (Large RVs cannot be accommodated at this campground.) Vault toilets, picnic tables, drinking water, a picnic area, boat landing, and fire rings are provided. Leashed pets are permitted.

Reservations, fees: Reservations are accepted

from April 2 to October 31 866/857-2757 or online at www.stayatmnparks.com ($8.50 non-refundable reservation fee) and can be made up to one year in advance. Reservations are not required the rest of the year. Sites are $12–24 per night. Open year-round, with limited facilities in winter.

Directions: From Birchdale, take Highway 11 east for 3.2 miles. Turn left on County Road 86. The park entrance is 1.6 miles ahead; follow signs to the campground.

Contact: Zippel Bay State Park, 218/783-6252, www.dnr.state.mn.us.

🔟 BIG FORK RIVER CANOE CAMPSITES
🛶🏊🏕🏠⛺

Scenic rating: 6

in Big Fork State Forest

BEST (

If you are more comfortable carrying a canoe on your shoulders than a backpack and want to dial up the adventure meter to the next notch, plop your paddle in the Big Fork River. Peppered with 11 water-access campsites throughout Big Fork State Forest, the Big Fork River makes for a classy canoe camping trip. This is a great option for canoeists who don't have the time or money to apply for a Boundary Waters Canoe Area Wilderness (BWCAW) permit but still want to access wilderness canoe camps.

The sites are hollowed into the thick forest that surrounds the river, spaced 0.5–2 miles apart. Campsites are rustic, primitive clearings that are irregularly maintained; you may encounter fallen trees or overgrown brush. All sites have ample river access for fishing and beaching canoes. I recommend bringing a well-stocked tackle box, as the Big Fork has snagged many a lure.

The state forest does not provide shuttle service, so you will need two vehicles or someone to pick you up downstream.

Campsites, facilities: There are 11 tent-only sites, five of which are directly on the river. All

sites are accessible only via water. Fire rings, water access, and a picnic table are provided; small wooden signs mark their locations along the water. Leashed pets are permitted.

Reservations, fees: Reservations are not accepted. Sites are first come, first served. There is no fee.

Directions: From Northome, take Highway 1 east for 6 miles. Turn right at the sign for the Big Fork River boat landing. A map of the area is highly recommended.

Contact: Big Fork State Forest, 218/999-7923, www.dnr.state.mn.us.

🔢 ARNOLD'S CAMPGROUND & RV PARK
🛶🏊🏕🏕♿🚐⛺

Scenic rating: 6

in International Falls

Arnold's is smack dab in the middle of International Falls, just 19 blocks south of the Canadian border. If you've ever been to International Falls, you know that the population of pine trees and people is about the same, which makes camping here nicer than you may think.

Arnold's feels like a peaceful park in the middle of the city. The well-spaced campsites are shaded by pine trees that keep traffic noise out. A nearby railroad track can sometimes be a nuisance, but isn't a reason to avoid the campground. The peak of the tourist season fills this campground up regularly in June, July, and August, so it pays to plan ahead if you want to camp here.

Arnold's makes a perfect base camp for enjoying International Falls. Supper clubs, restaurants, Rainy Lake fishing and boating, and of course Canada all lie within a few blocks in all directions. (Note that a passport and/or birth certificate are now required to gain reentry into the United States after visiting Canada.)

However, the location in the middle of town doesn't always deter wildlife from entering the campground. Use the same precautions with food and other belongings that you would in any other campsite.

Campsites, facilities: There are four tent-only sites and 24 RV sites. Electric, sewer, and water hookups are available at all RV sites. Picnic tables, fire rings, laundry facilities, playground, drinking water, shower facilities, and a dumping station are provided. All sites are wheelchair accessible. Leashed pets are permitted.

Reservations, fees: Reservations are accepted. Sites are $20 per day, $100 per week, and $300 per month. Children camp with their parents for free. Open from May 1 to October 31.

Directions: In International Falls, take Highway 11 to turn right on Keenan Avenue. Continue for 1 mile, turning right on Highway 53. The campground is three blocks ahead on the left.

Contact: Arnold's Campground & RV Park, 218/285-9100.

5 WOODENFROG CAMPGROUND

Scenic rating: 8

in Voyageurs National Forest

For a real taste of the north, it's hard to beat Voyageurs National Forest. Located just outside the park's boundary, Woodenfrog Campground occupies a peninsula on the western shore of Lake Kabetogama (say that three times fast!) and is one of two drive-in campsites that border this forest.

The trek up to Voyageurs National Forest is undertaken primarily by campers looking for quiet and solitude, great fishing, and water sports. The campground's abundant white and red pines form a shady cathedral that delivers the secluded northwoods feel unique to northern Minnesota, and every sunset can guarantee a water skier zooming past the beach, creating an almost clichéd postcard-perfect scene.

Angling is the real name of the game on Lake Kabetogama. Just above Echo Bay, boaters and anglers put in at Woodenfrog's boat

access point to catch walleye, trout, and bass. A lakeside hiking trail makes a loop around the entire campground, connecting the fishing dock, picnic area, beach, and boat access. The dense forest and mild temperatures around the lake make for choice hiking.

Although you will enjoy a peaceful camping experience any time you come to Voyageurs National Forest, the peak of the summer sees higher traffic and more crowded camping. Campsites are first come, first served, so make sure to get there early if camping in June, July, or August. Plan on packing some warm clothes, as well; the northern latitude and cold air from the lake can make evenings rather chilly, even during summer.

Campsites, facilities: There are 61 sites for tents and RVs. Large RVs are accommodated at all but three sites. A picnic area and picnic tables, water access and boat landing, swimming, public phone, dock, and two miles of nature trails are provided. Drinking water is available from May to early September. Campsites 43 and 26 are wheelchair accessible. Leashed pets are permitted.

Reservations, fees: Reservations are not accepted. Campers must self-register upon arrival. Sites are $12 per night. Open from May 1 to November 30.

Directions: From Orr take Highway 53 north for 30 miles to County Road 122/Gamma Road. Turn right and follow the signs for 6 miles to the campground.

Contact: Bear Head Lake State Park, 218/365-7229, www.dnr.state.mn.us.

6 ASH RIVER CAMPGROUND

Scenic rating: 7

in Kabetogama State Forest

Ash River Campground hugs the border of Voyageurs National Forest on the outskirts of Kabetogama State Forest. Ten miles south of Woodenfrog, the lake's other campground, the Ash River Campground is set on the headwaters of the Ash River as it exits Lake Kabetogama via Sullivan Bay.

Because the campground is situated at the lake's outlet, anglers have made this a particularly popular fishing spot in summer. During the day, the campground has an abandoned feel—most campers are out on the lake or along the river casting a line. The boat access has a fair amount of traffic on nice days, as boaters, kayakers, and canoeists can gain entry to the Ash River or Sullivan Bay on the lake from the campground's boat ramp.

The smaller of the two campgrounds, Ash River's campsites are heavily wooded with evergreens. The spaces between campsites are carpeted in a thick layer of fallen pine needles that add to the heavy silence of the forest. Camping here is on a first come, first served basis. If you are coming to fish, try to come the day before the weekend, or be ready to get up with the sun to secure your site.

Campsites, facilities: There are nine sites for tents and RVs. Picnic tables, fire rings, drinking water, water access, a dock, and vault toilets are provided. Some facilities are wheelchair accessible. Leashed pets are permitted.

Reservations, fees: Reservations are not accepted. Campers must self-register upon arrival. Sites are $12 per night. Open from May 1 to November 30.

Directions: From Orr, drive north on Hwy 53 for 26 miles to Ash River Road. Turn right and drive another 10 miles to the state forest sign marking the entrance to the campground.

Contact: Bear Head Lake State Park, 218/365-7229, www.dnr.state.mn.us.

⑦ TRAIL'S END CAMPGROUND

🏃 ⛺ 🎣 🚣 🚤 ❄ 🚐 ⛺

Scenic rating: 7

on Echo Lake near Buyck

Trail's End occupies the east shore of Echo Lake, just miles from the Canadian border.

The small campground has sites nestled in the woods, among pine, birch, and aspen trees. They overlook the lake and are serviced by a one-way access road. Trail's End is primarily known as a resort, supper club, and lake lodge; the modest campground is almost an afterthought, making it a quiet, shade-filled and secluded area that is still close to all the action. Near the water, a small wooden dock extends into the lake, setting the stage for watching sunsets. Large glacial rock deposits are scattered throughout the campground, giving the landscape a primal beauty.

A lakeside hiking trail and volleyball court attract regular use in nice weather. Boaters and anglers use the boat ramp and dock in the evenings to enjoy the beautiful scenery of Echo Lake. Things are still hopping here in winter when snowmobilers and cross-country skiers use the resort as a lodge. The Voyageurs Snowmobile Trail passes through the resort, connecting it to the popular Arrowhead Trail.

If traveling up north for a wilderness experience, you would do better to camp in one of the nearby state forests, but for a relaxed, comfortable place on a beautiful lake, Trail's End is the ticket.

Campsites, facilities: There are three tent-only sites and three RV sites. Full-service hookups are available for RVs. A central shower building provides showers, toilets, lavatories, drinking water, and laundry. Water access, swimming, hiking trails, outdoor volleyball, horseshoes, berry-picking, and snowmobile trails are available.

Reservations, fees: Reservations are accepted at 888/844-2257. Sites are $25 per night; a $30 deposit is required. There is a fee of $3 per pet, and $5 per person for more than two people. Open year-round.

Directions: From Buyck, take Crane Lake Road north for 4.3 miles. The campground and resort are on the right at 6310 Crane Lake Road.

Contact: Trail's End Campground, 888/844-2257, www.trails-end-resort.com.

🎟 ECHO LAKE CAMPGROUND
🏃🏊🛶🚣🏕🐕🚴🚐🏕

Scenic rating: 6

on Echo Lake near Ely

On a map, this campground looks like the ideal lakeside getaway. While it is definitely a getaway, it isn't so much lakeside. This single loop campground is near the southern shore of Echo Lake but is on elevated ground among the trees and away from the water. Protected by a thick stand of aspens, this woodsy campground turns its back to Echo Lake. A few sites have views of the water, especially in the early spring and late fall when the trees are leafless.

What it lacks in shoreline, it makes up for in privacy, shade, and activities. A swimming beach, a playground, fishing docks, hiking trails, and an interpretive program make it easy to occupy the whole family. Things can get a bit noisy here during the day, when families take advantage of all the facilities, but camping isn't always about quiet. Folks come here for fun, which any visitor will quickly learn. Campground traffic slows down in the fall, when people searching for quiet autumn hikes and turning leaves can enjoy a calmer atmosphere.

Campsites, facilities: There is one tent-only site and 23 sites for tents or RVs. There are no hookups or pull-through sites. Picnic tables, fire rings, grills, a swimming beach, boat launch, dock, hiking trail, playground, and community restrooms are provided. Quiet hours are 10 P.M.–6 A.M. Firewood is sold at the campground. Campers must use their site on the first night of reservation. Leashed pets are permitted.

Reservations, fees: Reservations must be made at least four days in advance at 877/444-6777. There is a maximum of two vehicles per site. Sites are $10 per night for tents and $20 per night for RVs. Open year-round.

Directions: From Orr, take St. Louis County Road 23 for 16 miles to Buyck. At Buyck, County Road 23 turns into County Road 24; continue on County Road 24 for 4 miles to the Echo Trail. Turn right onto Echo Trail and continue 0.8 mile to the Echo Lake Campground.

Contact: Superior National Forest, LaCroix Ranger District, 218/666-0020, www.fs.fed.us/r9/forests/superior.

🎟 BOUNDARY WATERS CANOE AREA WILDERNESS (BWCAW)
🏃🏊🛶🚣🎿🐕🏕

Scenic rating: 10

in the Superior National Forest along the Canadian border

BEST (

Dominating Minnesota's northeastern border, the Boundary Waters Canoe Area Wilderness is rife with canoe campsites in the deep wilderness area that extends north from Lake Superior to Canada's Quetico Provincial Park. Excellent fishing, quiet camping, and world-class canoeing all combine to make this one of the most legendary camping destinations in the world.

Secluded, primitive, rustic camping defines the BWCAW. Having a canoe, the endurance to carry your gear over mile-long portages, and the willingness to be dozens of miles from civilization are a must when camping here. Campers come to the BWCAW in all seasons, but mostly during summer and early fall when canoe camping is at its height. Motorized boats are not allowed, which has helped keep the BWCAW in pristine condition.

All of the BWCAW's campsites are accessible only by canoe in the summer, and only by snowshoes or skis in winter. Not all campsites and portages are well marked, or even marked at all. Keep a good map handy and scout out any shoreline areas you think might be your destination. It pays to be thorough when searching for unmarked portages and campsites in order to avoid circling the lake searching for an X on the map.

Note: A massive wildfire burned large

sections of the park in 1999, and some burn areas are still restricted.

Campsites, facilities: There are hundreds of primitive canoe-in campsites throughout the BWCAW. Primitive outdoor toilets and fire rings are provided. Campsites have water access, and many are located directly on the water, with room for swimming, fishing, hiking, and snowshoeing. Leashed pets are permitted.

Reservations, fees: Reservations are accepted at 877/550-6777 or online at www.recreation.gov ($10 nonrefundable fee). Sites are $16 per adult and $8 per child per night. Permits are required year-round for all day and overnight visits to the Boundary Waters Canoe Area Wilderness. (Different types of permits and related fees may apply.) From May 1 through September 30 there is a quota on the number of permits issued for each entry point, and reservations are required (a $12 nonrefundable reservation fee per permit is required). Overnight permits require a $32 deposit, regardless of group size.

Directions: The BWCAW permit stations are located in the towns of Grand Marais, Two Harbors, Ely, Chisholm, Tofte, Isabella, Buyck, Crane Lake, Finland, Babbitt, Tower, Beaver Bay, Cook, Aurora, and Duluth. Check the website for detailed directions to the entry point of choice.

Contact: Boundary Waters Canoe Area Wilderness, www.fs.fed.us/r9/forests/superior/bwcaw.

🔟 FALL LAKE CAMPGROUND
🚶 🏊 🛶 🚐 ⛵ 🐕 ♿ 🚍 ⛺

Scenic rating: 9

in Bear Island State Forest

BEST (

Fall Lake is an entry point to the Boundary Waters Canoe Area Wilderness (BWCAW). A small portion of the lake near the campground lies outside of the wilderness area, and traffic at the water access can be a little heavy during summer. Make sure you check out the camping loops before determining whether the campground is too crowded. Most people at the water access are heading into the BWCAW, leaving the quiet aspens of Fall Lake Campground behind. Although close to the lake, these campsites are not on the water.

Three overlapping loops winnow through the aspen forest that surrounds Fall Lake Campground. A paved walkway leads from the campground to the lakeshore and connects the three camping loops and the campground facilities. The Basswood, Lakeview, and Northlights loops spread out more than 60 campsites, keeping the integrity of the woodland and the quiet of the thick forest intact. Head to the Northlights loop for the walk-in-only sites; Basswood and Lakeview are drive-in-only sites for tents and RVs. Brand-new facilities were added in 2005 when the entire campground was renovated, making this a clean, safe, and friendly place to bring your family.

Note: If you venture across the lake or want to explore its shores, you will need a BWCAW permit, which is available by self-issue at the water access.

Campsites, facilities: There are 10 tent-only sites, five RV-only sites, and 51 sites for tents and RVs. All sites except 26, 33, and 41 have electricity available. There are five pull-through sites. Restrooms, showers, flush toilets, a swimming beach, boat ramp, picnic tables, fire grates, tent pads, and drinking water are provided. The camp store sells bait, firewood, and food and rents canoes. Some facilities are wheelchair accessible. Leashed pets are permitted.

Reservations, fees: Sites are $17 per night without hookups and $20–22 per night with electric hookups. One vehicle is permitted; additional vehicles are an additional $7 per night. Up to two vehicles are allowed per site. The maximum stay is 14 days. Open from May 1 to late September.

Directions: From Ely, take Highway 169 east to County Road 18 (Fernberg Road). Travel 4.5 miles to Fall Lake Road. Turn left and continue 1.5 miles to the campground entrance.

Contact: Fall Lake Campground, 218/365-2963, www.camprrm.com/Minnesota campgrounds.htm.

11 SAWBILL LAKE CAMPGROUND

Scenic rating: 8

near Tofte in the Superior National Forest

I always picture Sawbill Lake as the film set for *Land of the Lost.* Its sprawling ferns, glacial boulders, dark water, and heavy vegetation have a prehistoric feel to them. If you look out across the lake with the campground to your back you will see what northern Minnesota has looked like for thousands of years—undisturbed, glacially shaped wilderness.

The campground is a set of two overlapping loops that occupy the eastern shore of the lake, woven into a heavy stand of red and white pines. Although the lake is the main attraction, the campsites do not have water access or even much of a view of the water.

I personally consider this camping area to be a canoeist's paradise. You have the option to enter the BWCAW, or you can keep your paddles on the Superior National Forest side of the border. Sawbill Canoe Outfitters is on the same road that leads to the campground and offers canoe and equipment rentals, firewood, and BWCAW permits.

As at other BWCAW entry points, the lake access traffic often belies the level of campground use. Canoeists may be numerous during the day, but in the late afternoon the campground is often quiet and only half full. If you do decide to venture into the BWCAW while camping at Sawbill, make sure to fill out a self-issued day permit. Even if you don't canoe here, check out the canoe access area; it was a CCC project and is of historical interest.

Campsites, facilities: There are 45 sites for tents and RVs and six tent-only sites. There are no RV hookups. Picnic tables, fire rings and grills, drinking water, dump station, vault toilets, and a non-power-boat landing are provided. Leashed pets are permitted.

Reservations, fees: Reservations are accepted and must be made at least four days in advance at 877/444-6777 or online at www.recreation. gov ($10 nonrefundable fee). Sites are $14 per night. There is a maximum of two vehicles per site. Open from May 10 to October 1.

Directions: From Tofte, take County Route 2 north 22.8 miles to the campground.

Contact: Superior National Forest, Tofte Ranger District, 877/444-6777, www.forestcamping.com.

12 BAKER LAKE CAMPSITES

Scenic rating: 7

on Baker Lake north of Tofte

Baker Lake is used primarily as an entrance point to the Boundary Waters Canoe Area Wilderness. Most campers are in a rush to get their canoes in the water and head across the lake, but there are five nice little rustic sites here that make for good camping, whether you plan on heading into the BWCAW or not.

The campsites are looped along a gravel road through the dense pine forest on the southern shore of the lake. Each site is 100 feet or more away from the others, and all have excellent privacy, shade, and seclusion. Two sites have longer gravel driveways, making them even more private. Small RVs may be able to fit here, but these sites are made for tent camping.

Baker Lake has some undeveloped hiking trails along its shore that lead to fishing spots. There is also a boat ramp for canoes. The lake has excellent walleye, northern pike, and perch fishing. You can often catch your dinner here several nights in a row.

Campsites, facilities: There are five sites for tents only. A boat launch is available. Leashed pets are permitted.

Reservations, fees: Reservations are not accepted. There is no fee. Open year-round.

Directions: From Tofte, drive north on the Sawbill Trail for 17 miles. Turn right onto Forest Road 165 and drive for 5 miles to Forest Road 1272. The campground is 0.6 mile ahead at the end of the road.

Contact: Superior National Forest, Tofte Ranger District, 877/444-6777, www.forest-camping.com/dow/eastern/supcmp.htm.

13 CRESCENT LAKE CAMPGROUND

Scenic rating: 8

in Superior National Forest on Crescent Lake

Another of Arrowhead's small, little-used campgrounds, Crescent Lake is a remote and relatively unknown hideaway deep in the Superior National Forest. As such, it makes for a great weekend spot for fishing or for anyone who needs some fresh air and northwoods nature time.

All of the campsites are on the western side of the lake. Sites are spaced several dozen feet apart and are well shaded by the heavy pine forest. Most have steps leading right down to the water, and almost all have clear views overlooking the lake. Early risers are treated to the natural beauty of the northwoods sunrise across the lake, even though rousing yourself from the soft bed of pine needles below your tent is a challenge.

There is a fishing pier and a place to store trailers near the water. Most campers either fish for walleye, muskie, and northern pike or nap during the day. There is also a short 0.25-mile hiking trail through the woods and along the lakeshore at the foot of the campground.

Campsites, facilities: There are 20 sites for tents and RVs and 12 tent-only sites. There are no hookups or pull-through sites. Campsites 1, 2, 3, 4, and 5 are walk-in sites. Picnic tables, fire rings and grills, drinking water, boat ramp, and vault toilets are provided. Leashed pets are permitted.

Reservations, fees: Reservations are not accepted. Sites are $14 per night. Open from May 10 to October 11.

Directions: From Tofte, take State Route 2 north 16.9 miles to Forest Route 170. Turn right onto Route 170 and head east 6.7 miles to campground sign. At the sign, turn right into the campground.

Contact: Superior National Forest, Tofte Ranger District, 877/444-6777, www.forest-camping.com.

14 CLARA LAKE CAMPSITES

Scenic rating: 8

on Clara Lake north of Lutsen

The Clara Lake campground is an almost forgotten little camping spot. North of Tofte on the Caribou Trail, Clara Lake has just three rustic sites buried in the pine forest surrounding the lake. A boat ramp is about all you will find here. Some footpaths explore the shore of the lake, but this campground is clearly intended for people who want to get as far into the wilderness as they can, but still camp with their car nearby. Unless you plan on spending your time fishing or meditating in the woods, you will find little to do here besides take in the overgrown wilderness of northern Minnesota.

Campsites, facilities: There are three backcountry sites. There is no drinking water, so make sure to bring a water purification system. A boat launch and parking area are available. Leashed pets are permitted.

Reservations, fees: Reservations are not accepted; sites are available on a first come, first served basis. There is no fee.

Directions: From Tofte, drive northeast on Hwy. 61 for 10 miles. Turn left onto Caribou

Trail and drive 8.1 miles to Clara Lake Road. Turn left and continue for 0.7 mile. At 2 Mile Rd., turn right and drive for 2 miles to the end of the road and the campground.

Contact: Superior National Forest, Tofte Ranger District, 877/444-6777, www.forest-camping.com/dow/eastern/supcmp.htm.

15 IRON LAKE CAMPGROUND

Scenic rating: 8

on Iron Lake in the Superior National Forest

The Boundary Waters Canoe Area Wilderness might as well have extended its border the few short miles south it would have taken to include Iron Lake. There is little difference between the deep wilderness of the BWCAW and the deep wilderness of Iron Lake. Located more than 35 miles north of Grand Marais on the Gunflint Trail, Iron Lake is a small, overlooked camping area usually passed over by canoeists hungry for the portages of the BWCAW.

The seven campsites are sprinkled along a patch of the lake's north shore in thick brush. This part of the forest was consumed by wildfire in 2007. Camping is allowed here again, revealing the eager wildflowers, thick underbrush, and young trees that are quickly growing over the charred land. Some fallen trees and burnt snags still stand, so be careful when exploring the forest.

Because it is remote and not well-known as a camping destination, Iron Lake has excellent fishing; walleye and northern pike are particularly abundant. The carry-down boat access makes the lake accessible by canoe, and canoeing around the lakeshore will reveal ripe berry patches. Look for raspberries and wild blueberries in late summer.

Campsites, facilities: There are seven sites for tents and RVs up to 40 feet. Drinking water, vault toilets, a dump station, a carry-down boat access, canoe launch, and picnic tables are provided. Leashed pets permitted.

Reservations, fees: Reservations are accepted at 877/550-6777 or online at www.recreation.gov ($10 nonrefundable fee). Sites are $16 per night. Open year-round.

Directions: From Highway 61, drive north 36 miles on Gunflint Trail (County Road 12), then head east two miles on County Road 92. (Don't turn the first time you see County Road 92; you will turn at the second, west entrance.)

Contact: Iron Lake Campground, 800/280-2267.

16 FLOUR LAKE CAMPGROUND

Scenic rating: 8

on Flour Lake off Clearwater Road

If your family isn't quite ready for a full blown Boundary Waters Canoe Area Wilderness trip, but you still want to experience the remote northwoods, head to Flour Lake. About 30 miles north of Grand Marais, the Flour Lake campground is a little figure-eight loop of 37 campsites on the lake's north shore.

Campsites are not directly on the water, but all sites have lake access via two hiking paths on either end of the figure eight loop. A dense forest of pine and some mixed hardwoods crowds the campground, making each site feel like a little woodsy cathedral scooped out of the trees. Privacy here is excellent; most of the campsites aren't even connected by walking paths and are only linked by the access road.

A short but worthwhile hiking trail leads east from the campground, making a loop past a nearby lodge. At 0.25 mile down the trail, a lookout spot named Honeymoon Bluff offers a view of the treetops and some nearby lakes, giving perspective to the sea of forest that makes up the Arrowhead region. The trail is short but steep; winter campers also use it for a challenging cross-country ski route.

Flour Lake is really a group of several shallow bays, so wildlife is abundant along the water. Moose, beavers, eagles, and loons come to the lakeshore for feeding and nesting, and a pair of binoculars will serve you well. Bass and walleye fishing is decent, but I prefer the lake trout—Flour Lake has some of the best lake trout in the Arrowhead.

Campsites, facilities: There are 30 sites for tents and RVs and seven tent-only sites. There are no hookups or pull-through sites. Picnic tables, fire rings and grills, drinking water, vault toilets, a hiking trail, and a boat ramp are provided. Quiet hours are 10 P.M.–6 A.M. Leashed pets are permitted.

Reservations, fees: Reservations are accepted at 877/550-6777 or online at www.recreation. gov ($10 nonrefundable fee). Sites are $15 per night. Open from the weekend before Memorial Day through September 30.

Directions: From Grand Marais, take State Route 12 north 27 miles to the campground sign. Turn right and continue 2.2 miles to campground.

Contact: Superior National Forest, Gunflint Ranger District, 877/444-6777, www.flour-lakecampground.com.

17 EAST BEARSKIN LAKE CAMPGROUND

🚶 🛶 � 🚤 ❄ 🦌 ♿ 🚐 ⛺

Scenic rating: 8

on East Bearskin Lake in the Superior National Forest

East Bearskin Lake evokes the epic story of the old voyageurs and fur trappers that combed the Arrowhead region centuries ago—you can almost imagine the circumstance under which the lake got its name. Today, East Bearskin Lake is home to a small, quiet campground with fewer than 40 sites.

The campground makes a wide loop on the northwest shore of the lake, big enough to give most campsites their own mini-driveway and making this a very private campground. The lake is never far away, but the sites are surrounded by large pine trees and mixed hardwoods, giving them a deep-woods feel. If you don't have the time or equipment for a full-fledged Boundary Waters Canoe Area Wilderness trip, consider pitching your tent here. The flavor of the northwoods is strong, with thick forests, glacial boulders, and cold, blue water. Some of the campsites even have hike-in access for more of a backcountry experience.

Don't be surprised if the campground isn't as busy as the number of people on the lake would imply. Many locals come here to fish on the edge of the BWCAW, and canoeists often use the water access as an entry point into the wilderness area.

Campsites, facilities: There are 23 sites for tents and RVs and eight tent-only sites. There are no hookups or pull-through sites. RV length is limited to 59 feet. Picnic tables, fire rings and grills, vault toilets, a boat ramp, drinking water, and hiking and ski trails are provided. Some facilities are wheelchair accessible. Leashed pets are permitted.

Reservations, fees: Reservations are accepted at 877/550-6777 or online at www.recreation. gov ($10 nonrefundable fee). Sites are $18 per night. Open from the weekend before Memorial Day through September 30.

Directions: From Grand Marais, take State Route 12 north 26 miles to the campground sign (Forest Route 146). Turn right onto Route 146 and go 1 mile to another campground sign (Forest Route 142). Turn right and proceed to the campground.

Contact: Superior National Forest, Gunflint Ranger District, 877/444-6777, www.forest-camping.com.

18 TWIN LAKES CAMPSITES

🚶 🛶 🛶 🛶 🦌 ⛺

Scenic rating: 8

in Pay Bayle State Forest

The East Twin and West Twin Lakes are glistening northwoods lakes perfect for fishing, swimming, and clearing your mind. Secluded, rustic, and very quiet, these hike-in sites are several hundred feet apart from one another in the enchanting silence of the towering red and white pines that the Superior National Forest is famous for. The nearby lakes have fishing docks, swimming beaches, and undeveloped hiking paths. This campground gives you a real taste of the wildest parts of the Superior National Forest and Boundary Waters Canoe Area Wilderness, without having to fully commit to packing deep into the woods. You can park your car a few hundred feet away, walk in to your secluded rustic site, and let the northwoods work their magic. These sites are rarely used and you will often be the only camper here.

Campsites, facilities: There are three hike-in, tent-only sites. Picnic tables, fire rings, and garbage cans are provided. Swimming/water access and a dock are available. Leashed pets are permitted.

Reservations, fees: Reservations are not accepted. Sites are $12 per night. Open year-round, weather permitting.

Directions: From Grand Marais, drive north on the Gunflint Trail to South Brule Road. Turn left and drive 6 miles to Lima Mountain Road. Turn left again and drive 4 miles to the campground straight ahead.

Contact: Judge C. R. Magney State Park, 218/387-3039, www.dnr.state.mn.us.

19 TWO ISLAND LAKE CAMPGROUND

Scenic rating: 8

in the Superior National Forest

Like Devil Track Lake, Two Island Lake is away from the bustle of summer tourism but close enough to Grand Marais that you can enjoy the concerts, restaurants, and festivals the town hosts throughout the season.

Campsites stretch close to the water in a long loop, giving easy access via a footpath to the lake. Heavy tree cover provides shade throughout the campground. The 37 sites could easily accommodate twice that number, and instead offer a spacious, private feel to each area. The campground is kept particularly tidy and has very clean facilities.

Fishing is the biggest draw of Two Island. Walleye, bass, and northern pike keep anglers busy, but quality hiking and cross-country ski trails also make this lake a northwoods destination.

A more challenging option for canoe campers is to enter the lake on the Twin Lakes Canoe Route. Backcountry canoe-in campsites are available to paddlers who know how to find them or who have a good map. This option gives you more of a Boundary Waters Canoe Area Wilderness experience and eliminates the need for a wilderness permit. A short, four-mile drive west takes you to a footpath leading to Minnesota's highest point: Eagle Mountain. The sweeping view of the northwoods is worth the uphill trek.

Campsites, facilities: There are 26 sites for tents and RVs and 11 tent-only sites. There are no hookups or pull-through sites. Picnic tables, fire rings and grills, drinking water, vault toilets, hiking trails, and a boat ramp are provided. Leashed pets are permitted.

Reservations, fees: Reservations are not accepted. Sites are $15 per night. Open from the weekend before Memorial Day through Labor Day.

Directions: From Grand Marais, take State Route 12 north 3.5 miles to County Route 8. Turn left onto Route 8 and drive 5.6 miles to County Route 27. Turn right onto Route 27 and head 4.2 miles to the campground sign. Turn left into the campground.

Contact: Superior National Forest, Gunflint Ranger District, 877/444-6777, www.forest-camping.com.

20 DEVIL TRACK LAKE CAMPGROUND

Scenic rating: 8

on Devil Track Lake in the Superior National Forest

Grand Marais is a popular tourist town in the summer, and this campground is less than 10 miles away. If you want to do the north shore in style and save a little money at the same time, camping here is a great option. The campground's proximity to Grand Marais and Lake Superior makes it a hot spot.

Devil Track Lake has only 15 campsites, but they fill up fast. (You will need to make reservations at least one month in advance in summer.) Upon entering the campground, you will quickly see why it is such a sought-after spot: The campsites are enormous and are spaced hundreds of feet apart from each other; each site has its own driveway and room for a dozen tents, giving you awesome privacy. Trees separate the campsites, providing a dense forest, but only a small row of trees separates the sites from the lake, giving excellent waterfront views.

Devil Track Lake is good for sailing, water-skiing, and fishing, and you'll likely see all three happening during fair-weather visits. A hiking trail outlines the peninsula and some of the shoreline on either side of it. In the winter, the trail is a popular cross-country skiing spot.

Berry-picking in August is nothing short of divine on Devil Track. Bring a bucket and you will easily pick a pound or two of wild blueberries, raspberries, and blackberries.

Campsites, facilities: There are 14 sites for tents and RVs and one tent-only site. There are no hookups or pull-through sites. Picnic tables, fire rings and grills, drinking water, a swimming area, carry-down boat access, berry-picking areas, and vault toilets are provided. Leashed pets are permitted.

Reservations, fees: Reservations are accepted at 877/550-6777 or online at www.recreation.gov ($10 nonrefundable fee). Sites are $15 per night. Open from the weekend before Memorial Day through September 30.

Directions: From Grand Marais, drive north on the Gunflint Trail for 4 miles to County Road 8. Turn left and drive for 5.7 miles to County Road 57. Turn left and drive 2.7 miles to the campground.

Contact: Superior National Forest, Gunflint Ranger District, 877/444-6777, www.forest-camping.com.

21 CASCADE RIVER STATE PARK

Scenic rating: 10

on the Cascade River in the Superior National Forest

The Cascade River is one of the most appropriately named rivers in the state. Full of bubbling, thrashing waterfalls, foamy rapids, and craggy rock cliffs, this is a must-see for anyone visiting the north shore of Lake Superior.

The campground is less impressive than the river, but does the job. The clustered sites are somewhat crowded together and don't offer much privacy. The hike-in and backcountry sites are another story. Tourists flock to the wildly popular park, but the crowds stay within 0.25 mile of the highway, where the river makes a series of impressive falls and crashes before slipping into Lake Superior. Follow the hiking trails on either side of the river and you will see nary another camper for miles. The trail leaves the park and enters the Superior National Forest and the Superior Hiking Trail, where it links to backcountry and primitive sites that are private and remote.

There isn't much to fish for in this fast-moving, shallow river, but the hiking trails exceed all expectations. Minnesota is a generally flat state, but the Cascade River has peaks, valleys, cliffs, rock walls, and craggy drop-offs that will make your heart race. Park the RV and bring the family to view the falls near the lake, or take a small group of experienced backcountry campers up the foothills of the Sawtooth Range into the Superior National Forest.

Campsites, facilities: There are 40 sites for tents and RVs and five backpacking tent-only sites. RV length is limited to 35 feet, and there are four pull-through sites. Picnic tables, fire rings, and grates, vault and flush toilets, hiking and cross-country ski trails, a warming house, showers, and a dump station are provided. Leashed pets are permitted.

Reservations, fees: Sites are $12–24 per night. Reservations are accepted from April 2 to October 31 866/857-2757 or online at www.stayatmnparks.com ($8.50 non-refundable reservation fee) and can be made up to one year in advance. Reservations are not required the rest of the year. Open year-round, with limited facilities in winter.

Directions: From Grand Marais, drive southwest on Highway 61 for 10 miles. Turn right at the state park sign. Follow the signs to the park office and campground.

Contact: Cascade River State Park, 218/387-3053, www.dnr.state.mn.us.

22 GRAND MARAIS RECREATION AREA

Scenic rating: 5

in Grand Marais on Lake Superior

It might look like a cookie-cutter RV lot at first glance, but the Grand Marais Recreation Area campground isn't half bad. A short walk from downtown, the campground is right off of Highway 61, making trips to the Cascade River, the Gunflint Trail, and other nearby northwoods destinations a cinch.

I won't try to put lipstick on it—this is no wilderness experience. Grand Marais is a summer hot spot with live music nearly every weekend, art shows, a marina full of sailboats, and all manner of merriment. Campers come here to park their RV or pitch a tent so they can be close to the action.

The recreation area has an impressive 300 sites, but it's still a good idea to make reservations because this campground is the first to fill up in the summer. Past the first visible section of RV lots, a wooded hillside and waterfront area provide more private sites for tent camping. There are few to no trees, not much shade, and pretty crowded quarters, but if you want a convenient place close to town without shelling out for a hotel room, this is just the ticket.

Campsites, facilities: There are 256 sites for RVs and 44 tent-only sites. There are 152 RV sites with full water, sewer, and electric hookups; 104 RV sites have electric and water hookups. Picnic tables, fire rings and grills, a playground, a picnic area, pavilion, playground, public boat launch, and docks are provided. An indoor swimming pool, children's pool, Jacuzzi, flush toilets, dump station, showers, and sauna are also available. Some facilities are wheelchair accessible. Leashed pets are permitted.

Reservations, fees: Reservations are accepted at 800/998-0959 and are suggested for summer weekends. A $5 nonrefundable fee and a $20 deposit are required at the time of reservation. Sites are $23–40. Peak rates are July, August, and September; off-peak rates are May, June, and October. Open from May 1 to mid-October; the water is turned off from mid-October until May 1.

Directions: The park is in Grand Marais off Highway 61 (the North Shore Scenic Byway), on the right as you enter town (8th Avenue W), 110 miles from Duluth.

Contact: Grand Marais Recreation Area, 800/998-0959, www.grandmaraisrecreation-area.com.

23 DEVIL FISH LAKE CAMPGROUND

Scenic rating: 8

north of Hovland

Diamond in the rough, needle in the haystack, whatever you want to call it, Devil Fish Lake has that *je ne sais quoi* that only small Arrowhead region lakes have.

There are only five campsites here, strung along a single loop on the lake's south shore. The heavy woodlands give way to a small savanna-like clearing along the camping loop, giving this campground a breezy, sunshiney feel—which is nice considering it can be chilly up here in the Sawtooth range, even in the middle of summer. The sites are about 50 feet apart and enjoy large tent pad areas for several campers to spread out on. Each site has a short gravel driveway and is within walking distance of the lake.

Campsites, facilities: There are five sites for tents and RVs. Picnic tables, fire rings and grills, a vault toilet, water access, a boat ramp, and a dock are provided. Leashed pets are permitted.

Reservations, fees: Reservations are not accepted. Self-registration is required at the campground. Sites are $12 per night. Open year-round.

Directions: From Hovland, drive north on the Arrowhead Trail for 2.5 miles. Turn left onto Tower Road. In 1 mile turn right onto Tom Lake Road. Drive for 9.3 miles to Esther Lake Road. Turn left and drive 2.8 miles to the campground entrance on the right side of the road.

Contact: Grand Portage State Forest, 218/387-3039, www.dnr.state.mn.us.

24 ESTHER LAKE CAMPGROUND

Scenic rating: 7

south of Devil Fish Lake in Grand Portage State Forest

Esther Lake is one of my favorite spots when I really want seclusion but just don't feel like hiking in to get it. This little lake is nearly 20 miles away from the nearest town, and with only three sites the campground is never busy. The road in leads right to a boat access for canoeing, fishing, and swimming (if you like cold water), and the tightly knit forest makes the rest of the world just a memory.

Camping here is primitive. The fittingly small, three-site campground provides only the barest of bare necessities: Each site has a picnic table and fire ring. You'll need to bring drinking water or a water filtration system, toilet paper, and a spade for burying waste.

Campsites, facilities: There are three sites for tents and RVs. Picnic tables, fire rings, and grills, water access, a boat ramp, and a dock are provided. Leashed pets are permitted.

Reservations, fees: Reservations are not accepted. Sites are first come, first served. Sites are $12 per night. Open from May to October.

Directions: From Hovland, take the Arrowhead Trail (north) 11 miles to Esther Lake Road. Head left (west) 7 miles to Esther Lake.

Contact: Grand Portage State Forest, 218/387-3039, www.dnr.state.mn.us.

25 JUDGE C. R. MAGNEY STATE PARK

Scenic rating: 9

northeast of Grand Marais

Thank you, Judge Magney, from the bottom of my heart. You had the vision and ambition to protect and make available the wilds of the Lake Superior's north shore.

Judge Magney is no longer with us, but his legacy is. The former Minnesota state supreme court justice and Duluth mayor was a big fan of state parks. He aided in establishing 11 state parks and waysides along Lake Superior in the 1930s, including what became a memorial to him: Judge C. R. Magney State Park.

The park has the authentic quality of the Lake Superior National Forest and is a prime example of rugged northwoods charm. Although the park is divine, there is nothing special about the campground. A figure-eight campground loop sits just across the park road from the churning Brule River. The sites have some trees for privacy and aren't too crowded, but most of the park's charm lies outside of the campground along the Brule River.

The river has excellent fishing in spring and fall when the salmon are running. I like to fish, but my favorite feature of the Brule is Devil's Kettle, a massive, deep-wrought pool that lies below one of the many waterfalls cascading toward Lake Superior. Local legend says the kettle has no bottom, though I don't think anyone is willing to find out if it does or not. The fast-moving water is not for swimming.

Hiking trails along the river will treat you to waterfall views and bird-watching opportunities. In fall, hawks gather to migrate along this part of Lake Superior's shore. Seeing one hawk is always fun, but a cast of hawks is a real treat!

Campsites, facilities: There are 27 sites for tents and RVs. RV length is restricted to 45 feet. Picnic tables, fire rings and grills, showers, flush and vault toilets, and drinking water are provided. Hiking and snowshoeing trails run throughout the park. Leashed pets are permitted.

Reservations, fees: Sites are $12–24 per night. Reservations are accepted from April 2 to October 31 866/857-2757 or online at www.stayatmnparks.com ($8.50 non-refundable reservation fee) and can be made up to one year

in advance. Reservations are not required the rest of the year. Open from Memorial weekend through Labor Day (winter camping is not allowed at this park).

Directions: From Grand Marais, drive northeast on Highway 61 for 14 miles to the park entrance on the left side of the road.

Contact: Judge C. R. Magney State Park, 218/387-3039, www.dnr.state.mn.us.

26 SUPERIOR HIKING TRAIL LAKE WALK-IN

Scenic rating: 10

south of Hovland

The Superior Hiking Trail, known for its access to remote camping, stretches nearly 240 miles along the shore of mighty Lake Superior. Only one of those miles dips down to the lakeshore—luckily, this small stretch makes for some of the best camping on the entire trail.

The beachfront location is especially popular in summer and sits adjacent to a cusp of birch and pine trees filling the narrow area between the water and the highway. The campground is easily accessible from the highway, yet despite its proximity to the road, the lapping of Superior's waves provides a peaceful and pleasant soundscape that muffles nearby traffic. The primitive sites are situated fairly close together but enjoy a privacy created by the trees and undergrowth. Campfires and conversation from other campers will more than likely reach you after sunset, but the stunning view, especially on moonlit nights, is worth the crowd.

Campsites are nearly always full in the summer and early fall. For a good spot during those seasons, arrive mid-morning when campers from the night before are just leaving to hike the trail or head into town.

The cool water of the lake holds nighttime temperatures at bay during summer. With the right equipment, lake fishing beyond the breakers can be fruitful. If you get the itch to stretch your legs, you are in the middle of the state's longest hiking trail, spanning for days to the southwest and northeast.

Campsites, facilities: There are 10 tent-only sites. Fire rings are provided. There is no drinking water. Leashed pets are permitted.

Reservations, fees: Reservations are not accepted; sites are first come, first served. There is no fee. Open year-round.

Directions: From Grand Marais, drive northeast on Highway 61 for 10.5 miles toward Hovland. At County Road 14 turn right. The small dirt road cuts west to a small parking lot behind a row of a trees near the water.

Contact: Superior Hiking Trail Association, 218/834-2700, www.shta.org.

27 COTTONWOOD LAKE CAMPGROUND

Scenic rating: 4

north of Deer River in Bowstring State Forest

North of the small town of Deer River, Cottonwood Lake doesn't see much traffic. It is a camping area for just that: camping. The no-nonsense campground is made up of one loop on the southern shore of this tiny lake. You can catch a few sunfish in the shallow lake or cool off in the water, but don't expect much more than that.

Cottonwood Lake is a good place to bring the kids, a few fishing rods, and a picnic lunch for a simple summer afternoon. It's an adequate place for an overnight camping trip if you require a picturesque view.

Campsites, facilities: There are 10 sites for tents and RVs. Pull-through sites are available. Picnic tables, fire rings and grills, and a boat ramp are provided. Leashed pets are permitted.

Reservations, fees: Reservations are not accepted. Self-registration is required at the campground. Sites are $12 per night. Open year-round.

Directions: From Deer River, take Highway 6 north 4 miles to County Road 19. Turn right (east) and continue for 3 miles. Turn left (north) on County Road 48 for 1.5 miles then turn right (east) on County Road 160 and follow the signs on the left for 2.5 miles.

Contact: Hill Annex Mine State Park, 218/247-7215, www.dnr.state.mn.us.

28 CLUBHOUSE LAKE CAMPGROUND

Scenic rating: 7

east of Marcell in Chippewa National Forest

Red pine, red pine, red pine! Clubhouse Lake is surrounded by a pristine red pine forest. The whispering breeze, filtered sunlight, and soft, sound-absorbing pine needles create a cathedral-like quality here. The feeling of seclusion and the sweet smell of pine evoke a sense of a Minnesota long ago.

Sites are laid along a double loop that slices right through the pines. The tall pines with their upper branches and narrow trunks provide plenty of shade, but the openness under the canopy doesn't give a lot of privacy. The sites are spaced well enough apart that you won't be bumping elbows with your neighbors, but you'll definitely see them.

The Clubhouse Lake Campground is a simple, peaceful one. The view of the lake through the pines, the shady tree canopy, and the rustic setting provide a great place to relax, read a book, and leave the workaday world behind.

Campsites, facilities: There are 47 sites for tents and RVs. Picnic tables, fire rings and grills, drinking water, a sandy swimming beach, hiking trails, a playground, water access, and vault toilets are provided. Site 9 is wheelchair accessible. Leashed pets are permitted.

Reservations, fees: Reservations are accepted up to 240 days in advance at 877/444-6777 or online at www.recreation.gov ($10 nonrefundable fee). Sites are $16 per night. Open from May 1 to October 14.

Directions: From Marcell, drive east on County Road 45 for 5 miles. Turn left on Forest Road 2181 and drive for 3 miles to the campground entrance straight ahead.

Contact: Chippewa National Forest, 218/246-2123, www.fs.fed.us/r9/forests/chippewa/recreation/camping/marcell.php.

29 CHASE POINT CAMPGROUND

Scenic rating: 7

in Scenic State Park

Remember those scenic 1970s Minnesota postcards your great-aunt Mabel sent when you were a kid? Chances are they were all taken at Scenic State Park, one of Minnesota's most picturesque parks.

Stands of massive virgin red and white pines tower over sky-blue lakes. Amidst the glory is Chase Point Campground, set atop a hill above Coon Lake. The view from the hill is best, but if you want to get your feet wet, steps leads to the water and a boardwalk by the lake.

Scenic State Park is a good place to camp if you are an outdoorsperson who plans on spending most of your time on the trail, on the lake, or among the pines. The campground layout is a bit crowded, set in a grid pattern that was made for sleeping, not lounging in the shade. Although giant, century-old pine trees surround the lake, the campground itself is not very shaded.

Six lakes in the park are connected by hiking trails and park roads and have protected pine shorelands. They are also worth fishing. Walleye, northern pike, sunfish, and smallmouth bass linger in the shade pools created by the trees.

Campsites, facilities: There are 69 sites for tents and RVs and two backpacking tent-only sites. Electric hookups are available at 20 campsites. RV length is restricted to 50 feet. Picnic tables, fire rings and grills, drinking water, vault toilets, flush toilets, docks, water access, showers, and a dump station are provided. Backpacking sites have an unenclosed wilderness toilet and no drinking water. Campsite 26e is wheelchair accessible. Leashed pets are permitted.

Reservations, fees: Reservations are accepted from April 2 to October 31 866/857-2757 or online at www.stayatmnparks.com ($8.50 non-refundable reservation fee) and can be made up to one year in advance. Reservations are not required the rest of the year. Sites are $12–24 per night. Open year-round, with winter camping allowed at the 20 electric sites.

Directions: From Bigfork drive 7 miles east on County Road 7. Follow signs to the campground.

Contact: Scenic State Park, 218/743-3362, www.dnr.state.mn.us.

30 SCENIC STATE PARK CANOE CAMPSITES

Scenic rating: 8

in Scenic State Park

If you want to camp in Minnesota as it looked more than 200 years ago, point your bow toward these canoe campsites. The sites on Coon and Sandwick Lakes in Scenic State Park are set amid towering stands of virgin red and white pine trees that were growing here long before Minnesota became a state.

The campsites offer a primitive, rustic camping experience. Behemoth trees and sparkling lakes can be viewed from throughout the park, but these canoe campsites bring them to your feet, giving you more of a wilderness camping experience than the crowded campground on Coon Lake. Bring a water filtration system and toilet paper—there is no running water or electricity, and only wilderness toilets are provided.

You can access the sites from both Coon and Sandwick Lakes. You can also hike in to four of the sites; from the parking area, it makes for a 2.5-mile hike.

Campsites, facilities: There are five tent-only canoe-accessible sites. Drinking water is not provided. Wilderness toilets, picnic tables, and fire rings with grills are provided. Leashed pets are permitted.

Reservations, fees: Reservations are accepted from April 2 to October 31 866/857-2757 or online at www.stayatmnparks.com ($8.50 non-refundable reservation fee) and can be made up to one year in advance. Reservations are not required the rest of the year. Sites are $12–24 per night.

Directions: From Bigfork drive 7 miles east on County Road 7. Follow signs to the campground.

Contact: Scenic State Park, 218/743-3362, www.dnr.state.mn.us.

31 LOST LAKE FOREST CAMPGROUND

🚶 🛶 🎣 🐕 ♿ 🚐 ⛺

Scenic rating: 7

south of Bigfork in George Washington Forest

The Lost Lake Forest Campground is another state forest campground with huge, private campsites. Each of the 15 sites has its own driveway, a large clearing in the trees, and plenty of room for tents and RVs.

Hugging the southern shore of Lost Lake, the campground is heavily wooded on the western end, where the campsites have the added privacy of dense trees that gradually give way to sparser tree cover to the east. A fishing pier extends into the lake in the middle of the southern shore right off the campground, and the road has a spur to the east that leads to a boat ramp.

There are no established hiking trails, but there are footpaths that explore much of the lakeshore. The Herb Brandstrom All-Terrain Vehicle (ATV) Trail runs north and south about one mile to the west of Lost Lake and gives you access to dozens of miles of off-road trails. Fishing in Lost Lake is worthwhile; you can almost always catch a few pike or sunfish for dinner.

Campsites, facilities: There are 15 sites for tents and RVs. Picnic tables, fire rings and grills, vault toilets, drinking water, and water access are provided. There is one wheelchair-accessible site. Leashed pets are permitted.

Reservations, fees: Reservations are not accepted. Sites are $12 per night. Open year-round.

Directions: From Bigfork, take Scenic Highway/County Road 7 southeast 10 miles to County Road 340. Turn left (east) and drive about 7 miles to County Road 52. Then turn left (northeast) and follow the signs 2 miles to the campground.

Contact: Scenic State Park, 218/743-3362, www.dnr.state.mn.us.

32 OWEN LAKE FOREST CAMPGROUND

🏊 🛶 🎣 🐕 ♿ 🚐 ⛺

Scenic rating: 7

south of Bigfork in George Washington Forest

Owen Lake has one of the funkiest shapes I've ever seen; its bends and curves make it look more like a section of a wide river than a lake. Alternately surrounded by thick forests and swamps, the campground occupies a small peninsula that juts into the western end of the water.

As at other state forest campgrounds in this area, the campsites are large, private, and woodsy. The entire peninsula is covered in a thick forest of pine and hardwood, and although water surrounds you on both sides, you won't likely see it from your campsite.

Walking to the lake is no problem, though. There are no established hiking trails here, but there are well-worn footpaths that outline the entire peninsula near the water. There is no fishing pier, but there is a boat access about 0.5 mile south of the campground, and there are sufficient open areas along the shore to cast a line or go for a swim.

Campsites, facilities: There are 20 sites for tents or RVs and one walk-in tent-only site. Picnic tables, fire rings and grills, vault toilets, drinking water, and a swimming area are provided. Some facilities are wheelchair accessible. Leashed pets are permitted.

Reservations, fees: Reservations are not accepted. Sites are $12 per night. Open year-round.

Directions: From Bigfork, take Scenic Highway/County Road 7 southeast for 10 miles to County Road 340. Turn left and drive 7 miles to County Road 52. Turn left and follow the signs 2 miles to Owen Lake Campground Road, which leads directly to the campground.

Contact: Scenic State Park, 218/743-3362, http://www.dnr.state.mn.us/state_forests.

only limited facilities and no hookups, but the payoff is that hardly anyone ever camps here. Every time I have been to this campground I have been the only one there, without anyone even passing through.

There are no established hiking trails, but the tranquility of the water and the silent, spacious campground are worth the trip if you are just looking for a place to kick back and relax.

Campsites, facilities: There are 12 sites for tents and RVs and two walk-in tent-only sites. There are no hookups. Picnic tables, fire rings and grills, vault toilets, and drinking water are provided. Playground, fishing pier and swimming beach are available. There is one wheelchair-accessible site. Leashed pets are permitted.

Reservations, fees: Reservations are not accepted. Sites are $12 per night. Open year-round.

Directions: From Togo, take Highway 1 west for 4.5 miles. Turn right on Forest Road 542 and drive for 4 miles to the campground.

Contact: McCarthy Beach State Park, 218/254-7979, www.dnr.state.mn.us.

33 BUTTONBOX LAKE CAMPGROUND

Scenic rating: 7

west of Togo in George Washington Forest

Buttonbox Lake lies deep in the George Washington State Forest. It is a small, secluded campground with only 14 sites, not far from the Circle T All-Terrain Vehicle (ATV) Trail. If you aren't into off-road vehicles, don't fret. The trail passes far enough to the north that you will not be disturbed.

Some ATV riders camp at Buttonbox, but most head to the larger, more accommodating Thistledew Campground a few miles southeast of Buttonbox Lake. Buttonbox Lake is valuable for how unappreciated it is. There are

34 THISTLEDEW CAMPGROUND

Scenic rating: 6

west of Togo in George Washington Forest

Thistledew Lake lies at the end of a narrow country gravel road, almost halfway between Scenic and McCarthy Beach State Parks. The very definition of "off the beaten path," this quiet little lake is surrounded by whispering pine and maple trees.

Thistledew Lake is used more by local anglers than it is by campers, but the facilities are surprisingly well kept. Sites are shaded, roomy, and linked to a hiking trail that explores part of the lakeshore. The swimming beach isn't postcard perfect, but the lake is easily accessible and is good for swimming on a hot day.

Unlike most other campgrounds in the state, Thistledew is used more for winter camping than summer camping. A popular snowmobile trail passes right by the campground and provides an overnight stop for many a sled jockey.

Campsites, facilities: There are 21 sites for tents and RVs. Picnic tables, fire rings and grills, drinking water, vault toilets, a groomed snowmobile and cross-country ski trail, a dock, a swimming beach, boat ramp, and waste station are provided. Two campsites are wheelchair accessible. Leashed pets are permitted.

Reservations, fees: Reservations are not accepted. Sites are $12 per night. In winter, a ski pass is required for cross-country skiers. Open year-round.

Directions: From Togo, take Highway 1 west 4.5 miles. Turn left on Thistledew Road and continue for 0.5 mile. Turn left again on County Road 551 and drive 1.25 miles to the campground.

Contact: McCarthy Beach State Park, 218/254-7979, www.dnr.state.mn.us.

35 BEATRICE LAKE CAMPGROUND

Scenic rating: 8

in McCarthy Beach State Park, George Washington Forest

People come from all around to enjoy the sandy beaches at McCarthy Beach State Park, but there is another option for those looking for a more laid-back camping experience. The Beatrice Lake campground is an overflow camping area that is rarely used except on extremely busy summer weekends. If you would rather wander through pine tree forests than bury your toes in the sand, come to this secluded campground to avoid the crowds.

Sites are arranged in a single loop that circumnavigates a chunky peninsula jutting into Beatrice Lake. The rustic sites are several dozen feet apart, enveloped in birch and red pine trees; many have more birches than pines, allowing underbrush to grow under the forest canopy and giving these sites a more private enclosure.

The narrow road that leads to this campground is a particular treat. The path is lined with stately red pines and has a boulevard full of red pines running down the middle. The shady drive is a majestic way to enter this quiet campground.

Campsites, facilities: There are 27 sites for tents and RVs and three walk-in tent-only sites. Picnic tables, fire rings and grills, vault toilets, and hand pumps for water are provided. A boat landing is nearby. Hiking, biking, cross-country skiing, and snowmobile trails run throughout the park. Leashed pets are permitted.

Reservations, fees: Reservations are accepted from April 2 to October 31 866/857-2757 or online at www.stayatmnparks.com ($8.50 non-refundable reservation fee) and can be made up to one year in advance. Reservations are not required the rest of the year. Sites are $12–24 per night.

Directions: From Hibbing, drive north on Highway 169 for 4.1 miles to County Road 5. Turn left and drive 15.4 miles to McCarthy Beach Road. Take another left into the park and drive 1.4 miles to the campground.

Contact: McCarthy Beach State Park, 218/254-7979, www.dnr.state.mn.us.

36 SIDE LAKE CAMPGROUND

Scenic rating: 7

in McCarthy Beach State Park, George Washington Forest

How many campgrounds put you within a few dozen yards of two stately northwoods lakes? Add the Side Lake Campground to that list.

With the wide, sand beach of Sturgeon Lake to the west and the woodsy fishing waters of Side Lake to the east, this is one of the better campgrounds in the region for hiking, swimming, and fishing.

Located on an isthmus of land between Sturgeon and Side Lakes, the Side Lake Campground rations nearly 60 sites into three loops. While 60 sites may seem like a lot, the three loops are separated by several hundred feet, giving each loop a small campground feel. The campground is connected to a system of hiking and mountain biking trails that follow the pine ridges rising between the chain of lakes that make up the park.

Cross the road to Sturgeon Lake to go swimming on the impressively large, sandy beach. Full of soft white sand, McCarthy Beach State Park's beaches are frequently lauded by national magazines. If you want to get away to the coast but "keep it local," camp here and enjoy beaches unlike any others in the state.

Each lake has a boat launch and fishing pier. I recommend fishing in Side Lake, as there are fewer people and usually better catches. Sturgeon Lake also has more water skiers, motorboats, and swimmers, making fishing a bit more difficult.

Note: The Side Lake Campground has narrow roads and may not be suitable for some large motor homes. In addition, sites 4e, 7e, 20, 22, 23, 31, 32, 34, 35, 39, 40, 41, 42, 45, 49, and 51 have a sharp turning radius.

Campsites, facilities: There are 57 sites for tents and RVs. There are 18 RV sites with electric hookups. RV length is restricted to 45 feet. Picnic tables, fire rings and grills, drinking water, flush and vault toilets, showers, a fishing pier, playground, swimming beach and changing room, fish cleaning station, boat landing, and dump station are provided. Hiking, biking, cross-country skiing and snowmobile trails run throughout the park. Leashed pets are permitted.

Reservations, fees: Reservations are accepted from April 2 to October 31 866/857-2757 or online at www.stayatmnparks.com ($8.50 non-refundable reservation fee) and can be made up to one year in advance. Reservations are not required the rest of the year. Sites are $12–24 per night. Open year-round.

Directions: From Hibbing, drive north on Highway 169 for 4.1 miles to County Road 5. Turn left and drive 15.4 miles to McCarthy Beach Road. Take another left into the park and drive 1.4 miles to the campground.

Contact: McCarthy Beach State Park, 218/254-7979, www.dnr.state.mn.us.

37 HINSDALE ISLAND CAMPGROUND

Scenic rating: 8

in Kabetogama State Forest

BEST (

Lake Vermillion is a steely blue lake known for choppy waters, rocky shores, and primal beauty. The campsites on Hinsdale Island on Lake Vermillion are not for the faint of heart or weak of paddle. The rapacious lake can be an intimidating body of water, but the camping that awaits you is well worth the journey.

Camping means boating—these are water-access-only sites that require a canoe and a strong set of arms, or a boat with an outboard motor. The Hinsdale Island sites are beautiful, shaded shoreline campsites that are valued for their peace and quiet, excellent fishing, and primitive seclusion. Even with all sites occupied you are unlikely to see or hear other campers. The tall pines, soft forest floor, and regular breeze give Hinsdale Island an "edge of the world" quality.

You'll need an accurate map of the lake and the islands, as these first come, first served campsites are not well marked. Boat and canoe landings are the most visible signs from the water. Although you can secure your watercraft at these landings, make sure to bring sturdy rope because winds and high water can sweep your boat away.

Lake Vermillion's weather can be volatile—

and whatever is happening on the water is also happening on Hinsdale Island. Make sure to pack warm clothes, even in summer, as nighttime temperatures can be surprisingly chilly. Rain gear is another must, as are personal floatation devices.

Campsites, facilities: There are 11 primitive boat-in-only sites. Vault toilets, water access, swimming areas, and fire rings are provided. Leashed pets are permitted.

Reservations, fees: Reservations are not accepted. Campers must self-register upon arrival. There is no fee. Open from May 1 to November 30.

Directions: From Cook, drive north on County Road 24 for 3 miles to County Road 78. Turn right and drive 5.2 miles to County Road 540. Continue east for 4.3 miles to the public access at Timbuktu Marine.

Contact: Soudan Underground Mine State Park, 218/753-2245, www.dnr.state.mn.us.

38 HOODOO POINT CAMPGROUND

🧍 🚴 🏊 ⛏ 🚤 ⚓ 🐕 🚐 ⛺

Scenic rating: 6

north of Tower

Proximity to an airport probably isn't on the top of your northwoods campground checklist, but hear me out. Hoodoo Point is home to a 3,400-foot paved seaplane runway that draws some of the goofiest looking and most interesting planes in the country. The campground is a safe distance from the airstrip and offers an excellent vantage point for watching the crazy seaplanes come in from area lakes. Seaplane tours of the area are also available, which will give you a new and profound appreciation for the depth and breadth of the northwoods.

The campsites are wooded and set on a narrow peninsula that extends into one of Lake Vermillion's bays. A good number of sites have direct water access and are near the boat and fishing dock. The airport can create

a distracting amount of noise during the day, but chances are if you decide to camp here, you'll be interested in watching the planes come in. Nights are peaceful and quiet, just like at most other campgrounds in the area.

Campsites, facilities: There are 81 sites for RVs and 18 tent-only sites. Full RV hookups and pull-through sites are available. Picnic tables, fire rings and grills, flush toilets, showers, laundry, docks, mooring buoys, and a dump station are provided. Leashed pets are permitted.

Reservations, fees: Reservations are accepted at 218/753-6868 and must be made at least two days before visit. Sites are $18–32 per night. Open from mid-May to late October.

Directions: From Virginia, drive north on Highway 169 to the city of Tower. Take a left on Cedar Street for two blocks. Take a left on N. 3rd Street (turns into Hoodoo Point Road) and go about 1 mile. Follow signs to the campground on the left.

Contact: Hoodoo Point Campground, 218/753-6868, www.hoodoopoint.com.

39 MCKINLEY PARK CAMPGROUND

🧍 🚴 🏊 ⛏ 🚤 ⚓ 🐕 🏇 🚐 ⛺

Scenic rating: 8

on Lake Vermillion near Soudan

BEST (

Just a hop, skip, and a jump away from popular Soudan Underground Mine State Park, McKinley Park Campground is a family vacationing hot spot on the scenic southern shore of Lake Vermillion.

The campground is decked out with a playground, public beach, dock, boat landing, and even a fish cleaning station, so the summer months here are full of activity. The amazing sunsets from McKinley Park are the cherry on top. The campground lies on the eastern end of the lake, setting the stage for colorful evening skies and a deep orange setting sun. I would camp here just for the sunsets—and I have.

Hiking trails and the shoreline pass through

the pine forests of Lake Vermillion, but campsites are in a grassy, open area with only moderate privacy. Two walk-in campsites are available, but this is primarily a car and RV camping destination. Although comfortable, this campground is very active and a bit noisy during the height of the summer camping season. Expect campground neighbors almost anytime during the season. Bring your fishing rod, swimsuit, and barbecue grill—and expect everyone else to do the same.

Campsites, facilities: There are 15 tent-only sites and 50 RV sites. RV sites have electrical hookups; some pull-through sites are available. Picnic tables, drinking water, flush toilets, laundry facilities, a boat launch, docks, hiking and biking trails, a playground, dump station, fire rings, and showers are provided. Leashed pets are permitted.

Reservations, fees: Reservations are accepted at 218/753-5921. Sites are $25 per night for non-electric sites and $38 for electric sites. Rates are based on four people per site; there is a fee of $5 per each additional person over four per night. There is a two-night minimum on weekends and a three-night minimum on holiday weekends. Open from May 1 to September 30.

Directions: From Tower, drive 1 mile east on Highway 169. Turn left when you come to the Welcome to Soudan sign, then turn left again on McKinley Park Road in 0.1 mile. Drive 1.5 miles ahead to the campground.

Contact: McKinley Park Campground, 218/753-5921, www.mckinleypark.net.

40 BEAR HEAD LAKE STATE PARK

Scenic rating: 8

in Bear Head Lake State Park

Located near the Boundary Waters Canoe Area Wilderness (BWCAW), and just two hours north of Duluth, Bear Head Lake State Park is the "last call" for car camping before the thick wilderness to the north requires canoe- and backcountry-only camping. The campground is on pristine Bear Head Lake among the swaying red pine trees that dominate the Arrowhead Region.

Just below North Bay, the campground offers shaded, well-spaced sites along two wooded loops that maintains the private, hideaway feel campers seek in the northwoods. Its proximity to the BWCAW is apparent in the similarly isolated wilderness quality the areas share.

Encounters with wildlife are more the norm than the exception. Eagles nest in the tops of dead pines along the shores of the lake, raccoons regularly patrol the campsites, and sightings of moose, wolf, and black bear are not rare. A full, thriving forest of white and red pine, birch, aspen, and fir trees provides beautiful, wooded hiking trails.

Miles of shoreline lay in wait for you to explore by canoe, and catching fish is a near guarantee. Walleye, bass, crappie, and trout fill Bear Head Lake and make for excellent shore lunch. The campground area has a picnic and shelter building, a swimming beach, and the park's trails connect to the Taconite State Trail where snowmobilers and cross-country skiers have a heyday in the winter.

Campsites, facilities: There are 73 sites for tents and RVs, 26 RV-only sites with electric hookups, 4 backpacking tent-only sites, and 2 canoe-in tent-only sites. RV length limit is 60 feet. Picnic tables, fire rings, swimming beach, water access, drinking water, showers, flush toilets, vault toilets, and a dump station are provided. Some facilities are wheelchair accessible. Leashed pets are permitted.

Reservations, fees: Reservations are accepted from April 2 to October 31 866/857-2757 or online at www.stayatmnparks.com ($8.50 non-refundable reservation fee) and can be made up to one year in advance. Reservations are not required the rest of the year. Sites are $12–24. Open year-round, with limited facilities in winter.

Directions: From Tower, take Highway 169 east for 9 miles to St. Louis County Highway

128. Take Highway 128 south 7 miles to the contact station.

Contact: Bear Head Lake State Park, 218/365-7229, www.dnr.state.mn.us.

41 HERITAGE PARK AND CAMPGROUND

🚶 🚴 ⛵ 🛶 🎣 🐕 ♿ 🚐 ⛺

Scenic rating: 6

in Embarrass

Camping in town doesn't create the classic image of peaceful wilderness that we like to think of when we picture ourselves on vacation, but camping in Embarrass is an entirely different story. A two-hour drive north of Duluth, this small town lies in the middle of the protected wilderness north of Lake Superior.

Embarrass is a small town with a relaxed atmosphere, and its campground follows suit. The campground is on the eastern edge of town off a quiet gravel road and provides a very secluded, peaceful experience. Set on the curvy Embarrass River, the 18 sites are nestled among the whispering red and white pine trees that characterize the forests north of Lake Superior.

The campground is near several oxbows in the river where the current quickens slightly around the curves and carves out perfect fishing holes. The fishing is great, and the view is even better. A bog walk, paved hiking trails, and well-shaded, well-spaced campsites make this feel like a miniature state park.

Campsites, facilities: There are eight tent-only sites and 10 RV sites. RV sites have electric and water hookups. A picnic shelter, fire rings, dump station, drinking water, hiking and biking trails, bog walk, fishing piers, and shower house with flush toilets are provided. All sites and the paved hiking trails are wheelchair accessible. Leashed pets are permitted.

Reservations, fees: Reservations are accepted at 218/984-2084. Sites are $12 per night for tents and $18 per night for RVs. Open from May 1 to October 1.

Directions: From Embarrass, drive north on Highway 21 for 0.2 mile to Salo Road. Turn right and drive 0.5 mile to the Heritage Park entrance sign on the left side of the road. Turn left into the park and follow the gravel driveway to the camping area 0.3 mile straight ahead.

Contact: Heritage Park and Campground, 4789 Salo Road; City of Embarrass, 218/984-2084, www.embarrass.org.

42 MCDOUGAL LAKE CAMPGROUND

🚶 🏊 ⛵ 🎣 🏕 🐕 🚐 ⛺

Scenic rating: 7

near Isabella in the Superior National Forest

Good things come in small packages, and the McDougal Lake Campground is definitely a small package. Shady, isolated sites dot the northern shore of McDougal Lake, which marks the beginning of a short, one-mile hiking trail. Perched on the northeast corner of the lake, the campground sees beautiful summer sunsets that glow across the water; it's one of the best places in the state for stargazing. The open sky above the lake and the near total darkness give perspective to the enormous cosmos.

Two loops hold only 21 campsites buried in the heavy tree cover of the Superior National Forest. Evergreens, including several varieties of spruce, balsam, and red pine, surround the lake and campground, with some white birch scattered throughout the forest. Sites are not on the water, but several offer a clear view of the lake. Campers come here for peace and quiet, making this a nice spot for solo trips, couples looking for a romantic northwoods experience, or anyone seeking solitude in nature.

I highly recommend exploring the lake and forest via the hiking trail. Even though it's short, the trail has a lot to offer in terms of scenery. Remnants of wildfires in the not-too-distant past linger on some of the older trees; the once burnt area is now a bed of wildflowers and young growth. The trail also crosses a small, boggy swamp that occasionally sprouts pink lady's slipper orchids and wild blueberries.

Campsites, facilities: There are eight tent-only sites and 13 sites for tents and RVs. There are no hookups or pull-through sites. Picnic tables, fire grills and rings, vault toilets, drinking water, boat ramp, and a swimming beach are provided. Leashed pets are permitted.

Reservations, fees: Reservations are accepted and must be made at least four days in advance at 877/444-6777 or online at www.recreation. gov ($10 nonrefundable fee). Sites are $12 per night. There is a maximum of two vehicles per site. Open from May 10 to October 1.

Directions: From Isabella, take State Route 1 west 9.9 miles to the campground sign (Forest Route 106). Turn left onto Route 106 and go 0.5 mile to another campground sign. Turn right into campground.

Contact: Superior National Forest, Tofte Ranger District, 877/444-6777, www.forest-camping.com.

43 NINEMILE LAKE CAMPGROUND
🚶‍♂️🛶🚲🎣🐕🚐⛺

Scenic rating: 8

west of Tofte

Ninemile Lake is one of the Superior National Forest's most exciting campgrounds. The lake has a canoe access and a hiking trail that surrounds its shores, letting campers explore the many small islands, hidden bays, and small peninsulas that give the water so much character and mystery. A more developed hiking trail leads northeast through the dense hardwood forest that covers the area. Campers can also hike or drive about 0.5 mile north to Goldeneye Lake for more fishing and wildlife viewing.

The sites are arranged in a single loop on the lake's eastern shore. Sites 17–26 have direct access to the lake and views of the water. All sites enjoy plenty of tree cover, and there are

several dozen feet of space between neighboring sites. A footpath connects the camping area to the water.

Campsites, facilities: There are 22 sites for tents and RVs up to 50 feet (no hookups) and two tent-only sites. Picnic tables, fire rings and grills, vault toilets, drinking water, a boat ramp, and a hiking trail are provided. Boat, canoe, and paddleboat rentals are available. Leashed pets are permitted.

Reservations, fees: Reservations are not accepted. Sites are $12 per night. Campground services are provided from May 5 through November 1, but the campground is open year-round.

Directions: From Schroeder, take County Route 1 west for 6.1 miles to County Route 8. Continue straight on County Route 8 for 3.9 miles to County Route 7. Bear to the right onto Route 7 and go 4 miles to the campground sign. Turn left into the campground.

Contact: Superior National Forest, Tofte Ranger District, 877/444-6777, www.forest-camping.com.

44 TEMPERANCE RIVER STATE PARK
🚶‍♂️❄️🐕🚐⛺

Scenic rating: 10

in Temperance River State Park

BEST (

There are parts of Lake Superior's north shore that are a rock climber's paradise. Temperance River State Park is one of them. Its bare rock cliffs, cool lake breezes, and stunning views from high above the water draw hundreds of rock climbers—and spectators—each year.

The campground is divided into two parts: upper and lower. The upper camping area is nearer the park headquarters at the entrance of the park and has more modern shower, water, and toilet facilities. The lower campground is on the east side of the Temperance River and has a little over a dozen campsites, making it a less crowded option.

A hiking trail follows both sides of the river and links to the Lake Superior Hiking Trail, which heads north into the Sawtooth Range. If hiking, walk to the cliffs to the watch the rock climbers scaling the walls that rise up from the water. A footbridge crosses a busy little waterfall on the river. Cross-country skiing is a challenge here in the winter, as the terrain is quite hilly, but that doesn't stop dozens of skiers from hitting the trails every year.

Campsites, facilities: There are 52 sites for tents and RVs up to 50 feet; two sites are pull-through and 18 sites in the upper campground have electric hookups. There are also six cart-in tent-only sites (sites 31, 32, 33, 46, 47, and 48). Picnic tables, fire rings and grills, vault and flush toilets, showers, drinking water, water access, hiking trail, and a dump station are provided. Snowshoeing and snowmobiling are allowed in the park. Leashed pets are permitted.

Reservations, fees: Reservations are accepted from April 2 to October 31 866/857-2757 or online at www.stayatmnparks.com ($8.50 non-refundable reservation fee) and can be made up to one year in advance. Reservations are not required the rest of the year. Sites are $12–24 per night.

Directions: From Schroeder, drive northeast on Highway 61 for 1 mile to the Temperance River State Park sign on the right side of the road, immediately after crossing the Temperance River on Highway 61. Turn right into the park and drive 0.1 mile to the campground straight ahead.

Contact: Tettegouche River State Park, 218/226-6365, www.dnr.state.mn.us.

45 LAMB'S RESORT

🚶 🚴 🏊 🐴 🎣 🚐 ⛺

Scenic rating: 9

in Schroeder

With all the state forests, national hiking trails, and protected backcountry camping areas along the north shore, it is easy to overlook the more convenient, family-friendly campgrounds. Lamb's Resort near Schroeder is one of the nicer ones.

Lamb's is everything you want in a quaint northern Minnesota campground: family owned, quiet, and set on 60 acres of beautiful Lake Superior shoreline. Campsites are nestled among birches and pines; a footpath runs along the shore and links all of the sites to the water. A wooden fishing dock is good for dangling your feet in the lake or casting a line. Glacial boulders line parts of the shore as well, imparting a rugged northwoods feel. A small beach is available for swimming, if you can take the cold—the lake rarely rises above 55°F, even in summer!

Campsites, facilities: There are 50 tent-only sites and 25 sites for RVs. Full hookups are available. Picnic tables, fire rings and grills, flush toilets, a swimming beach, showers, drinking water, a playground, hiking and biking trails, and a dump station are provided. Leashed pets are permitted.

Reservations, fees: Tent sites are $22 per night and RV sites are $35 per night. Children stay free with parents. Open from mid-May to mid-October.

Directions: From Duluth, take Highway 61 north to Schroeder. There will be a large resort sign on lake side of highway. Turn into the driveway and stop at the office on the left.

Contact: Lamb's Resort, 218/663-7292, www.lambsresort.com.

46 MANITOU RIVER AND BENSEN LAKE

🚶 🏊 🎣 🐴 ⛺

Scenic rating: 7

in George Crosby Manitou State Park

Put on your hiking boots; the Manitou River and Bensen Lake backpacking sites are only accessible by foot. You'll have to hike at least 0.5 mile to camp, but real campers head to the 4.5-mile site deep in the woods.

All campsites are on either the river or the lake, so you won't have to carry water with you if you bring a purification system. The 21 sites are well separated; the trees and the distance between each site will make you feel like you are the only camper in the forest.

Hiking on the main trail is satisfying in itself and will give you a tour of all the campsites. Hiking off of the main trail near the water can be challenging if the underbrush is thick, but it makes for beautiful views. You can also find some awesome swimming holes and fishing spots if you are willing to get a little wet.

Campsites, facilities: There are 21 tent-only sites. Sites are 0.5–4.5 miles from the parking area. Fire rings, hiking trails, water access, and vault toilets are provided. Freshwater sources are available, but water purification is necessary. Leashed pets are permitted.

Reservations, fees: Reservations are not accepted. TSites are first come, first served and are limited to a one-night stay. There is no fee. Open year-round.

Directions: From Silver Bay, take Highway 61 east for 19 miles to Highway 1. Turn left and drive 7 miles to County Road 7. Take a right on County Road 7 and drive for 8 miles. Follow the signs into the park on the right.

Contact: George Crosby Manitou State Park, 218/226-6365, www.dnr.state.mn.us.

47 FINLAND CAMPGROUND
Scenic rating: 9

in Finland State Forest

During July and August, it seems like everyone and their brother is trying to camp at Tettegouche State Park. The Baptism River is a perennial favorite of Minnesotans from all over the state. If you don't have any luck reserving a campsite in the park, head upstream to the Finland Campground in adjacent Finland State Forest.

Given the crowds that are usually at Tettegouche, I think the upstream portions of the river are nicer, and they are certainly better for fishing. The sites here lie in a single loop along the eastern bank of the river in the thick pine and hardwoods that cover most of the north shore. You can hear the rushing water from all of the sites, a peaceful soundscape at night under a starry sky.

This is a state forest campground, so there are only basic facilities and no electricity, but that isn't much of a price to pay for a shoreside spot on one of Minnesota's most popular rivers. If you like to fish for salmon, head here in the early spring or late fall when they run upstream from Lake Superior. If you come at just the right time, you will see more salmon than you can shake a stick at!

Campsites, facilities: There are 39 sites for tents and RVs. Picnic tables, fire rings and grills, vault toilets, drinking water, and water access are provided. There are two wheelchair-accessible sites. Leashed pets are permitted.

Reservations, fees: No reservations are required. Sites are $12 per night. Campers should submit payment by completing a self-registration envelope and depositing it in the self-pay tube at the campground entrance.

Directions: From Finland, take County Road 6 east 0.5 mile.

Contact: Tettegouche State Park, 218/226-6365, www.dnr.state.mn.us.

48 ECKBECK CAMPGROUND
Scenic rating: 8

in Finland State Forest

The Baptism River's upstream campsites don't get a lot of attention—and you'll be glad they don't once you visit. Eckbeck Campground is one of the reasons why the Baptism is still one of my favorite rivers, despite how crowded its mouth can get in summer.

A simple, 30-site campground, Eckbeck

gives direct access to the river. The basic facilities and lack of electricity keep the big RVs and large camping groups away and let you enjoy the cascading river in a more primitive style. Birch trees encroach on the sites, giving them the cool, bright atmosphere that river birch impart. The northwoods of pine and hardwood quickly surround the campground loop, absorbing any traffic sounds from Highway 61 to the south.

Fishing is the best way to spend your time here—when the salmon are running, you can't beat the Baptism River for a good time. You can also catch several varieties of trout. Pick up some rocks in the river shallows to see what is hatching, then match your bait to it and you'll have dinner in no time. Hiking trails run along the river; they can be challenging at times, so make sure to bring your hiking boots and some water.

Campsites, facilities: There are 30 sites for tents and RVs. Picnic tables, fire rings and grills, vault toilets, drinking water, and water access are provided. There are five wheelchair-accessible sites. Leashed pets are permitted.

Reservations, fees: Reservations are not accepted. Sites are $12 per night. Submit payment by completing a self-registration envelope and depositing it in the self-pay tube at the campground entrance.

Directions: From Finland drive south on Highway 1 for 3 miles to the campground entrance on the left.

Contact: Tettegouche State Park, 218/226-6365, www.dnr.state.mn.us.

49 TETTEGOUCHE STATE PARK

Scenic rating: 10

in Tettegouche State Park

The crème de la crème of northwoods state parks, Tettegouche draws people from all over the country. The heavy northwoods, big glacial boulders, and rushing river combine to make this one of the most enchanting places in the state. Most come to see the cascades and waterfalls as the river heads toward Lake Superior.

Tree cover extends into the campground, providing plenty of shade and privacy. Sites are well spaced and removed enough from the parking lot that you can enjoy the birds and the gargle of the river. Although Tettegouche is tremendously popular, the campground isn't that big. Definitely make reservations at least one month ahead of time to secure a spot.

Hiking trails and a footbridge crisscross the river, giving great views of the cascades. In spring and fall, you will see lots of anglers in waders fly-fishing during the salmon runs. Come during the right weekend and you will see a river coursing with fish.

If you walk upstream a half mile or so where there are fewer people, you will have a good chance of spotting some wildlife. Kingfishers, beaver, raccoons, and deer all use the river and are often seen on its shores. You may even wake up to find deer tracks in your campsite.

Campsites, facilities: There are 28 sites for tents and RVs and six walk-in tent-only sites (sites 6, 7, 8, 23, 24, and 25 are walk-in). There are no hookups or pull-through sites. RV length is restricted to 60 feet. Picnic tables, fire rings and grills, showers, drinking water, and flush toilets are provided. Hiking, biking, cross-country skiing and snowmobile trails are in the park. Some facilities are wheelchair accessible. Leashed pets are permitted.

Reservations, fees: Reservations are accepted from April 2 to October 31 866/857-2757 or online at www.stayatmnparks.com ($8.50 non-refundable reservation fee) and can be made up to one year in advance. Reservations are not required the rest of the year. Sites are $12–24 per night. The drive-in campsites are available year-round.

Directions: From Silver Bay, take Highway 61 northeast for 4.5 miles. Follow the signs to the park office on the left.

Contact: Tettegouche State Park, 218/226-6365, www.dnr.state.mn.us.

50 TETTEGOUCHE LAKE SUPERIOR CART-IN

Scenic rating: 9

in Tettegouche State Park

BEST (

Another option at Tettegouche State Park is the section of cart-in sites south of Highway 61, positioned at the mouth of the Baptism River as it empties into Lake Superior.

This loop of campsites is wooded but still gives views of the massive lake. Even though you have to cart in your gear from the parking lot (the farthest campsite is 0.6 mile from the parking area), you don't get supreme privacy. The sites are within earshot of each other in a fairly small area. The view is worth it, though.

Sunrises here are absolutely resplendent. The long stretch of lake to the east goes on for miles, well beyond human sight. It's almost like watching a sunrise over the ocean, making it easy to see how the northwoods have cast their spell on so many travelers.

Campsites, facilities: There are 13 tent-only sites. Carts are provided to carry camping gear to the site. Picnic tables, fire rings and grills, vault toilets, drinking water, hiking trails, and water access are provided. Leashed pets are permitted.

Reservations, fees: Reservations are accepted from April 2 to October 31 866/857-2757 or online at www.stayatmnparks.com ($8.50 non-refundable reservation fee) and can be made up to one year in advance. Reservations are not required the rest of the year. Sites are $12–24 per night. Open year-round.

Directions: From Silver Bay, take Highway 61 northeast for 4.5 miles. Follow the signs to the park office on the left.

Contact: Tettegouche State Park, 218/226-6365, www.dnr.state.mn.us.

51 TETTEGOUCHE BACKPACKING CAMPSITES

Scenic rating: 7

along the Superior Hiking Trail

The world-famous Superior Hiking Trail winds through the northern portion of Tettegouche State Park in the Sawtooth Mountain Range. Although they aren't mountains by technical standards, they form an elevated ridge that follows much of the northern shore of Lake Superior. The Superior Hiking Trail follows the ridge for more than 200 miles; the portion that passes through Tettegouche is deep in the northwoods. In spring and autumn you can glimpse the lake, but in summer trees take over the view.

Large backpacking sites are scattered along the trail near Tettegouche. The Superior Hiking Trail generally makes enough room in its backpacking sites for several parties. There is a good chance you'll have to share a site if you are hiking on a summer weekend, but you won't often encounter a full campsite. Some sites have wilderness toilets and others don't. Make sure to bring drinking water and toilet paper.

Beautiful birch, spruce, balsam, and red pine are the trees of these campsites. Watching the stars from a backcountry site on the Superior Hiking Trail is an entirely new level of night-sky clarity that is hard to match.

Campsites, facilities: There are five tent-only sites. Picnic tables, fire rings and grills, vault toilets, hiking trails, and water access are provided. There is no drinking water. Leashed pets are permitted.

Reservations, fees: Reservations are not accepted; sites are first come, first served and are limited to a one-night stay. There is no fee. Open year-round.

Directions: From Silver Bay, take Highway 61 northeast for 4.5 miles. Follow the signs to the park office on the left.

Contact: Tettegouche State Park, 218/226-6365, www.dnr.state.mn.us.

52 WHITEFACE RESERVOIR CAMPGROUND

Scenic rating: 8

south of Hoyt Lakes on Whiteface Reservoir

Why does the land of 10,000 lakes need a reservoir? You'll be glad we have one when you visit the Whiteface Reservoir Campground. RVers come here with their families for the community and campground activities and facilities as much as they do for the view. If you come in summer, you can tell that many of these families have been coming here for years. The camaraderie is contagious, and you might just become a regular.

Divided into four loops, the campsites are close together and are not well shaded, but the park's activities will keep you too busy to notice. The reservoir has a 2.5-mile hiking trail, a large playground, an impressively large and sandy swimming beach, and a tidy boat ramp and dock.

Campsites, facilities: There are 51 sites for tents and RVs and one tent-only site. There are 24 sites with electric hookups and no pull-through sites. Picnic tables, fire rings and grills, a swimming beach, boat ramp, dock, camp supply store, vault toilets, drinking water, and a hiking trail are provided. Firewood, bait, boat rentals, ice, and some supplies are available at the camp store. The two fishing docks are wheelchair accessible. Leashed pets are permitted.

Reservations, fees: Reservations are accepted at 877/550-6777 or online at www.recreation. gov ($10 nonrefundable fee). Sites are $14–19 per night (electric hookups draw a higher rate). Open from early May through September.

Directions: From Hoyt Lakes, drive south on Highway 110 for 14 miles to Highway 16. Turn left onto Highway 16 and drive 5.2 miles to the reservoir campground sign at County Road 618. Turn left onto County Road 618 and continue 2.8 miles to the campground.

Contact: Superior National Forest, Laurentian Ranger District, 877/444-6777, www.forest-camping.com.

53 CADOTTE LAKE CAMPGROUND

Scenic rating: 8

south of Hoyt Lakes

You might be surprised that there is a campground out here—I know I was. Located in the middle of the boondocks south of Hoyt Lakes, Cadotte Lake is a skinny, isolated little lake surrounded by a spruce and aspen forest.

The campsites are spread throughout two loops on either side of a small swamp that extends into the lake's northwestern shore. The loops are separate from each other, giving each a small, woodsy feel. The heavy tree cover creates a shady, impenetrable canopy during summer and a dazzling gold and green landscape in fall when aspen leaves stand out against the spruce needles.

Cadotte Lake doesn't see much traffic. The opposite shore of the lake is private land, though only a handful of houses dot the shore. Swimming is good, as the campground has a wide, sandy beach. Fishing also proves fruitful; northern pike and some bass can frequently be caught around overhanging trees near the shore.

You may want to bring your own drinking water as the campground does not have running water, only a hand pump.

Campsites, facilities: There are 27 sites for tents and RVs. There are no hookups or pull-through sites. RVs are restricted to 55 feet in length. Picnic tables, fire rings and grills, drinking water, vault toilets, a swimming beach, and a boat ramp are provided. Leashed pets are permitted.

Reservations, fees: Reservations are not accepted. Self-registration is required at the campground. Sites are $12–14 per night. Open from early May through November.

Directions: From Hoyt Lakes, drive south on

Highway 110 for 14 miles to Highway 16. Turn left onto Highway 16 and drive 8.5 miles to the first campground sign. Turn left onto Bundle Lake Road and drive 0.5 mile to a second campground sign. Turn left at the second sign and drive 1 mile to the campground straight ahead.

Contact: Superior National Forest, Laurentian Ranger District, 877/444-6777, www.forestcamping.com.

54 SULLIVAN LAKE CAMPGROUND

Scenic rating: 8

in Finland State Forest

The Sullivan Lake Campground is the presidential suite of northwoods campgrounds. Located off of a small gravel road, the luxurious space this campground offers isn't readily apparent to passersby.

Campsites are beaded along Sullivan Lake's eastern shore. The country road that leads to the campground is far from any highways, and you'll usually be alone when you come here. Sites are pretty basic—just a picnic table, fire ring, and a tent clearing—but the large, secluded area the campground is spread over is priceless.

Little-used hiking trails follow the shore on either side of the campground and lead to open areas along the water that are good for fishing. You'll find mostly northern and sunfish in this lake, though the occasional walleye turns up if you are lucky.

Campsites, facilities: There are 11 sites for tents and RVs. Picnic tables, fire rings and grills, drinking water, vault toilets, boat ramp, and a hiking trail are provided. There is one wheelchair-accessible site. Leashed pets are permitted.

Reservations, fees: Reservations are not accepted. Sites are $12 per night. Submit payment by completing a self-registration envelope and depositing it in the self-pay tube at the campground entrance. Open year-round.

Directions: From Two Harbors, take County Road 2 north 27 miles to County Road 15. Turn left (west) on Forest Highway 11 and drive for 0.5 mile. Turn left into the campground.

Contact: Split Rock Lighthouse State Park, 218/226-6377, www.dnr.state.mn.us.

55 INDIAN LAKE CAMPGROUND

Scenic rating: 6

north of Duluth in Cloquet Valley State Forest

Indian Lake is one of the few campgrounds in the little-visited Cloquet Valley State Forest. The state forest is close to Lake Superior and the Superior National Forest, often playing second fiddle to the more popular outdoor and wilderness recreation facilities there. Camping here is definitely worthwhile, though.

The 25 sites are a little more than 100 feet from the lake's eastern shore, placed along two gravel drive loops amid the pines and hardwoods that surround the water. Each site has several trees and is at least 20 feet from neighboring campsites. Privacy is good here and the campground is usually not full, even during the summer. Campers can fish, swim, or explore the lakeshore on an undeveloped hiking trail.

Campsites, facilities: There are 25 sites for tents or RVs and four walk-in sites for tents only. Picnic tables, fire rings and grills, drinking water, and vault toilets are provided. Water access and a fishing dock are available. Some facilities are wheelchair accessible. Leashed pets are permitted.

Reservations, fees: Reservations are not accepted. Sites are $12 per night. Open from May to late October.

Directions: From Two Harbors, drive north on Highway 15 for 13 miles. Turn left at Wales Road and drive for 7.7 miles to Brimson Road.

Continue north for 2.5 miles and turn right onto Hopper Road. Turn left onto Indian Lake Road in 1.2 miles. The campground is less than 0.25 mile ahead on the left marked by a state forest sign.

Contact: Split Rock Lighthouse State Park, 218/226-6377, www.dnr.state.mn.us.

56 SPLIT ROCK LIGHTHOUSE STATE PARK

🚶 ⛵ 🛶 🎣 ❄ 🐎 ♿ ⛺

Scenic rating: 9

on Lake Superior in Split Rock Lighthouse State Park

BEST (

Home to one of the few remaining historic lighthouses left on the north shore, Split Rock Lighthouse State Park is one of Lake Superior's must-see parks. The cart-in camping and backpacking sites here give this park a backwoods feel, even though it is less than a mile from Highway 61, between the lake and the road.

The campsites are scattered throughout the hilly terrain that leads to the lake. A trail links all of the sites, which are set among a large grove of beautiful white birch trees. Sites nearest the parking lot are within earshot of each other, but visibility remains private. The farther in on the trail you go, the more privacy you will have. In spring and autumn when the leaves are off the trees, the campsites on the hill near the parking lot give great views of the lake.

Split Rock is a popular spot; it doesn't have a lot of sites and they fill up fast. Make reservations at least one month, or even up to 3–6 months, in advance to ensure a spot.

Hiking and fishing here are first-class. During the salmon runs in the spring and fall you can easily catch your limit in a few hours; I have lost count of the number of salmon dinners I've had in October at this park. Cross-country skiers sometimes brave the hills of Split Rock, but I wouldn't recommend it unless you really know what you are doing.

Campsites, facilities: There are 20 cart-in tent-only sites and four backpacking sites. Carts are available at the parking area. Sites range 0.5–2 miles from the campground parking lot. Two sites are accessible from Lake Superior for use by kayakers. Picnic tables, fire rings and grills, vault toilets, drinking water, showers, and water access are provided. There are two wheelchair accessible sites. Leashed pets are permitted.

Reservations, fees: Reservations are accepted from April 2 to October 31 866/857-2757 or online at www.stayatmnparks.com ($8.50 non-refundable reservation fee) and can be made up to one year in advance. Reservations are not required the rest of the year. Sites are $12–24 per night. Open year-round.

Directions: From Two Harbors, drive 20 miles northeast on Highway 61. Follow signs to the right.

Contact: Split Rock Lighthouse State Park, 218/226-6377, www.dnr.state.mn.us.

57 GOOSEBERRY FALLS STATE PARK

🚶 🚲 ⛵ 🎣 ❄ 🐎 ♿ 🚗 ⛺

Scenic rating: 10

in Gooseberry Falls State Park

Gooseberry Falls State Park is easily the most popular park on the north shore. Located just below the famous Gooseberry Falls, the campground is a quick exit off of Highway 61. After a massive remodeling in the late 1990s, Gooseberry has become a family friendly state park full of activities and sights for all ages.

The campground is made of four loops that extend north from Lake Superior. Rationed out into four sections, the sites don't feel crowded; the park did an excellent job of spacing its sites when the park was redesigned. Shade and privacy are both more than adequate, and hiking trails link all of the loops to the lake, to a paved biking trail near the shore, and to the trails that lead to the river and the falls.

Three sets of falls cascade down the river: upper, middle, and lower Gooseberry Falls. Hiking trails run like veins along the river shores, passing under the falls, crossing over boulders in the water, and lining each river bank. It is a great place to explore one of Minnesota's most beautiful northwoods rivers. Fishing here can be fun, but there are usually too many people to catch anything.

Campsites, facilities: There are 69 sites for tents and RVs up to 40 feet; there are no hookups but there are three pull-through sites. Picnic tables, fire rings and grills, drinking water, flush and vault toilets, showers, and a dump station are provided. Water access to the lake and river, hiking and cross-country skiing trails, and a warming house are available. There are two wheelchair-accessible campsites. Leashed pets are permitted.

Reservations, fees: Reservations are accepted from April 2 to October 31 866/857-2757 or online at www.stayatmnparks.com ($8.50 non-refundable reservation fee) and can be made up to one year in advance. Reservations are not required the rest of the year. Sites are $12–24 per night. Open year-round.

Directions: From Two Harbors, follow Highway 61 northeast approximately 13 miles to the park. Follow signs to the right.

Contact: Gooseberry Falls State Park, 218/834-3855, www.dnr.state.mn.us/state_parks.

58 INDIAN POINT CAMPGROUND

🚶 🚴 🏊 🛶 ⛵ 🚣 🎣 🏕 🥾 🚐 ⛺

Scenic rating: 5

south of Duluth near Spirit Mountain Ski Resort

Located on the St. Louis River, Indian Point Campground is hand-tailored for family vacations. The riverside campground is near the Lake Superior Zoo, close to the base of Spirit Mountain, and just minutes from downtown Duluth.

The RV sites are somewhat close together, but the tent sites have trees and brush that form borders between them. Because the campground is also a recreational area, the grounds can be noisy during the day, especially during the middle of the summer when people pack into Duluth for the Bayfront Blues festival and Fourth of July celebrations.

Campers can rent canoes and kayaks for use in the St. Louis River, swim at the beach, and jump from docks into the river. A birding trail also winds through the thick riverside forest, starting at the northeast corner of the playground area. Anglers enjoy fishing for walleye, bass, and northern pike in the river. The campground is also situated at the Munger Trail trailhead, one of the country's longest paved biking trails, stretching from Hinckley to Duluth and winding below majestic Spirit. Evenly paved, this wide, biking trail is perfect for all ages.

If you are in the Duluth area during tourist season and want to avoid pricey hotel rooms in the city, Indian Point is an affordable alternative for the more adventurously inclined.

Campsites, facilities: There are 50 sites for tents and RVs and 20 tent-only sites. The tent and RV sites feature electricity and water. Sites 1–7 have full hookups with 75-foot pull-throughs. Picnic tables, grills, and fire rings are all provided. Free wireless Internet, 24-hour laundry, coin-operated showers, a dump station, water pump, flush toilets, and a playground are available. Leashed pets are permitted.

Reservations, fees: Reservations are accepted at 800/982-2453. Sites are $21 per night for tents, $25 per night for electric-only sites, $28 per night for sites with water and electric, and $32 per night for full-hookup sites. Open year-round.

Directions: From Duluth, drive southwest on I-35 for 4.7 miles to Exit 251. Turn left at Exit 251 onto Highway 23 and continue for 1.3 miles to the campground entrance on the left side of the road at 75th Avenue W.

Contact: Indian Point Campground, 218/628-

4977 or 800/982-2453, www.indianpoint-campground.com.

59 JAY COOKE STATE PARK

🏃 🏊 🎣 🚣 🛶 🏇 🚴 🚐 🅿️

Scenic rating: 9

in Jay Cooke State Park

Jay Cooke State Park is everything that a state park should be. It has a wild, rapids-filled river, large glacial rock deposits, thick northwoods forests, and a swinging footbridge that crosses the water.

The campground is less exciting, packed with more than 80 campsites along a paved drive. There is a fair amount of shade from the birch and maple trees that are scattered throughout the sites, but privacy is limited. You will have to purchase firewood or bring your own, as the woods are sparse around the campsites.

But the park! I can't say enough good things about it. Kayakers shoot through the rapids, brave swimmers dive off of rock cliffs into deep pools of water, and winding trails lead deep into the woods to hike-in campsites and forested ridges full of wild berries and wildlife.

Hiking at Jay Cooke gives you views of the St. Louis River, wildflowers in forest meadows, and towering white pine trees. Fishing in the river is hit or miss. Anglers are always trying their luck at the dam just upstream in Carlton.

Campsites, facilities: There are 79 sites for tents and RVs, three walk-in tent-only sites, and four backpacking tent-only sites. There is one pull-through site. RV length is restricted to 60 feet. Picnic tables, fire rings and grills, vault and flush toilets, drinking water, hiking trails, and a dump station are provided. There is no drinking water at the backpacking sites. There are three wheelchair-accessible sites. Leashed pets are permitted.

Reservations, fees: Reservations are accepted

from April 2 to October 31 866/857-2757 or online at www.stayatmnparks.com ($8.50 non-refundable reservation fee) and can be made up to one year in advance. Reservations are not required the rest of the year. Sites are $12–24 per night. Open year-round.

Directions: From Carlton drive 3 miles east on Highway 210. The park is on the right side of the road, marked by a large wooden state park sign.

Contact: Jay Cooke State Park, 218/384-4610, www.dnr.state.mn.us.

60 HOFFMAN'S OAK LAKE CAMPGROUND

🏃 🏊 🎣 🚤 🚣 🏇 🤸 🚴 🚐 🅿️

Scenic rating: 5

in Grand Rapids

Camping doesn't always have to mean wilderness camping. Enter Hoffman's Oak Lake Campground, near the town of Kerrick. Hoffman's is perfect for family reunions and camping trips: Little kids run around with floaties, teenagers play beach volleyball, and a playground echoes with the laughter of youngsters. This place has family vacation written all over it.

The campground is laid out in a long, single loop, filled every summer with tents and RVs. Hoffman's packs a lot of sites into a relatively small area. Although there are plenty of open spaces and lakeshore areas, the actual sites are close together and have little shade. Trees line the campground but are not dispersed thickly throughout it.

It is worth noting that the Kerrick area has many restaurants, golf courses, and tourist activities during the summer, including a town celebration. If you want to enjoy the area, watch the kids have fun, *and* have a place to park your RV for the weekend, this is the right campground for you.

Campsites, facilities: There are 151 sites for RVs and eight tent-only sites. Full RV hookups and pull-through sites are available. Fire rings and grills, picnic tables, a playground, flush toilets, showers, laundry facilities, docks, a boat ramp, drinking water, a swimming beach, hiking trails, and a dump station are provided. Boats, motors, paddleboats, and pontoons are also available for rental. All campsites are wheelchair accessible. Leashed pets are permitted.

Reservations, fees: Reservations are accepted at 888/723-5218. Sites are $29 per night for tents and $35 per night for RVs. Open from May 1 to October 15.

Directions: From Kerrick, take a left on County Road 46 and travel 0.5 mile to County Road 56. Take a right and drive 2.5 miles to the campground.

Contact: Hoffman's Oak Lake Campground, 888/723-5218, www.oaklakerv.com.

MINNESOTA NORTHWOODS

© JAKE KULJU

BEST CAMPGROUNDS

Full of lakes, rivers, thick deciduous and pine

forests, gravel roads, small towns, and great fishing, the north-central region of Minnesota is responsible for much of the state's reputation as an "up north" state full of wilderness, harsh winters, and 10,000 lakes.

This author's hometown is in north-central Minnesota, and it is where he learned that this region is the best place for hiking boots, pup tents, canoes, and campfires to be fully appreciated. Coniferous and hardwood forests battle for real estate along the shores of countless sky-blue lakes, fish jump in the rays of the setting sun, and whitetail deer stand calmly at the edges of fields pensively chewing their dinners. If this seems a bit idyllic, it's because the northwoods are every bit as enchanting and legendary as they are made out to be by the lucky travelers, campers, and canoeists that have spent time here.

Bordered by the St. Louis and St. Croix Rivers to the east and the sweeping prairies to the west, the northwoods are home to the Brainerd Lakes Area, mythic Lake Mille Lacs, some of the largest stands of red and white pines on the continent, and the world's largest ball of twine!

The northwoods region embraces its longest season, winter, with enthusiasm. State parks remain open all year, most of them featuring sliding hills, warming houses, groomed cross-country ski trails, dog-sled routes, and winter camping areas. Several lake towns in this region also hold annual "Polar Bear Swims," where anyone brave enough to jump into a hole chopped into the ice gets a free pancake breakfast at the local VFW. There are few better places to find crazy winter fun than northern Minnesota.

The habitat here is mainly hardwood and pine forests, but many important wetlands are located here as well. The Rice Lake National Wildlife Refuge and Savanna State Park lie along one of the nation's busiest bird migration corridors and protect acres of marshes, lakes, and bogs. Pink lady's slippers (the protected state flower of Minnesota), pitcher plants, and peat moss all grow in abundance here, drawing bird watchers and wildflower enthusiasts from around the region. The lake effect of Lake Superior extends to the eastern portions of the region, as well, causing an extended autumn that draws every last drop of fall pigment out of the deciduous trees, making this one of the better leaf-changing observation areas in the state.

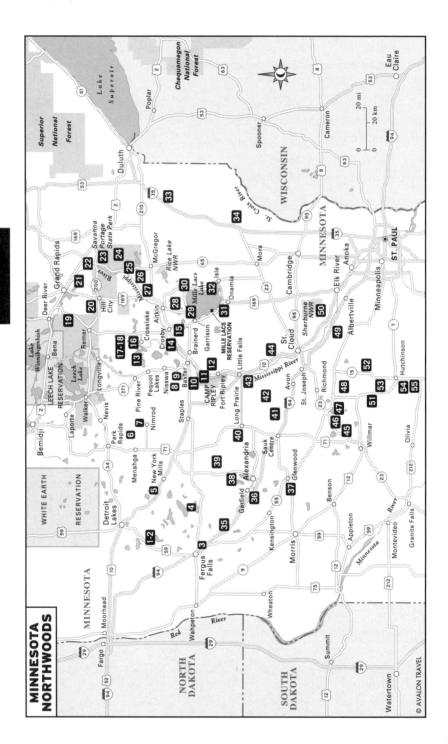

1 MAIN LOOP AND HOLLOW LOOP CAMPGROUNDS

Scenic rating: 9

in Maplewood State Park

Minnesota has many lovely places to visit in the autumn to see the changing leaves, but Maplewood State Park may be the loveliest. Abounding with (you guessed it) maple forests, this park turns all manner of reds, yellows, and bright oranges from late September through early November with a beauty so fierce it is hard to leave the park behind even after spending a full weekend camping here.

The campgrounds are in a series of four loops around Grass Lake. Hollow Loop is approximately 0.25 mile farther north from the Main Loop and offers a slightly more secluded and rustic camping experience. The sites are in some of the densest forest in the region, buried among the maples and hardwoods under a thick, rich canopy that provides copious shade throughout the summer and an amazing, blazing ceiling of orange and yellow during the fall.

Maplewood is a great year-round camping destination, with hiking and horse riding trails, a swimming beach, and many groomed cross-country ski trails in the winter.

Campsites, facilities: There are 71 sites for tents and RVs up to 50 feet; 32 sites have electrical hookups. There are also three backpacking sites, 24 equestrian sites, and one group campsite for up to 30 people. Picnic tables, fire rings, drinking water, flush toilets, showers, and a dump station are provided. Hiking and horse riding trails, snowmobile trails, cross-country ski trails, a warming house, fishing pier, swimming beach, and boat access are available. Some facilities are wheelchair accessible. Leashed pets are permitted.

Reservations, fees: Reservations are accepted from April 2 to October 31 at 866/857-2757 or online at www.stayatmnparks.com ($8.50 non-refundable reservation fee) and can be made up to one year in advance. Reservations are not required the rest of the year. Sites are $12–24 per night. Open year-round.

Directions: From Pelican Rapids, drive east for 7 miles on Highway 108. Turn right at the state park sign onto Park Entrance Road. The park office is 0.5 mile ahead.

Contact: Maplewood State Park, 218/863-8383, www.dnr.state.mn.us/state_parks.

2 LAKE LIDA CAMPGROUND

Scenic rating: 9

in Maplewood State Park

BEST (

Lake Lida is the largest of several lakes in Maplewood State Park. The campground is on the east shore of Lake Lida in the northwest section of the park; this is a more remote and secluded location than the Main Loop and Hollow Loop campgrounds.

An excellent swimming beach is about 0.5 mile up the road from the campground near a picnic area. A short hiking trail leads to Hallaway Hill Overlook atop a hill that gives a sweeping view of the park and the pristine lake. Maplewood's hiking and horse-riding trails, swimming beach, and cross-country ski trails are available to Lake Lida campers as well.

Campsites, facilities: There are 71 sites for tents and RVs up to 50 feet. There are also three backpacking sites and 24 horse sites. Picnic tables, fire rings, toilets, showers, and a dump station are provided. Hiking and horse-riding trails, snowmobile trails, cross-country ski trails, a warming house, fishing pier, swimming beach, and boat access are available. Some facilities are wheelchair accessible. Leashed pets are permitted.

Reservations, fees: Reservations are accepted from April 2 to October 31 at 866/857-2757 or online at www.stayatmnparks.com ($8.50 non-refundable reservation fee) and can be made up to one year in advance. Reservations are not required the rest of the year. Sites are $12–24 per night. Open year-round.

Directions: From Pelican Rapids, drive east for 7 miles on Highway 108. Turn right at the state park sign onto Park Entrance Road. The park office is 0.5 mile ahead.

Contact: Maplewood State Park, 218/863-8383, www.dnr.state.mn.us/state_parks.

❸ DELAGOON PARK CAMPGROUND

Scenic rating: 6

on Pebble Lake south of Fergus Falls

Delagoon used to be known as the $5 campground. If you had five bucks and a tent you could camp here. The park recently underwent some renovations, raising the price to $10, which is still a heck of a deal.

The park is a large, grassy expanse on the north shore of Pebble Lake just south of Fergus Falls. The campsites are on the east side of the park at the end of Delagoon Park Drive in a grass clearing. A large loop is lined with sites, and two smaller loops are attached to it closer to the water. The Central Lakes State Trail, a paved biking trail that stretches for 55 miles from Osakis to Fergus Falls, swoops past the campground just 150 feet to the east and within walking distance.

Campsites, facilities: There are 36 sites for tents and RVs; some sites have hookups. Picnic tables, fire rings, toilets, and garbage cans are provided. A playground, biking and hiking trail, boat ramp, and picnic area are available. Leashed pets are permitted.

Reservations, fees: Reservations are not accepted. Sites are $10 per night for tents and $20 per night for RVs. Open from mid-May to late September.

Directions: In Fergus Falls, drive south on Pebble Lake Road to Delagoon Park Drive, which leads directly to the campground.

Contact: Fergus Falls, 218/739-3205, www.ci.fergus-falls.mn.us.

❹ GLENDALOUGH STATE PARK

Scenic rating: 9

in Glendalough State Park

BEST (

Dancing on the line between northwoods forest and western prairie lies Glendalough State Park. The centerpiece of the park is majestic Annie Battle Lake, a 335-acre lake (nonmotorized boats only). Anglers will catch sunfish and bass here in abundance, as well as the occasional walleye.

The campground is made up entirely of cart-in sites near the western shore of Annie Battle Lake. The sites are all within 200 yards of the parking area, but are spread several dozen feet apart from each other with plenty of tree cover. The cart-in sites are in a thick grove of hardwoods adjacent to the water, surrounded on all other sides by the sweeping tallgrass prairie. Come here in the spring to see the wildflowers blooming like crazy, or in the fall to watch the forest leaves take on the bright pigments of autumn.

Several creeks run in and out of the lake and are great for kayaking and canoeing; bring your own or rent one at the park office. The hiking trails here are a real treasure as well, touring the blooming prairies, thick hardwood forests, and all of the five lakes within the park.

Campsites, facilities: There are 22 cart-in sites, three canoe-in sites, and two group campsites for up to 20 and 40 people each. Picnic tables, fire rings, flush and vault toilets, and showers are provided. Hiking trails, paved biking trails, cross-country ski trails, a canoe access, fishing pier, and swimming beach are available. Some facilities are wheelchair accessible. Leashed pets are permitted.

Reservations, fees: Reservations are accepted from April 2 to October 31 at 866/857-2757 or online at www.stayatmnparks.com ($8.50 non-refundable reservation fee) and can be made up to one year in advance. Reservations are not required the rest of the year. Sites are

$12–24 per night. Open year-round, with limited facilities in winter.

Directions: From Battle Lake, drive north on Highway 78 for 1.5 miles. Turn left onto County Road 16. The road leads directly to the park entrance in just under 2 miles.

Contact: Glendalough State Park, 218/864-0110, www.dnr.state.mn.us/state_parks.

5 GOLDEN EAGLE RV VILLAGE

Scenic rating: 6

east of Perham on Pine Lake

Located on the shores of sublime Pine Lake, Golden Eagle has a kind of summer camp atmosphere, with lots of fishing piers and docks, boaters, swimmers, planned summertime entertainment, and canoes—lots of canoes! You can tent camp here, but the prevailing atmosphere here is one of RVs, not just at a campground but at a village.

The 155 sites here manage to be well spaced and enjoy moderate tree cover, ranking this campground higher on the privacy scale for RV campgrounds than most other area RV parks.

Campsites, facilities: There are 155 sites for tents and RVs; some sites are pull-through and some have hookups. Picnic tables, fire rings, toilets, showers, and a dump station are provided. A hiking and biking trail, boat ramp, fishing boat rental, dock, canoes, playground, outdoor pool, and laundry facilities are available. Some facilities are wheelchair accessible. Leashed pets are permitted.

Reservations, fees: Reservations are accepted at 218/346-4386. Sites are $26 per night. Open from May to October.

Directions: From Perham, drive 2 miles southeast on County Road 80. Turn left onto Highway 10. In 0.7 mile, turn left onto Minnesota Street and drive for 1.6 miles. Turn left onto Golden Eagle Road. In 0.5 mile veer to the right onto Loon Lane. When the road becomes Loon Lane, the campground is 0.3 mile ahead on the left. Turn left onto Golden Eagle Road into the campground.

Contact: Golden Eagle RV Village, 218/346-4386, www.goldeneaglervvillage.com.

6 HUNTERSVILLE FOREST LANDING CAMPGROUND

Scenic rating: 8

on the Crow River near Itasca State Park

Itasca State Park is a must-see place in Minnesota, but all the traffic and hubbub at the Mississippi headwaters can leave some campers looking for a respite from the crowds. Huntersville Forest Landing Campground is less than half an hour away to the southeast in the Huntersville State Forest. The campground is near the Crow Wing River State Canoe Route and the Shell River.

There are only 24 campsites scattered along the landing road as it approaches the Crow Wing River. The sites are in a savanna of grass and trees on an eastward bend in the river. Pines and mixed hardwoods press in on the bend in the river, providing shade and copious amounts of privacy between campsites. The cleared areas have plenty of room for several tents.

Hunters seek ruffed grouse here during the fall and early winter, so make sure to wear blaze orange if you plan on camping during the hunting season.

Campsites, facilities: There are 24 sites for tents and RVs up to 30 feet. Picnic tables, fire rings, vault toilets, and garbage cans are provided. A boat ramp, hiking trail, swimming beach, and snowmobile trails are available. Some facilities are wheelchair accessible. Leashed pets are permitted.

Reservations, fees: Reservations are not accepted. Self-registration is required at the campground. Sites are $12 per night. Open from May to late December.

Directions: From Menahga, drive east on

Stocking Lake Road for 4 miles. Turn left onto County Road 23 and drive 1 mile to 380th Street. Turn right and drive 3 miles to 199th Avenue. Turn right and drive 1 mile to the state forest sign. At the sign, turn left onto the Huntersville Forest Road. The campground is 2 miles ahead on the left just past the Y in the road.
Contact: Huntersville State Forest, 218/266-2100, www.dnr.state.mn.us/state_forests/sft00025/index.html.

⑦ CROW WING RIVER CAMPGROUND
🏊 🛶 � 🎣 🐕 🚐 ⛺

Scenic rating: 5

northeast of Nimrod

The Crow Wing River is full of awesome camping spots all along its sandy-bottomed banks—this just isn't one of them. A patch of grass and gravel on the river's east bank near Nimrod, it does the trick but it isn't pretty.

The modest campground has no trees and no privacy, but the facility has a swimming beach and does rent canoes. The Crow Wing River is great for swimming and fishing, which you will have direct access to here. Luckily, it doesn't cost much for tent campers to stay here.
Campsites, facilities: There are 15 sites for tents and RVs. Picnic tables, fire rings, toilets, showers, and a dump station are provided. A swimming beach, canoe rental, and boat ramp are available. Leashed pets are permitted.
Reservations, fees: Reservations are accepted at 218/472-3250. Sites are $13 per night for tents and $18 per night for RVs. Open from late April to October.
Directions: From Nimrod, drive east on County Road 12 across the bridge over the Crow Wing River for 0.3 mile. Turn left onto County Road 18/Huntersville Road. The campground is 1.5 miles ahead on the left. A large wooden sign marks the spot.
Contact: Crow Wing River Campground, 218/472-3250.

⑧ ROCK LAKE CAMPGROUND
🥾 🏊 🛶 🚎 🎣 🐕 ♿ 🚐 ⛺

Scenic rating: 8

in Pillsbury State Forest

Rock Lake is a small Pillsbury State Forest lake northwest of Brainerd near Gull Lake. The city of Brainerd and its lakes area have rapidly become one of Minnesota's most popular outdoor recreation areas. Pillsbury State Forest protects the northwest part of this region and provides secluded wilderness camping at Rock Lake, something that is becoming harder and harder to find in the Brainerd lakes area.

Within driving distance of Gull Lake and Crow Wing State Park, the Rock Lake Campground is convenient for exploring the many nature-oriented activities in the area or just enjoying the seclusion and quiet of the quaint northwoods. The sites are in a wide, wooded loop on the west shore of the lake, and some sites have a lake view. The campground is connected to a state forest hiking trail, and a footpath leads to the lake. Swimming and fishing are both excellent here, both from shore or out in the lake. Take note that you can RV camp here, but only with a modestly sized rig.
Campsites, facilities: There are 48 sites for tents and RVs up to 30 feet; 13 sites are lakeside. Picnic tables, fire rings, drinking water, vault toilets, and garbage cans are provided. Hiking trails, a swimming beach, fishing area, and boat ramp are available. There are seven wheelchair-accessible sites. Leashed pets are permitted.
Reservations, fees: Reservations are not accepted. Self-registration is required at the campground. Sites are $12 per night. Open from mid-May to October.
Directions: From Pillager, drive west on Highway 210 for 0.6 mile. Turn right onto County Road 1. In 6 miles, turn left onto Orchard Park Lane. The campground is 1.5 miles ahead on the left side of the road. A wooden state forest sign is posted at the entrance.
Contact: Crow Wing State Park, 218/825-3075, www.dnr.state.mn.us/state_forests.

9 GULL LAKE DAM CAMPGROUND

Scenic rating: 7

on Gull Lake northwest of Brainerd

The Army Corps of Engineers (ACOE) maintains this recreation area and dam site on the Gull Lake outlet. The area is a hub for boating, water-skiing, swimming, and especially fishing below the dam, which is both popular and rewarding. Many people park their RVs here for the season to enjoy the clean, modern facilities and for access to Gull Lake and the greater lakes area.

The 39 campsites are very private, spread throughout the entire recreation area along the park's campground road. Several of the sites are connected via footpaths through the trees, and many are adjacent to the Gull Lake Outlet and swimming area.

Campsites, facilities: There are 39 sites for tents and RVs. Picnic tables, fire rings, toilets, showers, and a dump station are provided. A swimming beach, playground, hiking trail, boat ramp, and fishing area are available. Some facilities are wheelchair accessible. Leashed pets are permitted.

Reservations, fees: Reservations are accepted at 877/444-6777 or online at www.recreation.gov ($10 reservation fee). Sites are $26 per night. Open from May to late September.

Directions: From Brainerd, drive west on Highway 210. Turn right onto Highway 371 and drive for 5 miles to County Road 125. Turn left and drive for 3 miles to Gull Lake Dam Road. In 0.1 mile, stay to the right on E. Gull Lake Drive. The recreation area is just 200 feet on the right side of the road.

Contact: Gull Lake Dam, 218/829-3334, www.mvp.usace.army.mil/recreation/default.asp?pageid=65.

10 CROW WING RIVER CANOE CAMPSITES

Scenic rating: 8

on the Crow Wing River in Crow Wing River State Park

BEST (

The Crow Wing River is a shallow, winding river in Hubbard County that slowly makes its way to the Mississippi in Crow Wing State Park. This is one of Minnesota's State Scenic Canoe Routes, filled with heavy pine and hardwood forests, abundant wildlife, and scores of waterfowl that take advantage of the river's shallow waters (the channel is seldom deeper than three feet but is still suitable for canoe traffic).

The 90-mile river has dozens of rustic wilderness campsites along its shores. The sites are little more than small clearings among the trees on the riverbank. They are at least one mile apart from each other, with room for several tents and canoes to be pulled onto shore. Aside from a fire ring, a picnic table, and a rustic toilet, these sites have little else other than the occasional short footpath that explores the surrounding wilderness.

When camping here, make sure to bring your own water or water filtration system. The sites have no electricity or drinking water.

Campsites, facilities: There are 16 canoe-in sites for tents only. Picnic tables, fire rings, and vault toilets are provided. Leashed pets are permitted.

Reservations, fees: Reservations are accepted from April 2 to October 31 at 866/857-2757 or online at www.stayatmnparks.com ($8.50 non-refundable reservation fee) and can be made up to one year in advance. Reservations are not required the rest of the year. Sites are $12–24 per night. Open year-round.

Directions: From Brainerd, drive south on Business Highway 371 for 6 miles. Merge onto Highway 371 S and drive for 2.7 miles to State Park Road. Turn right and drive for 1 mile to the park office.

Contact: Crow Wing State Park, 218/825-3075, www.dnr.state.mn.us/state_parks.

11 CROW WING CAMPGROUND

Scenic rating: 9

in Crow Wing State Park

The view over the Mississippi River from lofty Chippewa Lookout is reason enough to come to Crow Wing State Park. The pine-forested park has much more to offer than this one great view, including historic buildings, a state canoe route, choice cross-county skiing, and abundant wildlife. The park is established at the junction of the Mississippi and Crow Wing Rivers, with the wing-shaped Crow Wing Island its namesake landmark.

The campground is burrowed into the northwestern region of the park, set in the heavy pine and hardwood forest that surrounds the Mississippi River. The campground sits atop a ridge on the river's southern shore, and wooden steps lead down to the water for fishing, hiking, and wildlife-viewing. The sites are spaced up to 20 feet apart, and each has a short gravel driveway and large tent pad area. The campground is located on a hiking trail system that leads north along the river and south to famous Chippewa Lookout high above the water.

The park enjoys a rich history as a Native American village and as a frontier town along the Red River to St. Paul oxcart route more than a century ago.

Campsites, facilities: There are 59 sites for tents and RVs up to 45 feet; 12 sites have electrical hookups. There is also one group campsite for up to 75 people. Picnic tables, fire rings, flush and vault toilets, showers, and a dump station are provided. Hiking trails, a paved bike trail, boardwalk, cross-county ski trail, boat ramp, swimming beach, and fishing area are available. There are two wheelchair-accessible sites and a wheelchair-accessible trail. Leashed pets are permitted, with limited facilities in winter.

Reservations, fees: Reservations are accepted from April 2 to October 31 at 866/857-2757 or online at www.stayatmnparks.com ($8.50 non-refundable reservation fee) and can be made up to one year in advance. Reservations are not required the rest of the year. Sites are $12–24 per night. Open year-round.

Directions: From Brainerd, drive south on Business Highway 371 for 6 miles. Merge onto Highway 371 S and drive for 2.7 miles to State Park Road. Turn right and drive for 1 mile to the park office.

Contact: Crow Wing State Park, 218/825-3075, www.dnr.state.mn.us/state_parks.

12 CROW WING LAKE CAMPGROUND

Scenic rating: 6

on Crow Wing Lake south of Brainerd

Crow Wing Lake Campground is on the eastern shore of Crow Wing Lake, just 0.25 mile off of Highway 371. The campground is on a wooded parcel of land that overlooks the water, and the 100 campsites are spread out over a large area full of trees and with plenty of space between. There are four fishing docks, a hiking trail that tours the campground, and an outdoor pool.

The campground definitely attracts more RV campers than tent campers, providing full hookups and large spots for big-rig RVs. It is just minutes south of beautiful Crow Wing State Park and is a handy camping spot for people who want to visit the park but want more creature comforts than a state park campground offers.

Campsites, facilities: There are 100 sites for tents and RVs. Picnic tables, fire rings, toilets, showers, and a dump station are provided. A playground, hiking trail, canoes, docks, fishing boat rental, pontoon rental, boat ramp, outdoor pool, laundry facilities, dish-washing station, pet-washing station, off-leash pet park, wireless Internet access, and camp store are provided. Some facilities are wheelchair accessible. Pets are permitted.

Reservations, fees: Reservations are accepted at 218/829-6468. Sites are $39–51 per night. There's a two-night minimum on weekends, a three-night minimum on holidays. Open from May to October.

Directions: From Brainerd, drive south on Highway 371 for 12 miles. Turn left at Crow Wing Camp Road. The campground is straight ahead in 0.2 mile.

Contact: Crow Wing Lake Campground, 218/829-6468, www.crowwingcamp.com.

13 HIGHVIEW CAMPGROUND & RV PARK

Scenic rating: 5

on Ossawinnamakee Lake near Breezy Point

No bones about it, this is an RV park of the truest variety. You can pitch a tent here, but will be charged only four dollars less than the full RV price. On the southeastern shore of Ossawinnamakee Lake (say that three times fast!), Highview has nearly 150 sites and all the fixings of a truly accommodating RV park. A camp store and laundry facility make Highview a self-sustaining village where you could spend all summer if you wanted to, and lots of campers do; there are seasonal camping spots for long-term visitors.

The sites are in a large grassy clearing in the middle of a thick mixed-hardwood forest. There is little privacy between RVs, but you can find some sites nearer the lake that have trees. The swimming beach and water sports available here are a real blast, especially if you like water-skiing, boating, or canoeing. The campground also has paddleboats for use.

Campsites, facilities: There are 148 sites for tents and RVs. Picnic tables, fire rings, toilets,

showers, and a dump station are provided. A swimming beach, playground, boat ramp, fishing boat rental, dock space, canoe rental, laundry facilities, and a camp store are available. Some facilities are wheelchair accessible. Leashed pets are permitted.

Reservations, fees: Reservations are accepted at 218/543-4526. Sites are $32 per night for tents and $36 per night for RVs. A two-night minimum stay is required on weekends ($30 deposit), with a three-night minimum stay on holiday weekends ($50 deposit). Open from May to October.

Directions: From Breezy Point, drive east on County Road 11 for 2.1 miles. Turn left onto County Road 39 and drive for 0.6 mile to Old County Road 39. Veer left here and continue for 0.2 mile to the campground on the left side of the road.

Contact: Highview Campground & RV Park, 218/543-4526, http://highviewcampground.com.

14 PORTSMOUTH BAY CAMPGROUND

Scenic rating: 10

in Cuyuna Country State Park

Cuyuna Country State Park is Minnesota's newest state park, and its campground is still getting on its feet. There are only 17 rustic sites here for now, with vault toilets and no electricity. The seclusion, heavy tree cover, privacy, and proximity to acres upon acres of forest and lakes make this little-known campground a kind of needle in the haystack, especially as camping in the Brainerd Lakes area can get crowded in the summer. Outdoor recreation has exploded in this area in the last 10 years, and all the ATV riders and motorboaters haven't fully discovered this recreation area.

The Cuyuna Lakes State Trail passes through the park, providing access to more than six miles of paved biking and hiking. What really makes this park a gem is the fact that it has been closed off to the public for decades as an abandoned mining area. Huge pit mines have been grown over with wild, untamed forest, and the massive pits, some hundreds of feet deep, have filled with clear northwoods water. The DNR has begun stocking many of them with game fish, making this area a rare, almost unexplored wilderness in the middle of one of the state's most popular recreation areas.

Campsites, facilities: There are 17 sites for tents and RVs (no hookups) and one group campsite for up to 25 people. Picnic tables, fire rings, drinking water, vault toilets, and garbage cans are provided. A paved hiking and biking trail, picnic area, fishing pier, and boat ramp are available. Leashed pets are permitted.

Reservations, fees: Reservations are not accepted. Sites are $12 per night. Self-registration is required at the campground. Open from May to late September.

Directions: From Ironton, drive north on County Road 30 for 0.7 mile. Turn right into the Portsmouth Bay campground at the wooden sign.

Contact: Cuyuna Country State Park, 218/546-5926, www.dnr.state.mn.us/state_parks.

15 CROSBY MEMORIAL PARK CAMPGROUND

Scenic rating: 6

on Serpent Lake in Crosby

Crosby is known as the "Antiquing Capital" of Minnesota. My grandmother, mother, and aunts used to make a day of driving to Crosby, searching the dozens of antiques shops lining Main Street for good finds. Crosby Memorial Park on the northwestern shore of Serpent Lake is anything but antique.

The park is located on the south side of town, just two blocks away from Main Street. The modern campground's modest sites are in a woodsy patch of the park near the water. The sites themselves are large enough for an RV and a tent, and each has at least one tree, which increases the privacy factor by several degrees. The campground is popular with RV campers who come to enjoy the small-town charm of Crosby for a weekend but don't want to rough it tent camping. Surprisingly for a small town, the park can get noisy, especially during the summer months when locals come to enjoy the swimming beach and fishing pier.

Campsites, facilities: There are 20 sites for tents and RVs. Picnic tables, fire rings, toilets, showers, and a dump station are provided. A playground, fishing pier, swimming beach, and softball field are available. Some facilities are wheelchair accessible. Leashed pets are permitted.

Reservations, fees: Reservations are accepted at 218/546-5021. Sites are $20 per night. Open from mid-May to mid-October.

Directions: In Crosby, drive south on Highway 210 for 0.25 mile. Turn left into the park at 4rd Street SW.

Contact: City of Crosby, 218/546-5021.

16 GREER LAKE CAMPGROUND

Scenic rating: 7

on Greer Lake north of Crosby

Deep in the Crow Wing State Forest, Greer Lake is folded into the dense woods near Cuyuna State Recreation Area. Used primarily as a public boat landing, the campground is very secluded and rarely used. The sites are located at the end of Greer Lake Road in an arc through the trees about 100 feet from the lake. There are oodles of shade, privacy, and seclusion here. More often than not you will be among just a handful of campers, if not the only one—especially if you come here during the week or in the off-season.

Campers have access to the Bass Lake

Nature Trail from the campground, as well as the many lakes and hiking trails spread throughout the state forest. Having a map of the area is a must if you plan on venturing out from Greer Lake and taking advantage of the many trails that winnow through its woods.

Campsites, facilities: There are 31 sites for tents and RVs. Picnic tables, fire rings, drinking water, toilets, and a garbage can are provided. A boat ramp, dock, and fish cleaning station are provided. Leashed pets are permitted.

Reservations, fees: Reservations are not accepted. Self-registration is required at the campground. Sites are $12 per night. Open year-round.

Directions: From Crosby, drive north on Highway 6 for 12 miles to County Road 36. Turn left and drive for 3 miles to County Road 114. Turn left and drive for 1.4 miles.

Contact: Cuyuna State Recreation Area, 218/546-5926, www.dnr.state.mn.us/state_forests/facilities/cmp00010/index.html.

17 LITTLE PINE RV PARK

Scenic rating: 6

on Roosevelt Lake in Land O'Lakes State Forest

Little Pine RV Park is a small RV campground in the Land O'Lakes State Forest. The park is about a half hour from mighty Leech Lake, the Mississippi River, and Whitefish Lake, not to mention that it is right on Roosevelt Lake and enjoys a beautiful view of water and woods.

The lakes region is notorious for large RV parks lacking in character, but happily, this isn't one of them. The sites are sunk into the trees along the shoreline and are connected via a footpath to the swimming beach and boat landing. Campers can rent pontoons and fishing boats or just fish from the dock.

Land O'Lakes State Forest is a beautiful swatch of pine and hardwoods, full of wildlife,

in the center of the state. There are several day-use areas in the forest, and the Duck Lake State Wildlife Area is just a 15-minute drive south of the campground.

Campsites, facilities: There are 25 sites for RVs. Picnic tables, fire rings, toilets, showers, and a dump station are provided. A swimming beach, dock, boat ramp, pontoon rental, and laundry facilities are available. Some facilities are wheelchair accessible. Leashed pets are permitted.

Reservations, fees: Reservations are accepted at 218/763-2942. Sites are $20 per night. Open from May to late September.

Directions: From Emily, drive south on Highway 6 for 0.7 mile. The campground is on the left side of the road between Dahler and Emily Lakes about 0.3 mile past Dahler Avenue.

Contact: Little Pine RV Park, 218/763-2942.

18 CLINT CONVERSE CAMPGROUND

Scenic rating: 8

on Washburn Lake

The Clint Converse Campground makes a Minnesotan proud of the state forest service. This idyllic campground is nice and small, divided into two loops on the south shore of Washburn Lake. It is secluded, heavily forested, private, and an excellent outdoor recreation spot. The campground is adjacent to hiking trails that explore the state forest, great fishing on Washburn Lake, and a wonderful, sandy swimming beach. It is close to dozens of other north country lakes.

The sites are well-spaced and heavily shaded amid the dense pine and hardwood forest that surrounds Washburn Lake. A boat ramp gives access to the eastern arm of the lake, but by traveling north and around the large peninsula boaters and anglers have access to the lake's much larger western section.

Campsites, facilities: There are 31 sites for tents and RVs. Picnic tables, fire rings, drinking water, vault toilets, and a garbage can are provided. A swimming beach, fishing area, hiking trails, and a boat ramp are available. Leashed pets are permitted.

Reservations, fees: Reservations are not accepted. Sites are $12 per night. Self-registration is required at the campground. Open year-round, with limited facilities in winter.

Directions: From Outing, drive north on Highway 6 for 2 miles to Lake Washburn Road. Turn left and drive for 2 miles. The campground is on the right side of the road marked by a wooden state forest sign.

Contact: Cuyuna State Recreation Area, 218/546-5926, www.dnr.state.mn.us/state_forests/facilities/cmp00033/index.html.

19 SCHOOLCRAFT CAMPGROUND
🚶 🛶 ⛵ 🐕 🚐 ⛺

Scenic rating: 8

in Schoolcraft State Park

Schoolcraft State Park operates under the mantra of simplicity. An evergreen-forested slice of land on the Upper Mississippi River, the park is named after the avid explorer who feverishly searched for the headwaters of the mighty river. He came close, declaring what is now Cass Lake to be the source.

The park is in a very rural area on the river, giving it a "middle of nowhere" quality. The campground is very quiet and private, with dozens of trees peppered between the sites. Even during the summer you may find yourself alone or with just one or two other campers, especially if you come during the week.

The hiking trail here is especially worthwhile. There are stands of virgin pine untouched by the logging frenzy of the 19th century. Some trees are estimated to be more than 300 years old, giant specimens of evergreen along the nation's longest river.

Campsites, facilities: There are 28 sites for tents and RVs up to 40 feet. There is also one canoe-in site and one tent-only group campsite for up to 50 people. Picnic tables, fire rings, vault toilets, and garbage cans are provided. A hiking trail, boat access, and picnic area are provided. Leashed pets are permitted.

Reservations, fees: Reservations are accepted from April 2 to October 31 at 866/857-2757 or online at www.stayatmnparks.com ($8.50 non-refundable reservation fee) and can be made up to one year in advance. Reservations are not required the rest of the year. Sites are $12–24 per night. Open year-round, with limited facilities in winter.

Directions: From Deer River, drive east on Highway 2 for 2.5 miles. Turn right onto County Road 11. In 5 miles, turn right onto County Road 18 and drive for 2.8 miles. The road becomes 124th Street NE and continues for 0.6 mile to 88th Avenue. Turn left and drive for 2 miles to Schoolcraft Lane NE. The park and campground are 1 mile ahead. The road ends in a loop just before reaching the river.

Contact: Schoolcraft State Park, 218/247-7215, www.dnr.state.mn.us/state_parks.

20 HILL LAKE PARK CAMPGROUND
🚶 🚲 ⛵ 🏊 🛶 🐕 🎣 ♿ 🚐 ⛺

Scenic rating: 6

in Hill City

Hill City is one of those cinematic small towns that somehow managed to hold onto the charm and energy small-town America had long ago. Its lovely city park was dedicated to the town in the 1920s and lies on the western shore of beautiful Hill Lake.

The campsites line a gravel drive that leads through the park to the lake and fishing pier. There is no tree cover, which is unfortunate because all other aspects of this park are perfect. A shady picnic area, sandy swimming beach, and woodsy hiking trail all add up to a real charmer of a park. With no privacy or shade between sites, camping here isn't as enjoyable as just visiting.

Campsites, facilities: There are 30 sites for tents and 10 sites for RVs (partial hookups). Picnic tables, fire rings, toilets, showers, and a dump station are provided. A swimming beach, playground, hiking and biking trail, and boat ramp are available. Some facilities are wheelchair accessible. Leashed pets are permitted.

Reservations, fees: Reservations are accepted at 218/697-2301. Sites are $15 per night for tents and $20 per night for RVs. Open from mid-May to mid-October.

Directions: In Hill City, drive east on Park Avenue for 0.1 mile to the city park and campground.

Contact: Hill City City Hall, 218/697-2301, www.hillcitymn.com.

21 MISSISSIPPI RIVER CANOE CAMPSITES

Scenic rating: 9

on the Mississippi River between Grand Rapids and Brainerd

BEST (

The Mississippi River begins to gain some steam as it flows south from Grand Rapids toward Brainerd. The winding river is still slow moving, but several feet wider, holding more water than its extreme upper regions.

The waterway is peppered with small canoe campsites. Each of these dozen or so sites is accessible only by canoe from the river. The sites are marked by small wooden numbered signs and are very primitive, with just a fire ring and a clearing for a tent or two; some may have picnic tables and vault toilets. Many of the sites have a rural-nowhere feel to them, far from cities and country roads that can't reach the floodplain surrounding the muddy river.

Campsites, facilities: There are approximately 10 sites for tents only located along the river from Grand Rapids to Brainerd. Picnic tables, fire rings, and vault toilets may be provided. There is no drinking water, so bring your own or a filtration device. Leashed pets are permitted.

Reservations, fees: Reservations are not accepted. There is no fee. Open year-round.

Directions: Access to the river is available at Crosby, Aitkin, Grand Rapids, and Crow Wing State Park. An accurate map of the river and the locations of these sites is essential. Contact the Minnesota Department of Natural Resources at info@dnr.state.mn.us for maps.

Contact: Minnesota Department of Natural Resources, 218/308-2372, www.dnr.state. mn.us/watertrails/mississippiriver/one.html.

22 JACOBSON CAMPGROUND

Scenic rating: 6

in Jacobson on the Mississippi River

Jacobson is a small river community in one of the northwoods' most rural areas. The Mississippi is particularly unwieldy here, making repetitive and dramatic oxbows that stack upon each other for miles. The campground is just upstream from the Highway 200 bridge near its intersection with Highway 65, the most prominent landmark of the village.

The campground is in a little park, which is really more of a small clearing in the trees along the riverbank. Sites are rustic; an outhouse, some picnic tables, and tent pads are all you will find here. Canoeists often camp here on their way downriver, and it is close to Savanna Portage State Park and Pokegama Lake in Grand Rapids, known for its fishing.

Campsites, facilities: There are 10 sites for tents. Picnic tables, fire rings, pit toilets, and a garbage can are provided. A hiking trail, a boat ramp, an artesian well, and an ATV trail are available. Leashed pets are permitted.

Reservations, fees: Reservations are not accepted. Sites are $12 per night. Self-registration at the campground is required. Open from May to late October.

Directions: From the intersection of Highways 65 and 200, drive west on Highway 200 for 0.25 mile. The campground is on the right side of the road just after crossing the bridge over the river.

Contact: City of Jacobson, 218/752-6690, http://jacobsonnews.com/index.cfm?CID=24.

23 HAY LAKE CAMPGROUND
Scenic rating: 8

southeast of Jacobson

Savanna Portage State Park is perennial favorite of campers from all around the state, but for an even more remote camping experience in the Savanna Portage State Forest, head up to Hay Lake.

The small camping loop has only 20 sites on remote Hay Lake just south of Jacobson. The little lake is actually quite the fishing hole, producing pike, walleye, bass, and crappie. The sites are spaced several dozen feet apart on the wooded south shore of the lake. A small clearing on the water provides a swimming beach and canoe landing, along with a dock for fishing. This is becoming a better-known spot, but you can still usually find the campground unoccupied on weekdays or during the off-season.

Campsites, facilities: There are 20 sites for tents and RVs. Picnic tables, fire rings, drinking water, vault toilets, and garbage cans are provided. A swimming beach, boat ramp, dock, hiking trails, fishing area, and canoe landing are available. Leashed pets are permitted.

Reservations, fees: Reservations are not accepted. Self-registration is required at the campground. Sites are $12 per night. Open from May to late October.

Directions: From Jacobson, drive south on Highway 65 for 2.5 miles. Turn left onto Hay Lake Road and drive for 2.3 miles to a T in the road. Turn right and continue on Hay Lake Road for another 0.25 mile to the campground at the end of Hay Lake Road, marked by a wooden state forest sign.

Contact: Savanna Portage State Park, 218/426-3271, www.dnr.state.mn.us/state_forests/facilities/cmp00047/index.html.

24 SAVANNA PORTAGE CAMPGROUND
Scenic rating: 10

in Savanna Portage State Park

BEST (

Savanna Portage State Park is possibly the state's perfect park. The park and state forest that contain it lie along a historical portage trail used by voyageurs in the 1700s. Beautiful Loon Lake is stocked with trout and rife with wildlife. A mile-long bog boardwalk trail tours one of the state's largest peat bogs, where you can find lady's slippers, pitcher plants, and other rare orchid family and bog flora. A hiking trail explores the continental divide that lies in the center of the park, diverting water on one side to the Mississippi River and on the other to Lake Superior.

The campground is on Lake Shumway's southern shore, a picturesque northwoods lake circumnavigated by a hiking trail. The two-loop campground is well shaded, though the sites are a bit close together. The heavy tree cover and peaceful lake make up for it, as well as the fact that the campground in this remote park usually isn't full.

The backpacking sites that branch throughout the park make for wonderful weekend hiking trips, some of them deep in the bog, some high atop the continental divide with stunning views overlooking the surrounding state forest.

Campsites, facilities: There are 61 sites for tents and RVs up to 55 feet; four sites are pull-through and 18 sites have electrical hookups.

There are also six backpacking sites, one canoe-in site, and one group campsite for up to 30 people. Picnic tables, fire rings, drinking water, flush and vault toilets, showers, and a dump station are provided. Hiking and mountain-biking trails, cross-country ski trails, a bog boardwalk, playground, fishing piers, canoe rental, and swimming beach are available. Leashed pets are permitted.

Reservations, fees: Reservations are accepted from April 2 to October 31 at 866/857-2757 or online at www.stayatmnparks.com ($8.50 non-refundable reservation fee) and can be made up to one year in advance. Reservations are not required the rest of the year. Sites are $12–24 per night. Open year-round, with limited facilities in winter.

Directions: From McGregor, drive north on Highway 65 for 11 miles to County Road 14. Turn right and drive for another 11 miles straight into the park.

Contact: Savanna Portage State Park, 218/426-3271, www.dnr.state.mn.us/state_parks.

25 AITKIN LAKE RESORT AND CAMPGROUND

Scenic rating: 6

on Aitkin Lake north of McGregor

Aitkin Lake is a small, secluded lake with a single development on it: Aitkin Lake Resort. The lake feeds into the much larger and more popular Big Sandy Lake, famed for its walleye, water-skiing, and big blue bays.

The campground at Aitkin Lake sits at the end of a long gravel drive that leads to the eastern shore of the lake. Campsites are lined up along the lakeshore, most of them just across the driveway from the water. There are several docks for boats, fishing, and swimming, and a boat ramp provides access to Aitkin Lake and Big Sandy Lake. The channel leading to Big Sandy is just a few hundred feet south of Aldrich's, marked by buoys.

There are lots of trees, plenty of shade, and a quiet, peaceful atmosphere up on Aitkin Lake. It is perfect for campers who want the amenities of a resort and the seclusion of a small campground.

Campsites, facilities: There are 40 sites for tents and RVs; some sites have hookups. Picnic tables, fire rings, flush toilets, showers, and a dump station are provided. A hiking and biking trail, playground, canoe rental, fishing boat rental, and boat ramp are available. Some facilities are wheelchair accessible. Leashed pets are permitted.

Reservations, fees: Reservations are accepted at 218/363-2610. Sites are $18.50 per night for tents and $28 per night for RVs. Open from mid-May to September.

Directions: From McGregor, drive north on Highway 65 for 13 miles. Turn right onto Aitkin Lake Road. The resort is 1.2 miles ahead at the end of the road.

Contact: Aitkin Lake Resort and Campground, 218/426-3327, www.aitkinlakeresort.com.

26 LIBBY DAM RECREATION AREA

Scenic rating: 6

on Big Sandy Lake

BEST (

Libby Dam is actually the Sandy Lake and Dam Recreation Area, maintained by the Army Corps of Engineers (ACOE), but the locals know it as Libby Dam. I grew up in this area and used to love coming here to camp, swim, and fish. The recreation area has a swimming beach, boat access to Big Sandy and Aitkin Lakes, a historical cemetery, and a boat house that was once the northernmost lock and dam system on the Mississippi. The fishing here is great, especially below the dam where several types of fish—including pike and walleye—cluster in the swirling waters looking for food.

The campsites are strung along a long, wide loop that passes into the oak and maple forests filling the park. The dam was built at the outlet of Big Sandy Lake, where the Sandy River travels about 0.5 mile to its confluence with the Mississippi. The bottomland forest here is thick and shady, and the campsites are very private, each with its own gravel driveway and complete tree cover. Another set of campsites (about half of them) is much closer to the water, in an open, grassy area. These sites enjoy less privacy but have a better view of the lake and waterfront areas.

Big Sandy is popular for walleye fishing, water skiing, and motorboating. The recreation area also has a bike trail that passes through the park, a large playground, and a volleyball court.

Campsites, facilities: There are 59 sites for tents and RVs. Picnic tables, fire rings, toilets, showers, and a dump station are provided. A hiking and biking trail, swimming beach, playground, three boat ramps, fishing docks, and laundry facilities are available. Some facilities are wheelchair accessible. Leashed pets are permitted.

Reservations, fees: Reservations are accepted at 877/444-6777 or online at www.recreation. gov ($10 reservation fee). Sites are $14 per night for tents and $22 per night for RVs. Open from mid-May through November.

Directions: From McGregor, drive north on Highway 65 for 13 miles. Turn right into the recreation area at the South Entrance park sign.

Contact: Sandy Lake and Dam Recreation Area, 218/426-3482, www.mvp.usace.army. mil/navigation/default.asp?pageid=148.

27 BERGLUND PARK CAMPGROUND

Scenic rating: 6

on the Mississippi River in Palisade

Palisade is a quaint little river town along the Upper Mississippi as it winds its way toward Aitkin. Within minutes of a dozen area lakes, including the popular Big Sandy Lake, this is a good spot if you are looking to go easy on the wallet while still being close to all the action. The campground has just nine sites in a small city park on the river's north bank. Each site has a short gravel driveway and several trees for shade, though most of the park is an open grassy area. The Soo Line Trail and Highway 232 cross the river on either side of the campground, which makes a handy fishing hole, especially when the water is a little higher during late spring.

Campsites, facilities: There are nine sites for tents and RVs. Picnic tables, fire rings, toilets, showers, and a dump station are provided. A boat ramp and picnic area are available. Some facilities are wheelchair accessible. Leashed pets are permitted.

Reservations, fees: Reservations are accepted at 218/927-7364. Sites are $15 per night. Open from mid-May to late-October.

Directions: From the intersection of Highway 10 and Highway 5 in Palisade, drive west on Highway 10 for 0.1 mile. The campground is on the left just off Great River Road.

Contact: Berglund Park Campground, 218/927-7364.

28 HICKORY LAKE CAMPGROUND

Scenic rating: 6

on Hickory Lake

Hickory Lake Campground is pure class. From the efficient campground design and beautiful spot on Hickory Lake to the gorgeous flower gardens and sandy swimming beach, this is a campground with style. I would say you'll feel right at home here, but this might actually be nicer!

The sites are well spaced, have ample privacy and good tree cover, and are close to the central area of the campground where the outdoor pool, playground, and game room are. They are also close to Hickory Lake, the beach, and fishing and boating docks.

There are more than 100 lakes in a 15-mile radius from the campground, and mighty Mille Lacs, which has two state parks—Mille Lacs Kathio and Father Hennepin—is straight down Highway 169.

Campsites, facilities: There are 56 sites for tents and RVs (full hookups). Picnic tables, fire rings, toilets, coin showers, and a dump station are provided. An outdoor pool, swimming beach, playground, boat ramp, fishing boat rental, canoe rental, coin laundry, wireless Internet, and a camp store are available. Some facilities are wheelchair accessible. Leashed pets are permitted.

Reservations, fees: Reservations are accepted at 218/927-6001 (a one-night deposit is required). Sites are $42–$59 per night. There is a $5 fee per pet per night. Two- and three-night minimums may apply on holiday weekends. Open from May 1 to September 30.

Directions: From Aitkin, drive south on Highway 169 for 7 miles. The campground is on the left directly off of the highway shortly after passing between Hickory and Little Pine Lakes just past Township Road 1096.

Contact: Hickory Lake Campground, 218/927-6001, www.hickorylakecampground.net.

29 WILDERNESS OF MINNESOTA CAMPGROUND
🚶 ⛵ 🐕 🚴 🛶 🚐 ⛺

Scenic rating: 4

on Lake Mille Lacs near Garrison

Everything adds up for this to be an alluring camping spot, but the real thing doesn't quite deliver on the promise. While the small, residential community is located on the shores of stunning Lake Mille Lacs, the campground itself is on a patch of treeless grass and gravel across Highway 169 from the water. Traffic is less than 100 feet away from the camping area, which provides no privacy or shade. For a quick overnight, this place will do in a pinch, but it's not a destination in and of itself.

Campsites, facilities: There are 99 sites for tents and RVs. Picnic tables, fire rings, toilets, showers, and a dump station are provided. A hiking trail, outdoor pool, playground, and laundry facilities are available. Leashed pets are permitted.

Reservations, fees: Reservations are accepted at 320/692-4347. Sites are $25 per night for tents and $36 per night for RVs. Open from mid-May to mid-September.

Directions: From Garrison, drive north on Highway 169 for 0.5 mile. A campground sign will direct you to turn left. Follow the campground road for 250 feet, then turn right at the next campground sign to the registration office.

Contact: Wilderness of Minnesota Campground, 320/692-4347.

30 PETE'S RETREAT
🚴 ⛵ 🐕 🚴 🦽 🚐 ⛺

Scenic rating: 6

in Malmo

Pete's Retreat is part campground, part retreat center, and part amusement park. Located just two blocks from Lake Mille Lacs, Pete's Retreat is a full-service campground and RV park in a heavily wooded piece of land just north of Malmo. There are nearly 100 campsites here dispersed throughout heavy tree cover and along gravel drives that probe deep into the shady forest. About a dozen of the sites cluster close to the parking area, but many more are very private, with plenty of trees, and enjoy up to 50 feet of space between each other. The camping areas are large enough for an RV and at least two tents.

Pete's Retreat has regularly scheduled weekend events that include hay rides, carnival-themed weekends, and Halloween. Recreation is emphasized here, with volleyball courts, basketball, a BMX bike track, outdoor pools, and awesome playgrounds. A public boat access to Lake Mille Lacs is just across the highway, less than 0.5 mile away.

Campsites, facilities: There are 96 sites for tents and RVs up to 120 feet. Pull-through sites and full hookups are available. Picnic tables, fire rings, toilets, showers, and a dump station are provided. An outdoor pool, hot tub, game room, bike track, playground, Internet access, and a camp store are available. Some facilities are wheelchair accessible. Leashed pets are permitted.

Reservations, fees: Reservations are accepted at 866/578-7275 (one night's deposit is required). Sites are $32–50 per night. There is a $5 fee per pet per night. A two-night minimum stay is required on weekends, a three-night minimum stay on holiday weekends. Open from mid-May to October.

Directions: In Malmo, drive north on Highway 47 for 0.25 mile. The campground is on the left side of the road just before County Road 80.

Contact: Pete's Retreat Family Campground & RV Park, 320/684-2020, www.petes retreat.com.

31 MILLE LACS KATHIO CAMPGROUNDS

Scenic rating: 9

in Mille Lacs Kathio State Park

Mille Lacs Kathio State Park may be Minnesota's single most significant archaeological area. In the 1970s, archaeologists discovered ancient Native American village sites along Ogechie Lake. Wooden walls, stoneware, and wild-rice pits, along with dozens of other artifacts, were unearthed. Today, an interpretive hiking trail tours the sites, educating visitors about the history of Native Americans in the area and the significance of this area to their culture.

There are two campgrounds in the park— Ogechie Campground, adjacent to the interpretive trail that leads to the ancient villages, and Petaga Campground, farther south along the Rum River as it flows from Lake Mille Lacs. There are 70 well-spaced sites between the two campgrounds, both protected by heavy tree cover, and private camping areas with large tent pads. The park also has several backpacking sites along the hiking club trail in the north section of the park; these offer supreme privacy and seclusion in the park's hardwood (mostly maple) forest.

A tall observation tower in the park rises high above the treetops, with views of nearby Lake Mille Lacs and the rolling forest that covers the region.

Campsites, facilities: There are 70 sites for tents and RVs up to 60 feet; three sites are pull-through, and 22 sites have electrical hookups. There are also three walk-in sites, four backpacking sites, 10 equestrian sites, and two tent-only group campsites for up to 15 and 45 people each. Picnic tables, fire rings, drinking water, flush and vault toilets, and showers are provided. Hiking and cross-country ski trails, a boardwalk, a playground, canoe access and rentals, a sliding hill, warming house, and swimming beach are available. There are two wheelchair-accessible sites. Leashed pets are permitted.

Reservations, fees: Reservations are accepted from April 2 to October 31 at 866/857-2757 or online at www.stayatmnparks.com ($8.50 non-refundable reservation fee) and can be made up to one year in advance. Reservations are not required the rest of the year. Sites are $12–24 per night. Open year-round, with limited facilities in winter.

Directions: From Onamia, drive west on Highway 27 for 1.7 miles. Turn right onto County Road 26. In 5.4 miles, turn left onto Kathio State Park Road by the wooden state park sign. The park office is 2.1 miles ahead.

Contact: Mille Lacs Kathio State Park, 320/532-3523, www.dnr.state.mn.us/state_parks.

32 FATHER HENNEPIN STATE PARK

Scenic rating: 9

in Father Hennepin State Park

BEST (

Father Hennepin State Park is a sleepy little strip of lakeshore on the south side of Lake Mille Lacs. Pine, birch, and maple forests all meet here, giving three distinct habitats a chance to express themselves. A superb hiking trail tours each wooded area and leads past the swimming area out to Pope Point, a lookout spot over the lake. On a clear day, Pope Point views include one of the last nesting places of the endangered common tern. The swimming area is adjacent to the fishing piers and boat access point. Fishing from shore or the pier proves surprisingly fruitful.

The campground sits in a maple-forested area. Some of the sites are in a clearing along the park road, but the choicest ones lie on the lakeshore with footpaths that lead directly to the water beneath the trees.

Lake Mille Lacs is wildly popular for its famed walleye fishing. Father Hennepin State Park has an amazing stretch of real estate on this very valuable lake, giving campers and hikers a chance to fully enjoy it and imagine what the area once looked like before heavy settlement.

Campsites, facilities: There are 103 sites for tents and RVs up to 60 feet; 41 sites have electrical hookups. There are also six group campsites for up to 12, 15, 20, and 25 people each. Picnic tables, fire rings, flush and vault toilets, drinking water, showers, and a dump station are provided. Hiking trails, cross-country ski trails, a playground, warming house, fishing pier, swimming beach, and boat access are available. There are four wheelchair-accessible sites. Leashed pets are permitted.

Reservations, fees: Reservations are accepted from April 2 to October 31 at 866/857-2757 or online at www.stayatmnparks.com ($8.50 non-refundable reservation fee) and can be made up to one year in advance. Reservations are not required the rest of the year. Sites are $12–24 per night. Open year-round, with limited facilities in winter.

Directions: From Wahkon, drive northeast on Highway 27 for 2.5 miles. Then turn left onto Father Hennepin Park Road into the park. The park office is 0.1 mile ahead.

Contact: Father Hennepin State Park, 320/676-8763, www.dnr.state.mn.us/state_parks.

33 MOOSE LAKE STATE PARK

Scenic rating: 8

in Moose Lake State Park

BEST (

Moose Lake State Park is a reminder that the best things come in small packages. This compact state park delivers a first-class northwoods camping experience without being part of a sprawling state forest or wildlife management area. Hiking trails traverse the hardwood forest, the tall, silent red pine grove, and the shores of Echo Lake with its exquisite swimming beach. The beach and the lake bottom here are a gradual, sandy descent into the water, making this one of the finest state park beaches in north-central Minnesota. The Willard Munger Trail, which extends from Hinckley all the way to Duluth, is the longest paved bike trail in the country and is just two miles west of the park.

The campground is on the eastern shore of Echo Lake in three small loops. There are only 33 sites in the park, making each loop feel like a small, private camping area in the thick patch of forest that huddles around water.

The Moose Lake area is the agate capital of the Midwest. The town holds an annual agate festival, and the state park has an agate museum and shop in it. Campers at the state park often travel the gravel roads and old train tracks looking for agates, which exist in high quantities in this part of the state.

Campsites, facilities: There are 33 sites for tents and RVs up to 60 feet; 20 sites have electrical hookups. There are also two walk-in sites and one tent-only group campsite for up to 45 people. Picnic tables, fire rings, flush and vault toilets, and showers are provided. A wheelchair-accessible trail, hiking trail, cross-country ski and snowmobile trail, playground, fishing pier, and swimming beach are available. There are two wheelchair-accessible sites. Leashed pets are permitted.

Reservations, fees: Reservations are accepted from April 2 to October 31 at 866/857-2757 or online at www.stayatmnparks.com ($8.50 non-refundable reservation fee) and can be made up to one year in advance. Reservations are not required the rest of the year. Sites are $12–24 per night. Open year-round, with limited facilities in winter.

Directions: From Moose Lake, drive east on County Road 137 across I-35 for 0.5 mile. The state park entrance is on the right, marked by a large wooden sign.

Contact: Moose Lake State Park, 218/485-5420, www.dnr.state.mn.us/state_parks.

34 BANNING CAMPGROUND

Scenic rating: 9

in Banning State Park

Banning State Park lies on the turbulent and magnificent Kettle River. A large rock quarry operated here in the early 20th century. Remains of the stone buildings still stand along the river where huge boulders were taken from the earth. The river here is full of rapids, white water, and sheer cliffs. The campground sits on top of a pine forested hill several hundred yards from the water but is connected via a hiking trail to all of the best sites along the river, including Wolf Creek Falls.

Landmarks along the river carry names like Dragon's Tooth, Hell's Gate, and Deadman Trail, which themselves paint a picture of the powerful nature of the river. The Kettle River is also a State Scenic River, frequented by adventurous kayakers and canoeists brave enough to take on the churning waters. For landlubbers, the hiking trails here are awesome, touring both sides of the river and delivering hikers to spectacular overlooks of the river and its rapids.

Campsites, facilities: There are 33 sites for tents and RVs up to 50 feet; 11 sites have electrical hookups. There are also four canoe-in sites and one backpacking site. Picnic tables, fire rings, drinking water, flush and vault toilets, and showers are provided. A wheelchair-accessible trail, hiking trail, paved biking trail, cross-country ski and snowmobile trail, fishing area, boat ramp, canoe access, and picnic area are available. Some facilities are wheelchair accessible. Leashed pets are permitted.

Reservations, fees: Reservations are accepted from April 2 to October 31 at 866/857-2757 or online at www.stayatmnparks.com ($8.50 non-refundable reservation fee) and can be made up to one year in advance. Reservations are not required the rest of the year. Sites are $12–24 per night. Open year-round, with limited facilities in winter.

Directions: From the intersection of I-35 and Highway 23, drive south on Highway 23 for 0.1 mile. A highway sign direct drivers to the park on the left. Follow the state park road for 1 mile to the park entrance. A state park sign directs drivers to turn right. The park office is 1 mile ahead on the gravel road.

Contact: Banning State Park, 320/245-2668, www.dnr.state.mn.us/state_parks.

35 INDIAN MOUNDS RESORT AND CAMPGROUND

Scenic rating: 7

on Pelican Lake

Indian Mounds sits on the end of a long, winding peninsula that extends for more than a mile into scenic Pelican Lake. Considering its prime location and excellent resort facilities, camping here is a real deal for tent campers. Indian Mounds is primarily a resort, with a small seven-site campground. The sites are tucked into a shady grove of oak, maple, and pine trees that provide excellent shade and more than ample privacy. Footpaths explore the shoreline of the peninsula, and campers can use the resort's canoes, paddleboats, and fishing dock.

Campsites, facilities: There are seven sites for tents and RVs. Picnic tables, fire rings, toilets, showers, and a dump station are provided. A hiking and biking trail, swimming beach, canoes, dock space, fishing boat rental, a boat ramp, playground, and camp store are available. Leashed pets are permitted.

Reservations, fees: Reservations are accepted at 218/948-2201. Sites are $32 per night. There is a $5 fee per pet per night. Open from May to October.

Directions: From Fergus Falls, drive south on I-94 for 21 miles. Take Exit 77 onto Highway 78 and turn left. In 4.2 miles, turn right onto County Road 82 and drive for 2.7 miles to County Road 19. Turn right onto County Road 19 and drive 0.5 mile to County Road 57. The campground is 2.5 miles ahead at the end of the peninsula on the right side of the road.

Contact: Indian Mounds Resort and Campground, 218/948-2201, www.indianmounds-resort.com.

36 OAK PARK KAMPGROUND

Scenic rating: 6

near Garfield

Surrounded by grassy fields and wetlands, Oak Park is an oasis of trees in the midst of lakes and grass. The park is adjacent to the Douglas Area Trails system and is near sizable Elk Lake.

The campground sits on the border of the large grove of oak trees from which the park gets its name. The sites are arranged in three narrow loops that are peppered with oak trees. A hiking trail tours the forest, but there is more to do in the campground than in the woods. A game room and outdoor pool are well maintained and nice to use on rainy days. This campground has more of a rest-and-relaxation atmosphere than an outdoors one, which is just the ticket if you want to catch up on your afternoon naps.

Campsites, facilities: There are 45 sites for tents and RVs. Picnic tables, fire rings, toilets, showers, and a dump station are provided. A hiking trail, game room, outdoor pool, laundry facilities, and a camp store are available. Some facilities are wheelchair accessible. Leashed pets are permitted.

Reservations, fees: Reservations are accepted at 320/834-2345. Sites are $25 per night for tents and $40 per night for RVs. Open from May to October.

Directions: From Exit 97 on I-94, drive east on County Road 8 for 0.25 mile. The campground is on the left side of the road, the third left from the freeway.

Contact: Oak Park Kampground, 320/834-2345.

37 BARSNESS PARK CAMPGROUND

Scenic rating: 6

in Glenwood

Lake Minnewaska is a paradox of outdoor preservation. Beautiful Barsness Park and its campground are book-ended by two large golf courses on the east side of the lake, while a state wildlife area lies just a few miles north. These two different takes on outdoor recreation make Barsness Park a convenient place to stop—close to 36 holes of golf or a pristine state wildlife area. Shady Barsness Park itself is a large, undeveloped patch of forest on the water, crisscrossed with hiking and biking trails, and stamped with tennis courts, a swimming beach, and playground.

The campsites sit in a little clearing amid a hardwood forest that looks like the trees will close in on it any second. Prodigious shade and a sense of seclusion make this a wonderfully woodsy campground. The sites are only about 10 feet away from each other, but all the trees and the "hidden away" feeling of the campground loop make up for it.

Campsites, facilities: There are 50 sites for tents and RVs (full and partial hookups). Picnic tables, fire rings, toilets, showers, and a dump station are provided. A swimming beach, playground, tennis court, and hiking trail are available. Leashed pets are permitted.

Reservations, fees: Reservations are accepted at 320/634-5433. Sites are $15 per night for tents, $20–30 per night for RVs. Open from May to October.

Directions: In Glenwood, drive south on Highway 104 for 0.25 mile to Barsness Park. Turn left into the park after the ball fields.

Contact: Barsness Park Campground, 320/634-5433.

38 LAKE CARLOS CAMPGROUND

🚶 ⛱ 🏊 🛶 ❄ 🏕 ♿ 🚐 ⛺

Scenic rating: 9

in Lake Carlos State Park

Like much of north-central Minnesota, Lake Carlos State Park was shaped by glaciers from the last ice age that left behind the vast blanket of lakes and wetlands we enjoy today. The park is an abundant collection of peat bog, wetland, and lake habitat within a larger hardwood forest.

There are two campgrounds in the park. One campground is on the north shore of Lake Carlos, set in two narrow loops that are absolutely packed to the gills with nearly 100 campsites. A smaller, more secluded campground lies farther north on the heavily wooded hilltop that rises to the more open grassland area in the northern section of the park.

Campsites, facilities: There are 121 sites for tents and RVs up to 50 feet; 81 sites have electrical hookups. There are also seven equestrian sites for up to 30 people and two group campsites for up to 35 and 50 people each. Picnic tables, fire rings, drinking water, flush and vault toilets, showers, and a dump station are provided. Hiking and horse trails, cross-country ski trails, a warming house, boat ramp, and swimming beach are available. Two sites and some facilities are wheelchair accessible. Leashed pets are permitted.

Reservations, fees: Reservations are accepted from April 2 to October 31 at 866/857-2757 or online at www.stayatmnparks.com ($8.50 non-refundable reservation fee) and can be made up to one year in advance. Reservations are not required the rest of the year. Sites are $12–24 per night. Open year-round, with limited facilities in winter.

Directions: From Alexandria, drive north on Highway 29 for 8.2 miles. Turn left onto County Road 38 NE and drive 1.2 miles. Veer to the left to stay on County Road 38 for another 0.2 mile into the park on the north side of Lake Carlos.

Contact: Lake Carlos State Park, 320/852-7200, www.dnr.state.mn.us/state_parks.

39 LAZY DAYS CAMPGROUND

🚴 ⛱ 🏕 🚣 ♿ 🚐 ⛺

Scenic rating: 4

northeast of Miltona

Lazy Days is surrounded by a vibrant and robust lakes area, full of heavy woods, beautiful sky-blue lakes, and excellent fishing. None of this is in this campground, however, which makes this area much more appealing than your campsite. Sites are laid on a square grid in an open grass clearing with no trees, no shade, and no privacy. A BMX bike track and outdoor pool are unique amenities, but if you are looking for a cozy lakeside campground, best look elsewhere.

What the campground lacks in a view, it makes for in spirit, though. Monthly pancake breakfasts, a Christmas in July celebration, and a Labor Day weekend Halloween party are some of the events and entertainment the campground hosts hold each summer to keep things lively.

Campsites, facilities: There are 99 sites for tents and RVs (full hookups); some sites are pull-through. Picnic tables, fire rings, toilets, showers, and a dump station are provided. A bike track, heated outdoor pool, playground, and camp store are available. Some facilities are wheelchair accessible. Leashed pets are permitted.

Reservations, fees: Reservations are accepted at 218/943-3000. Sites are $32 per night. There is a $2 fee per pet per night. Open from May to October.

Directions: From Miltona, drive east on County Road 14 for 3 miles. Turn left onto County Road 3. In 2 miles, turn left onto County Road 36. The campground is on the right side of the road in 0.5 mile.

Contact: Lazy Days Campground, 218/943-3000, http://lazydaysmiltona.com/LDM/Home.html.

40 CAMP RNL RV PARK & CAMPGROUND

Scenic rating: 5

north of Long Prairie

Camp RNL is your basic RV park in a field. The campground consists of six long loops, adjacent to each other in a clearing just north of the Long Prairie and across the highway from the Long Prairie River. A grove of trees

buffers the western end of the camping loop, but the sites have no shade or privacy.

The campground is just across the road from one of Minnesota's State Scenic Canoe Routes, and there is an access point in town for canoes. The river is a lazy, beautiful tributary of the Crow Wing River, lined with oak and aspen forest. Some areas of the river enjoy a complete tree canopy from overhanging oaks on both banks. Lake Osakis is a 15-minute drive to the west for good fishing, though you can find northern pike and walleye in the river as well.

Campsites, facilities: There are 28 sites for tents and RVs. Picnic tables, fire rings, toilets, showers, and a dump station are provided. Some facilities are wheelchair accessible. Leashed pets are permitted.

Reservations, fees: Reservations are accepted at 320/732-2517. Sites are $18 per night for tents and $22 per night for RVs. Open from mid-April to late October.

Directions: From Long Prairie, drive north on Highway 71 for 0.6 mile. The campground is on the left side of the road just after County Road 58.

Contact: Camp RNL RV Park & Campground, 320/732-2517.

41 BIRCH LAKE CAMPGROUND

Scenic rating: 7

on Big Birch Lake

Big Birch Lake is well known for its crappie, bass, and walleye fishing. The state forest campground seems to have been built for anglers, with more than half of its sites right on the water.

The campground loop is full of shaded, private sites, each with a small gravel driveway and a large camping area. Birch, oak, and aspen trees blanket the lakeshore and give each campsite a woodsy, secluded feel. The only drawback is that noise from motorboats can reach an irritable pitch during the summer weekends. Unlike many state forest lakes, Big Birch Lake permits motorboats, and many people take advantage of it.

Campsites, facilities: There are 29 sites for tents and RVs. There are also five walk-in sites and one group campsite. Picnic tables, fire rings, drinking water, vault toilets, and garbage cans are provided. A hiking trail, boat ramp, dock, and fishing area are available. Some facilities are wheelchair accessible. Leashed pets are permitted.

Reservations, fees: Reservations are not accepted. Self-registration is required at the campground. Sites are $12 per night; the group site is $50 per night. Open from mid-May to October.

Directions: From Sauk Centre, drive east on County Road 17 for 8.3 miles. Turn left onto Birch Lake Road and drive for 2 miles to the state forest campground sign. Turn right and drive for 1.1 miles to the parking area and water access. The campground is on the left side of the parking area.

Contact: Charles A. Lindbergh State Park, 320/616-2525, www.dnr.state.mn.us/state_forests/facilities/cmp00006/index.html.

42 CEDAR LAKE MEMORIAL PARK CAMPGROUND

Scenic rating: 6

on Cedar Lake west of Upsala

Cedar Lake Memorial Park is a convenient campground for exploring the surrounding lakes area, most notably the Birch Lakes State Forest and Oak Ridge State Wildlife Area. Two other wildlife areas are within driving distance of this campground.

The park is on the southeastern shore of Cedar Lake in a grove of oak and maple. The campground has 66 sites that are close together, but the ample tree cover provides shade and

a semblance of privacy. The swimming beach is quite nice, and spending time on the lake is why most people come here to camp. The park rents canoes and paddleboats and has a game room and camp store for convenience.

Campsites, facilities: There are 66 sites for tents and RVs. Picnic tables, fire rings, toilets, showers, and a dump station are provided. A swimming beach, canoes, boat ramp, playground, and camp store are provided. Some facilities are wheelchair accessible. Leashed pets are permitted.

Reservations, fees: Reservations are accepted at 320/573-2983. Sites are $20 per night. Open from May to late September.

Directions: From Upsala, drive west on 1st Avenue for 1.3 miles. Continue west on Abaca Road for 1.4 miles. Turn right into the park about 0.1 mile after 20th Avenue.

Contact: Cedar Lake Memorial Park, 320/573-2983, www.cedarlakecampground.com.

43 CHARLES A. LINDBERGH CAMPGROUND

Scenic rating: 9

in Charles A. Lindbergh State Park

Not everyone knows it, but Charles Lindbergh, the famous aviator, grew up in northern Minnesota. His family's estate is maintained by the Minnesota State Park system. Lindbergh learned how to fly here and actually managed the property himself for several years in his father's absence when he was a young man. The park features the Mississippi River as it begins to gain steam and swell into a rolling waterway on its way south to Brainerd. It also has a crash site in a field on the western side of the park where Lindbergh lost control on one of his early flights.

The campground sits underneath a towering cathedral of red pines, one of the most beautiful such groves along the Upper Mississippi. The sites are in the northern section of the park along Pike Creek before it enters the Mississippi. The two loops hold just 38 sites, each very private and well-shaded among the pines. A historical WPA-era stone water tower and picnic shelter are close to the river and are the start of a hiking trail that leads to the water.

Campsites, facilities: There are 38 sites for tents and RVs up to 50 feet; 15 sites have electrical hookups. There are also two cart-in sites and one tent-only group campsite for up to 30 people. Picnic tables, fire rings, flush and vault toilets, showers, and a dump station are provided. Hiking and cross-country ski trails, a fishing area, boat ramp, warming house, and playground are available. Some facilities are wheelchair accessible. Leashed pets are permitted.

Reservations, fees: Reservations are accepted from April 2 to October 31 866/857-2757 or online at www.stayatmnparks.com ($8.50 non-refundable reservation fee) and can be made up to one year in advance. Reservations are not required the rest of the year. Sites are $12–24 per night. Open from April to October.

Directions: From Little Falls, drive southwest on Lindbergh Drive SW for 1.6 miles. The park entrance is on the right side of the road, marked by a wooden state park sign. The campground is 0.25 mile ahead.

Contact: Charles A. Lindbergh State Park, 320/616-2525, www.dnr.state.mn.us/state_parks.

44 BENTON BEACH CAMPGROUND

Scenic rating: 7

on Little Rock Lake

Benton Beach is a cheerful 30-acre county park on Little Rock Lake. The campground's 44 sites are spread over an area the size of two city blocks, and are bisected by a gravel road. The wooded area is shady and serene, about 0.25 mile from the lake and recreation

building. The sites are close together but usually aren't all taken, except on summer holidays or particularly busy weekends.

The park is used more as a day-use area than a campground. It features a disc golf course, softball field, and a conference center that overlooks the water, and it maintains a well-kept swimming beach, recreation building, and playground. Campers also have access to a boat ramp and fishing dock. The atmosphere is quiet and close here; you will probably smell your neighbor's bratwurst cooking on the grill, but you won't mind because they'll probably offer you one.

Campsites, facilities: There are 44 sites for tents and RVs. Picnic tables, fire rings, toilets, showers, and a dump station are provided. A hiking trail, playground, swimming beach, and boat landing are available. Some facilities are wheelchair accessible. Leashed pets are permitted.

Reservations, fees: Reservations are not accepted. Self-registration is required at the campground. Sites are $20 per night. Open from Memorial Day to Labor Day.

Directions: From Rice, drive southeast on Highway 10 for 0.5 mile to 125th Street NW. Turn left and drive 2.5 miles. Turn right onto Benton Beach road marked by the campground sign. The campground is 0.25 mile ahead.

Contact: Benton Beach Campground, 320/968-5291, www.co.benton.mn.us/Parks/bentonbeach.htm.

45 KANDIYOHI COUNTY PARK #5

Scenic rating: 7

on Green Lake north of Spicer

Green Lake is the darling of Kandiyohi County. The glacial lake is hundreds of feet deep, famed for its walleye fishing, and lauded for its clean, clear waters. The county park campground is on the northeastern shore of the lake right on the water. A paved trail for biking and hiking passes through the park and circles the lake, providing a connection to the nearby Glacial Lakes State Trail.

A grove of oak, maple, and some evergreens shades the cluster of campsites. Each site has plenty of tree cover and is connected via footpaths to the water. The county road passes just a few dozen feet away from the park, but there is usually little traffic on it, especially at night.

The swimming beach and water access point here are well maintained. Swimming in Green Lake is wonderful—its deep, clear water makes it one of the cleanest lakes in the state, something the locals are very proud of.

Campsites, facilities: There are 54 sites for tents and RVs; nine sites are tent-only, and some sites have hookups. Picnic tables, fire rings, flush toilets, showers, and a dump station are provided. A paved hike/bike trail, playground, boat ramp, swimming beach, laundry facilities, and a camp store are available. Leashed pets are permitted.

Reservations, fees: Reservations are accepted for stays of seven days or longer at 320/796-5564. Stays less than seven days are first come, first served. Sites are $22 per night for tents and $33 per night for RVs. Open from early May to September.

Directions: From Spicer, drive north on Highway 23 for 2 miles. Turn right onto N. Shore Drive. The campground is on the right in 3.5 miles on County Park Road.

Contact: Kandiyohi County Park, 320/796-5564, www.kandipark5.com.

46 HIDE-AWAY CAMPGROUND

Scenic rating: 7

northeast of New London

The phrase "family camping" may be overused, but it accurately describes the Hide-Away Campground north of New London.

Located right on Long Lake, the campground has dozens of trees, a fun swimming area with a dock and anchored raft, a tennis court, and a playground. If you have children and want to take them to a campground full of safe and fun outdoor activities, this is a sure bet.

The Glacial Lakes State Trail and popular Green Lake are just a few miles away. Long Lake has decent fishing, but if you are on the hunt for walleye, drive over to Green Lake, which is famous for above-average numbers of the state fish.

Campsites, facilities: There are 40 sites for tents and RVs; full hookups available. Picnic tables, fire rings, toilets, showers, and a dump station are provided. A hiking trail, swimming beach, canoes, fishing boat rental, a dock, boat ramp, playground, and tennis court are available.

Reservations, fees: Reservations are accepted at 320/354-2148. Sites are $28 per night. Self-registration is required at the campground. Credit cards are not accepted. Open from May to late September.

Directions: From New London, drive northeast on Highway 23 for 2.7 miles. Turn right onto 199th Avenue/County Road 31. Turn left at the campground sign onto the gravel driveway. The registration office is 0.8 mile ahead.

Contact: Hide-Away Campground, 320/354-2148, www.hide-awaycampground.com.

47 LAKE KORONIS REGIONAL PARK

Scenic rating: 6

on Lake Koronis south of Paynesville

Lake Koronis is a midsized, pristine lake just south of Highway 23 near Paynesville. It is has a fair amount of development around it, but much of its shores are still wooded with pine and mixed-hardwood forests. The regional park on the lake's south side is one of the best access points for fishing and water-skiing. A quaint 43-site campground is nestled into the trees near the shore.

The sites are woven into the trees in two winding loops. The entire campground is connected to the beach by a paved walking and biking path. The abundance of shade from the many trees here makes this a cool, relaxing spot, especially on hot summer days spent on the lake.

Campsites, facilities: There are 43 sites for tents and RVs. Picnic tables, fire rings, toilets, showers, and a dump station are provided. A paved hiking and biking trail, boat ramp, and playground are available. Some facilities are wheelchair accessible. Leashed pets are permitted.

Reservations, fees: Reservations are accepted at 320/276-8843. Sites are $16 per night for tents and $20 per night for RVs. Open from May to late September.

Directions: From Paynesville, drive southwest on Highway 23 for 2.6 miles. Turn left at Tri County Road NE. In 2 miles, turn left onto County Road 20. Drive for another 1.7 miles to the campground on the left side of the road.

Contact: Lake Koronis Regional Park, 320/276-8843.

48 CLEAR LAKE CAMPGROUND

Scenic rating: 6

on Clear Lake

Clear Lake is one of the few isolated lakes in central Minnesota. While there are ponds and small lakes in the area, it is a good 15-minute drive in any direction before you come upon another sizable lake.

Clear Lake Campground is a no-frills RV park on the lake's northeastern shore. Maples, oaks, and aspens surround the lake and shade the camping area. Each site has several trees

and more privacy than many similarly sized RV parks.

There is decent trout fishing on the stream that connects Clear Lake to tiny Mud Lake in Sportsmen Park, which is just a block away from the campground across County Road 2. Campers also have access to a boat ramp and dock for fishing and water-skiing.

Campsites, facilities: There are 50 sites for RVs. Picnic tables, fire rings, toilets, showers, and a dump station are provided. A fishing dock, boat ramp, playground, and volleyball court are available. Leashed pets are permitted.

Reservations, fees: Reservations are accepted at 320/764-2592. Sites are $30 per night. Open from May to October.

Directions: From Forest City, drive north on County Road 2 for 5.5 miles. Turn left onto 657th Avenue. The campground is immediately to the right opposite the lake just after passing Sportsmen Park.

Contact: Clear Lake Campground, 320/764-2592.

49 LAKE MARIA CAMPGROUND

Scenic rating: 8

in Lake Maria State Park

Lake Maria State Park preserves more than 1,500 acres of Big Woods forest northwest of the Twin Cities. Big Woods are a mixture of oak, basswood, and maple, forming a thick-canopied, shady forest habitat that once covered much of south-central Minnesota.

The campsites are spread throughout the park, clustered around the half dozen lakes amid the forest. The sites are several hundred feet apart; sites on the Big Wood Loop trail in the northern section of the park are more secluded and are up to a mile apart from each other and the main hiking trail. Many of the sites are on small lakes, but the marshy, undeveloped areas around them make fishing and swimming impossible. For water recreation, hike to Lake Maria, which has a beach and fishing pier.

The park is a wonderfully unchanged chunk of forest home to ospreys, the endangered Blanding's turtle, and eagles whose nests can be seen throughout the park. The boardwalk travels through a particularly marshy area, where there are several nests high in the dead trees standing in the water, and where you will have the greatest chance of seeing the bright yellow spots of the little Blanding's turtle. I almost always see a marsh hawk when I camp here, and egrets, loons, and swans are also commonly sighted. During the migratory seasons, the lakes and marshes here are overrun with birds. The park has recorded more than 200 species of them.

Campsites, facilities: There are 17 backpacking sites for tents only; they require a one-mile walk from the parking area. There are also two tent-only group campsites for up to 50 people. Picnic tables, fire rings, flush and vault toilets, and drinking water are provided. Hiking and biking trails, a boardwalk, cross-county skiing trails, a groomed skate-ski trail, warming house, skating rink, and fishing pier are available. Leashed pets are permitted.

Reservations, fees: Reservations are accepted from April 2 to October 31 at 866/857-2757 or online at www.stayatmnparks.com ($8.50 non-refundable reservation fee) and can be made up to one year in advance. Reservations are not required the rest of the year. Sites are $12–24 per night. Open year-round, with limited facilities in winter.

Directions: From Monticello, drive west on County Road 39 NE for 5.7 miles to County Road 111. Turn right and drive for 0.7 mile to the state park sign on the left side of the road. Turn left and drive 0.25 mile to the park office.

Contact: Lake Maria State Park, 763/878-2325, www.dnr.state.mn.us/state_parks.

50 ANN LAKE CAMPGROUND

Scenic rating: 8

on Ann Lake west of Zimmerman

The Ann Lake campground is a popular horse camp and horse-riding area in the northwoods; the campground has more than 30 sites specifically designed for horse camping. There are also two regular—and wheelchair accessible—sites. There is a beautiful three-mile nature trail that explores the lake and the surrounding forest engulfing the campground. The trail leads to the sandy swimming beach and a convenient fishing area. In the winter the trails are groomed for cross-country skiing.

Campsites, facilities: There are 30 sites for tents and RVs, 15 equestrian sites, and four group campsites. Picnic tables, fire rings, drinking water, toilets, and garbage cans are provided. A hiking trail, cross-country ski trail, swimming beach, and a picnic area are available. Some facilities are wheelchair accessible. Leashed pets are permitted.

Reservations, fees: Reservations are not accepted. Self-registration is required at the campground. Sites are $12–16 per night; the group sites are $50 per night. Open from May to November.

Directions: From Zimmerman, drive west on County Road 4 for 6 miles. Turn left onto 168th Street. Turn left and drive for 1.5 miles on the gravel road, following signs to the Ann Lake Recreation Area. The campground is adjacent to the parking area in the park.

Contact: Lake Maria State Park, 763/878-2325, www.dnr.state.mn.us/state_forests/facilities/cmp00046/index.html.

51 LAKE RIPLEY CAMPGROUND

🚶 🚴 ⛱ 🏊 🛶 🏕 🎣 ♿ 🚐 ⛺

Scenic rating: 7

on Lake Ripley south of Litchfield

Lake Ripley Campground is just south of Memorial Park in Litchfield on the eastern shore of Lake Ripley. The campsites are squeezed between the water and Lake Ripley Drive on a strip of land about 75 feet wide and 0.75 mile long.

The sites are all on the water and are close to the sandy swimming beach. Camping here is very affordable for tent campers, and the facilities are clean and well maintained; the shower house, beach, and boat ramp are first-rate. Camping here also puts you close to the Madsen State Wildlife Area, just a few miles north of Litchfield.

Campsites, facilities: There are 32 sites for tents and RVs. Picnic tables, fire rings, toilets, showers, and a dump station are provided. A swimming beach, playground, hiking and biking trail, and dock are available. Some facilities are wheelchair accessible. Leashed pets are permitted.

Reservations, fees: Reservations are accepted at 320/693-7201. Sites are $15 per night for tents and $17 per night for RVs. Open from mid-April to mid-October.

Directions: From Litchfield, drive south on Highway 22 for 1.2 miles. Turn right onto Lake Ripley Drive. The campground is in the city park on the right in about 0.2 mile.

Contact: Lake Ripley Campground, 320/693-7201.

52 LAKEDALE CAMPGROUND

⛱ 🏊 🏕 🎣 🚐 ⛺

Scenic rating: 5

on Spring Lake north of Dassel

Just north of Dassel, the Lakedale Campground is in a small park that hugs that north shore of Spring Lake. The campsites are in an open grassy area interspersed with large, shady oak and maple trees. Long Lake is about 100 feet away, just across the road, so you have easy access to two of the area's fishing lakes. The park also features a swimming beach, ball fields, and a fishing dock.

Campsites, facilities: There are 45 sites for tents and RVs. Picnic tables, fire rings, toilets, showers, and a dump station are provided. A swimming beach, boat ramp, and fishing dock are available. Leashed pets are permitted.

Reservations, fees: Reservations are accepted at 320/275-3334. Sites are $22 per night. Open from May to late September.

Directions: From Dassel, drive north for 1.5 miles on County Road 4. Turn right onto 242nd Street. The campground is about 500 feet ahead on the left.

Contact: Lakedale Campground, 320/275-3334.

53 PIEPENBURG COUNTY PARK

🚶 🏊 ⛱ 🏕 🎣 🚐 ⛺

Scenic rating: 8

on Belle Lake near Hutchinson

If you are wondering if there are still any big, beautiful lakes in Minnesota that aren't overrun with development and chopped into real estate, Belle Lake is your answer. Piepenburg County Park is stuck to the side of Belle Lake like a happy little barnacle, full of wildflower fields; groves of oak, maple, and basswood trees; a lovely swimming beach; and shady campsites.

The campground is situated about 100 feet from the lake, connected to the swimming beach by a gravel drive and by a footpath that follows close to the shore. Take note that the mosquitoes here in early June are nearly unbearable. A wetland extends along the inlet inside of the park that is a swarming ground for the critters. Later in the summer the red-winged blackbirds, blue herons, wetland wildflowers, and whitetail deer outnumber the bugs and make this park an enchanting place to visit.

Campsites, facilities: There are 35 sites for tents and RVs. Picnic tables, fire rings, toilets, showers, and a dump station are provided. A swimming beach, hiking trail, playground, and volleyball court are available. Leashed pets are permitted.

Reservations, fees: Reservations are accepted at 320/587-2082. Sites are $15 per night for tents and $23 per night for RVs. Open from May to October.

Directions: From Hutchinson, drive north on Highway 15 for 5 miles. Turn left onto County Road 60. In 1.3 miles turn right onto County Road 12 and drive for 0.3 mile to Belle Lake Road. Turn left and drive 1.5 miles to the park entrance at Piepenburg Park Road. Turn right and drive 0.1 mile to the park office.

Contact: Piepenburg County Park, 320/587-2082.

54 WEST RIVER PARK CAMPGROUND

🧍🚴🛶🚤🏕️🛶♿🚐⛺

Scenic rating: 6

in Hutchinson

If you are from Minnesota, you know who Les Kouba is. And if you don't, you soon will after visiting Hutchinson. The beloved painter is well known throughout the state for his beautiful nature-based artwork. Kouba is from Hutchinson, and the parkway that leads to West River Park on Otter Tail Lake is named after him. While a city park isn't as pristinely wild as most of Kouba's paintings, it has its own charm.

The park is a large open grassy expanse lined with oak and maple trees on the north shore of the lake. The campground lies directly on the Luce Line Trail, a state recreational paved bike and hiking path that stretches for

63 miles all the way to the Twin Cities area. The sites are laid on a grid of planted trees in the center of the park. There isn't a lot of privacy between them, but the park itself is fairly private—situated right on the lakeshore and removed from the essence of the town.

Campsites, facilities: There are 47 sites for tents and RVs. Picnic tables, fire rings, toilets, showers, and a dump station are provided. A hiking trail, biking trail, boat ramp, and playground are available. Some facilities are wheelchair accessible. Leashed pets are permitted.

Reservations, fees: Reservations are accepted at 320/234-4494. Sites are $10 per night for tents and $15 per night for RVs. Open from April to mid-October.

Directions: In Hutchinson, cross over Otter Lake heading north. Turn right onto Highway 7. The campground is on the right side of the road at Les Kouba Parkway in 0.3 mile.

Contact: West River Park, 320/234-4494, www.explorehutchinson.com.

55 LAKE MARION PARK CAMPGROUND

🧍🛶🚤🏕️🛶🚐⛺

Scenic rating: 6

south of Hutchinson

Lake Marion Park lies on the western shore of Lake Marion in a thick grove of hardwoods. Surrounded by farmland, the lake and its grove of trees are an oasis of shade in the open fields south of Hutchinson.

Campsites are arranged in a single, large loop about 100 feet from the water. The loop is in a lightly treed area just east of the heavier grove of trees on the lake's shore. Each site has a short gravel driveway and at least one tree. Privacy from tree cover isn't exemplary here, but the sites are well spaced. A short hiking trail and cross-country ski trail system lie between the loop and the lake. A large fishing pier extends several dozen yards into the lake, providing excellent fishing.

Campsites, facilities: There are 45 sites for tents and RVs. Picnic tables, fire rings, toilets, showers, and a dump station are provided. A hiking trail, playground, cross-country ski trail, fishing pier, and boat ramp are available. Leashed pets are permitted.

Reservations, fees: Reservations are accepted at 320/328-4479. Sites are $15 per night for tents and $23 per night for RVs. Open from May to October.

Directions: From Brownton, drive east on Division Street for 1.1 miles to Highway 15. Turn right and drive 4 miles to the park. The campground is on the left side of the road just past 115th Drive.

Contact: Lake Marion Park, 320/328-4479.

THE PRAIRIES

© KERSTIN HANSEN

BEST CAMPGROUNDS

❰ **Families**
Lake Shetek State Park, **page 141.**

❰ **Fishing**
Lake Shetek State Park, **page 141.**

❰ **Lakeshore Campgrounds**
Lake Shetek State Park, **page 141.**

❰ **Tent Camping**
Sakatah Lake State Park, **page 152.**

❰ **Views**
Glacial Lakes State Park, **page 133.**
Sibley State Park, **page 135.**
Lac qui Parle State Park, **page 135.**
Blue Mounds State Park, **page 155.**

The broad sweep of the Great Plains comes to

a gentle rest in southwestern Minnesota. The wildflowers and prairie grasses gather around the slight undulations and sky-reflecting lakes near the Dakotas, then begin to mingle with the shrubs and trees that mark the hazy, ever-changing border between forest and prairie.

At this edge of the prairie, trees, lakes, and grasslands share a constantly changing habitat. The weather is the prime factor, giving grasses and wildflowers a stronghold in drier years, trees and shrubs an advantage during years of higher rainfall.

Among this landscape's many intriguing features is the subtlety of elevation. Even slight changes in elevation dramatically change your view. Climbing a small hill can let you see for miles into the distance. Standing on a rock outcropping or cliff edge in Blue Mounds State Park will open a panorama so vast you'll think you are standing on the buttes of Oklahoma or the rolling prairies of Nebraska.

The large lakes of the prairie lie open to the sky, reflecting the endless openness of the wide plains. The lakes in these grasslands are especially precious, providing respite from the hot summer days in the form of cool breezes and afternoon swims. The water draws wildlife, including herons, cranes, foxes, whitetail deer, raccoons, and opossums.

Despite being the prairie region of the state, southwestern Minnesota has its share of wooded areas. Oases of trees, usually clustered around lakes and rivers, dot the landscape, bringing shade and shelter to parts of the wide-open countryside. The loss of wild grazing animals, including the buffalo of centuries past, along with human intervention, has reduced the grasslands, which have given ground to trees and shrubs in many areas. Much of the prairie has been lost.

Lac qui Parle, Upper Sioux Agency, and Blue Mounds State Park are invaluable parks that embody the Minnesota prairie lands and protect them from development. You can find flowering cacti in Blue Mounds State Park in the height of summer, observe thousands of migrating waterfowl on Lac qui Parle in the spring and autumn, and enjoy the rolling hills laden with wildflowers and prairie grasses in Upper Sioux Agency State Park. Many a camper has awoken to the sound of buffalo grazing just a few feet away from their tent on dewy summer mornings in these parks.

The lonely country highways and vast skies of southwestern Minnesota can give you a profound sense of isolation and beauty. Lying on your back and staring at the seemingly empty blue sky will reveal that it is full of circling hawks, flitting sparrows, and hungry kestrels flying hundreds of feet above the earth. The starry skies at night are unrivaled in splendor, making this a prime camping destination. The prairies aren't just for summer recreation, though. Cross-country skiers, winter campers, and snowshoers are all welcome in the state parks of the region. Many have groomed ski trails with warming shelters, and nearly everyone knows about the big sledding hill in Upper Sioux Agency State Park.

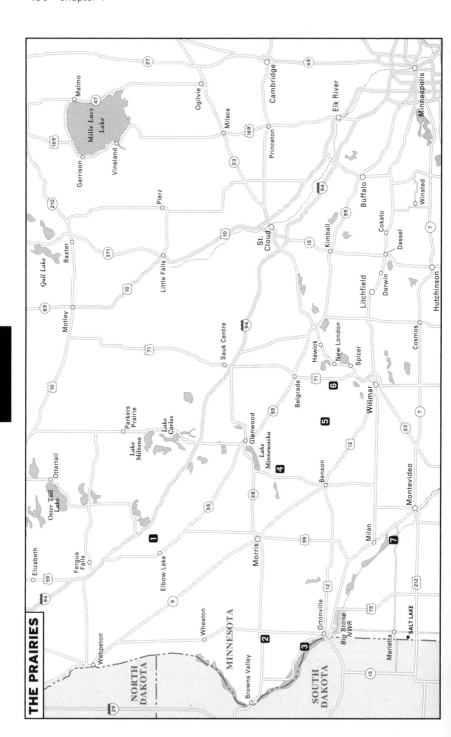

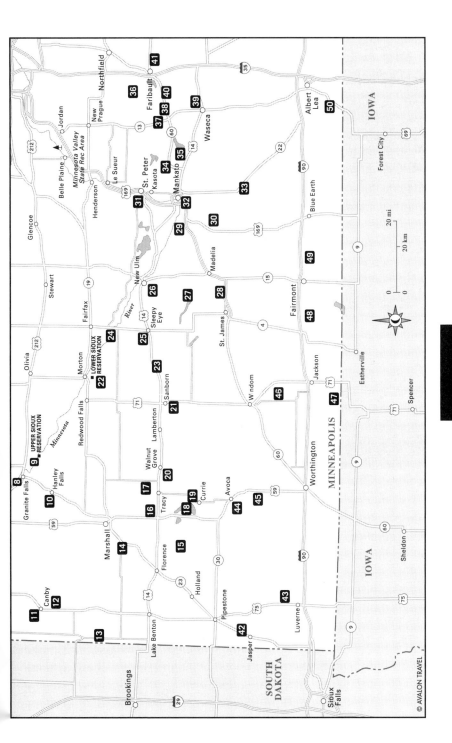

◼ TIPSINAH MOUNDS CAMPGROUND

🚶 🏊 🛶 ⛺ 🎣 🐕 🚣 ♿ 🚐 ⛺

Scenic rating: 7

on Pomme de Terre Lake

Tipsinah Mounds Campground sits on the southern shore of Pomme de Terre Lake. Surrounded by a sea of farmland and prairie, this shady knoll is covered in towering oak trees that fill the small peninsula as it extends gently into the water. The campground is adjacent to the Pomme de Terre State Wildlife Management Area, with no other private land or developments on this side of the lake.

The campsites are arranged in two loops. A large loop on the eastern side of the park is crowded and unsheltered by the park's many trees, but a smaller loop to the west and nearer the water is protected by dozens of large oaks, and the sites are several dozen feet apart from one another.

This is a recreational hot spot, with a sandy swimming beach, several docks and fishing piers, a new playground, and hiking trails that explore the shoreline. Campers can also rent canoes and paddle across the lake to fish or just to spend some time on the water.

Campsites, facilities: There are 50 sites for tents and 25 sites for tents and RVs; partial and full hookups are available. Picnic tables, fire rings, drinking water, showers, toilets, and a dump station are provided. A playground, hiking trail, swimming beach, canoe rental, fishing docks, fishing boats, boat ramp, game room, and a camp store are available. Some facilities are wheelchair accessible. Leashed pets are permitted.

Reservations, fees: Reservations are accepted at 218/685-5114 (a one-night deposit is required). Sites are $18 per night for tents and $25–27 per night for RVs. Holiday weekends require a three-night minimum stay. Open from May to October.

Directions: From the city of Elbow Lake, drive east on Highway 79 for 4 miles. Turn left onto Tipsinah Mounds Road and drive 0.6 mile to the campground straight ahead.

Contact: Tipsinah Mounds Park, 218/685-5114, www.tipsinahmoundscampground.com.

◼ TOQUA PARK CAMPGROUND

🏊 ⛺ 🐕 🚐 ⛺

Scenic rating: 6

on East Toqua Lake near Graceville

A big lake, a small town, and a nice park—if that sums up what you are looking for in a camping experience, then Toqua Park Campground is for you. A fine example of one of southwestern Minnesota's ubiquitous county parks, Toqua Park is on the southern edge of Graceville on Toqua Lake.

The campsites are close to the highway and town, but the little park does a good job of delivering a quiet campground on a beautiful lake. It's as much a day-use park as a campground; Toqua Park's campsites surround two softball diamonds and a swimming beach that are regularly used by locals.

The sandy beach is easily accessible from the campground, as are the softball diamonds. Organized softball games are usually scheduled at the park on summer weekends, creating a cheerful, sporting atmosphere.

Campsites, facilities: There are 12 campsites for tents and RVs (with electric hookups). Picnic tables, fire rings, drinking water, flush toilets, showers, softball diamonds, horseshoe pits, a swimming beach, boat access, and a dump station are provided. Leashed pets are permitted.

Reservations, fees: Reservations are accepted at 320/748-7411. Sites are $8–15 per night. Open May to October.

Directions: From Graceville, drive south on Highway 75 for 0.5 mile along East Toqua Lake. Turn right into the park and follow signs to the campground.

Contact: Big Stone County Toqua Park, 320/748-7411, cigraceville@mchsi.com.

3 BIG STONE LAKE STATE PARK

🚶 🏊 🚣 ⛵ 🛶 🏇 ♿ 🚐 ⛺

Scenic rating: 9

in Big Stone Lake State Park

When Minnesotans talk about going to the border, they are usually referring to the Canadian border—but the South Dakota border is just as fun, and quite a bit warmer. Big Stone Lake State Park hugs 26 miles of the Minnesota–South Dakota border on Big Stone Lake. The Minnesota River is sourced from this lake, making its dramatic journey to St. Paul through southern Minnesota.

Sites are spread throughout the park within two campgrounds. The Bonanza Area in the northern section of the park, as you might surmise from its name, has the more adventurous camping. The park's picnic area, boat launch, and primitive camping area are located there. The Meadowbrook Area in the southern section of the park has a drive-in camping loop along with more modern facilities.

Campsites, facilities: There are 37 sites for tents and RVs up to 48 feet; 10 sites have 30-amp electric hookups. There is also one group hike-in, tent-only campsite available through September for up to 20 people. Picnic tables, fire rings, showers (available seasonally), flush and vault toilets, a boat ramp, swimming beach, and a dump station are provided. Some facilities are wheelchair accessible. Leashed pets are permitted.

Reservations, fees: Reservations are accepted from April 2 to October 31 at 866/857-2757 or online at www.stayatmnparks.com ($8.50 non-refundable reservation fee) and can be made up to one year in advance. Reservations are not required the rest of the year. Sites are $12–24 per night. Open year-round, with limited facilities in winter.

Directions: From Ortonville, take Highway 7 north for 7 miles. Turn left into the state park and follow signs to the campground.

Contact: Big Stone Lake State Park, 320/839-3663, www.dnr.state.mn.us/state_parks.

4 GLACIAL LAKES STATE PARK

🚶 🚲 🏊 🚣 ⛵ 🛶 🏇 ♿ 🚐 ⛺

Scenic rating: 9

in Glacial Lakes State Park

BEST (

Glacial Lakes State Park is one of the few areas in Minnesota that can still give you a true prairie experience. The rolling landscape is covered with rich, natural prairie grasses and flowers, a thick blanket that once covered more than a third of the state. Colorful birds, flowers, and animals thrive here from early spring to late fall, proving that the grasslands are as full of life as any ecosystem on earth.

Despite being in the middle of one of Minnesota's largest patches of prairie, the campgrounds are shade-filled and roomy. Campsites are divided into two areas: the Lower Campground and the Oak Ridge Campground. Each camping area consists of a single loop in an oasis of trees and undergrowth that offer privacy and shade. The Lower Campground lies on the north shore of Mountain Lake, with more direct access to the lake. Privacy here is excellent, as the campground loop is populated by a dense oak, maple, and aspen forest that engulfs the lake's northern shore. The more remote Oak Ridge Campground has a better view of the surrounding prairie, though it is farther from the recreational facilities. The four backpacking sites let you actually camp in the prairie and give an unparalleled grasslands camping experience. On clear nights, the sky here seems endlessly full of stars, and the sounds of the frogs and crickets fill the whole county with their song. A horse camping area is available near the eastern parking lot.

Glacial Lakes State Park is popular with horseback riders, as horse trails run throughout the park and there are two horse camping areas. Mountain Lake, in the northeast portion of the park, is accessible to campers for fishing, swimming, and canoeing. A large picnic deck gives one of the best overlooks in the park, sweeping across the lake and surrounding prairie.

Campsites, facilities: There are 37 sites for tents and RVs up to 45 feet; one site (39) is pull-through and 14 sites have electric hookups. There are also four backpacking sites, eight equestrian sites, and one group site for up to 50 people. Picnic tables, fire rings and grills, drinking water, flush and vault toilets, showers (available seasonally), and a dump station are provided. Hiking, biking, and horseback riding trails, boat rentals, a fishing pier, swimming beach, and boat ramp are available. Some facilities are wheelchair accessible. Leashed pets are permitted.

Reservations, fees: Reservations are accepted from April 2 to October 31 866/857-2757 or online at www.stayatmnparks.com ($8.50 non-refundable reservation fee) and can be made up to one year in advance. Reservations are not required the rest of the year. Sites are $12–24 per night. Oak Ridge Campground is open from April to August; Lower Campground is open year-round, with limited facilities, but requires hike-in/ski-in in winter.

Directions: From Starbuck, drive south on Highway 29 for 3 miles. Continue south on County Road 41 to the park entrance. Follow signs to the campground.

Contact: Glacial Lakes State Park, 320/239-2860, www.dnr.state.mn.us/state_parks.

5 MONSON LAKE CAMPGROUND

Scenic rating: 9

in Monson Lake State Park

Southwestern Minnesota is primarily prairie land, but little pockets of forest and wetland dapple the landscape as well. Monson Lake State Park is one of the best examples of forest in the prairie.

The modest campground sits in a tight loop near Monson Lake's southeastern shore. The

park is a quiet place—the lapping waves of the lake and rustling leaves of the oaks, maples, and aspens will usher you to sleep most nights. Plenty of tree cover keeps the sites shady.

The wooded lake and wetland act as a magnet for migrating birds, drawing thousands of pelicans, grebes, herons, ducks, and geese during the spring and fall. Songbirds fill the trees in the summer, making bird-watching unavoidable. A hiking trail connects the campground with the nearby lake, touring through the shoreline and delving into the forest. You can also rent a canoe and paddle across the lake to a short portage that connects to nearby West Sunburg Lake. Anglers will have luck catching walleye, bass, and sunfish in both lakes.

Campsites, facilities: There are 20 sites for tents and RVs up to 70 feet; six sites have electric hookups (20-, 30-, and 50-amp). Picnic tables, fire rings and grills, flush and vault toilets, showers (available seasonally), and drinking water are provided. Firewood and a fishing pier are available. Leashed pets are permitted.

Reservations, fees: Reservations are accepted from April 2 to October 31 at 866/857-2757 or online at www.stayatmnparks.com ($8.50 non-refundable reservation fee) and can be made up to one year in advance. Reservations are not required the rest of the year. Sites are $12–24. Open from May through October.

Directions: From Sunburg, drive west on E. Front Street for 0.8 mile, turning left onto 180th Avenue. In 0.5 mile, turn right onto 30th Street NE and continue 1 mile. Turn left onto County Road 95 and drive 1.8 miles to the park entrance on the right side of the road. Turn right into the park and drive 0.1 mile to the park office.

Contact: Monson Lake State Park, 320/366-3797, www.dnr.state.mn.us.

6 SIBLEY STATE PARK

🚶🚴🏊🛶🚐🛶❄🏕♿🚐⛺

Scenic rating: 9

in Sibley State Park

BEST (

Sibley State Park occupies the prairie foothills of western Minnesota, where farmland, grassland, and forest mix with lakes, wetlands, and hilltops. This is one of the most diverse habitats in the region; campers can pitch their tents on wooded lakeshores, climb atop hills with vast overlooks that stretch over miles and miles of farmland, and watch wetlands blossom with flowers and wildlife alike all in one trip.

The campground is a set of two loops on the north shore of Lake Andrew. Named Lakeview Campground, all sites have a view of the water and access to the swimming beach just a few dozen feet from the camping area via a footpath. The hiking and skiing trails connect the campground to the entire trail system that runs winds for dozens of miles through the hills and dales of the park.

Hikers and cross-country skiers will especially enjoy Sibley's intricate and well-maintained trail system. A cornucopia of trails connect the campground to all ends of the park, leading hikers to the top of the breathtaking Mount Tom overlook tower and to the shores of Lake Andrew. The trails are groomed for good skiing in the winter, as well. A canoe route connects several local lakes with a series of portages that begin in the park, and a paved bike trail tours Lake Andrew's north shore.

Campsites, facilities: There are 132 sites for tents and RVs up to 70 feet. Picnic tables, fire rings, toilets, showers, and a dump station are provided. Hiking and cross-country skiing trails, a swimming beach, a fishing pier, sliding hill, and warming house are available. Some facilities are wheelchair accessible. Leashed pets are permitted.

Reservations, fees: Reservations are accepted from April 2 to October 31 at 866/857-2757 or online at www.stayatmnparks.com ($8.50 non-refundable reservation fee) and can be made up to one year in advance. Reservations are not required the rest of the year. Sites are $12–24. Open year-round.

Directions: From New London, drive west on County Road 40 for 3.1 miles. Turn right onto Highway 71. In 1 mile, turn left into the park on Sibley Park Road. The park office is 1.6 miles ahead.

Contact: Sibley State Park, 320/354-2055, www.dnr.state.mn.us/state_parks.

7 LAC QUI PARLE STATE PARK

🚶🏊🛶🚐🛶❄🏕♿🚐⛺

Scenic rating: 9

in Lac qui Parle State Park

BEST (

Lac qui Parle was named the "Lake That Speaks" many hundreds of years ago by the Dakota Indians who once populated its shores. Its name is still relevant today. Thousands of birds use the lake as a stopping point along one of the nation's largest bird migratory corridors.

The campground is divided into upper and lower sections. The two-loop Upper campground is closer to the park's recreation area, office, and main road. Its cart-in sites are accessed via the western parking area (within 400 feet of the parking area) and offer more shade and privacy. The single-loop Lower campground has fewer sites that are more spread out, giving campers more privacy, shade, and quiet.

A historical fort and preserved mission sites remain in the park and are of interest. Informational tours are available, and park rangers give tours during the summer. Trails for hiking and horseback riding are accessible from both campgrounds, though the canoe access is located on a park road away from the camping areas. Anglers will have luck with walleye, northerns, and crappie.

Campsites, facilities: There are 43 sites for tents and RVs up to 60 feet (partial hookups) in Upper campground; eight sites are pull-through and three of these have hookups.

There are also three cart-in sites and two tent-only group sites for up to 50 people each. Lower campground has 24 sites for tents and RVs up to 50 feet (partial hookups). Picnic tables, fire rings and grills, drinking water, flush and vault toilets, showers, and a dump station are provided. A visitors center, historical site, swimming beach, boat and canoe access, firewood, cross-country ski trails and a warming hut (in winter) are available. There are two wheelchair-accessible sites in Upper campground. Leashed pets are permitted.

Reservations, fees: Reservations are accepted from April 2 to October 31 at 866/857-2757 or online at www.stayatmnparks.com ($8.50 non-refundable reservation fee) and can be made up to one year in advance. Reservations are not required the rest of the year. Sites are $12–24. Lower campground is open year-round, with limited facilities in winter; Upper campground is open from May to October.

Directions: From Watson, take Highway 59 north for 0.5 mile. Turn left on County Road 13 and follow signs to the campground.

Contact: Lac qui Parle State Park, 320/734-4450, www.dnr.state.mn.us/state_parks.

8 GRANITE FALLS MEMORIAL PARK CAMPGROUND

Scenic rating: 6

in Granite Falls on the Minnesota River

The Minnesota River takes a lot of sharp turns, but few are sharper than the one it makes in Granite Falls. Here the river makes a nearly 90-degree turn to the east, sending it on its way to Mankato.

Memorial Park is across the river from town in a grove of cottonwood trees that hugs the river's south bank. There are just 22 sites scattered among the trees, with shade and privacy aplenty. An awesome overlook of the river valley is just a half mile away in town on the other side of the river.

Campsites, facilities: There are 10 tent sites and 12 sites for RVs (hookups). Picnic tables, fire rings and grills, drinking water, toilets, showers, and a dump station are provided. A hiking trail, playground, and boat ramp are available. Leashed pets are permitted.

Reservations, fees: Reservations are accepted at 320/564-3011. Sites are $5 per night for tents and $7 per night for RVs. Open from May through October.

Directions: From Granite Falls, drive south on Highway 67 for 0.5 mile. Take a left to stay on Highway 67 after crossing the river. The park entrance is on the left.

Contact: Granite Falls Memorial Park, 320/564-3011, www.granitefalls.com.

9 UPPER SIOUX AGENCY CAMPGROUND

Scenic rating: 9

in Upper Sioux Agency State Park

The words winter and camping don't go together for most people, but Upper Sioux Agency State Park may start changing minds. A major cross-country skiing, snowshoeing, and snowmobiling destination, this park is as popular in winter as it is during summer—not in the least because of its humongous sliding hill that draws people from all over the county after a good snow.

The campground is a figure-eight loop filled with well-spaced, shady campsites. There are also three walk-in sites near the parking lot on the western end of the loop and six rustic campsites in the Riverside campground, clustered around the Minnesota River near the boat ramp. Trees huddle near the river and campground, forming a nice canopy. The rustic sites are first come, first served and have the best privacy and most tree cover; the campground enjoys ample shade as well.

Cross-country skiing and showshoeing trails winnow through the park's open prairie and wooded slops. Bluffs, bottomlands, forests, and prairie all meet here, making hiking, skiing, or any outdoor activity a lesson in landscape diversity. Wildlife is abundant and you will be treated to sightings of turtles, raccoons, whitetail deer, and groundhogs.

Campsites, facilities: There are 34 sites for tents and RVs up to 60 feet; 14 sites have electric hookups (30- and 50-amp). There are also three walk-in sites, six rustic sites, and 45 equestrian sites. Picnic tables, fire rings, drinking water (unavailable at walk-in or rustic sites), flush and vault toilets, and showers (available seasonally) are provided. A sliding hill with warming house (in winter), horseshoe pit, canoe rental, playground, and a volleyball court are available. Some facilities are wheelchair accessible. Leashed pets are permitted.

Reservations, fees: Reservations are accepted from April 2 to October 31 at 866/857-2757 or online at www.stayatmnparks.com ($8.50 nonrefundable reservation fee) and can be made up to one year in advance. Reservations are not required the rest of the year. Sites are $12–24. Open year-round, with limited facilities in winter.

Directions: From the town of Granite Falls at the intersection of Highways 212 and 23, drive south on Highway 23, about one block to Highway 67. Turn left on 67 and go 8 miles to the park entrances. The first of the park's three entrances will take you to the horse rider campground. The second entrance takes you to the main park entrance. The last entrance takes you to the campground.

Contact: Upper Sioux Agency State Park, 320/564-4777, www.dnr.state.mn.us/state_parks.

This big facility primarily acts as a museum, threshing show site, and informational touring ground that chronicles early-20th-century machinery's role in Minnesota's past and present.

The campground is tucked behind the five big buildings that house all number of tractors, one-lungers, tools, gas engines, and other implements and oddities of the farming trade. You will usually find RVs filling the small campground, especially during weekends when shows and organized activities are happening at the museum. Camping here is perfect if you plan on taking a tour and spending all day in the museum facilities, but offers few opportunities for outdoor recreation.

Campsites, facilities: There are 12 sites for tents and RVs; six sites are pull-through (full hookups). Picnic tables, fire rings and grills, drinking water, toilets, and a dump station are provided. A playground is available. Leashed pets are permitted.

Reservations, fees: Reservations are accepted at 507/768-3522. Sites are $10 per night for tents and $15 per night for RVs. Open from May through September.

Directions: From Hanley Falls, drive north on 2nd Avenue E for 0.2 mile to 1st Avenue E. Turn right and drive 1 block to 1st Street N. Turn left and drive 2 blocks to the park and campground entrance on the left side of the road.

Contact: Minnesota Machinery Museum Campground, 507/768-3522, www.mnmachinerymuseum.com.

🔟 MINNESOTA MACHINERY MUSEUM

Scenic rating: 5

in Hanley Falls

Field trip! The campground at the Minnesota Machinery Museum is almost an afterthought.

1️⃣1️⃣ LAKE SYLVAN PARK CAMPGROUND

Scenic rating: 6

on Lake Sylvan in Canby

Camping in southwestern Minnesota can often pose a privacy problem. Campers used to the heavy woods and forests of northern and central Minnesota may find more solace at Lake Sylvan. This small, peaceful campground is no wooded oasis, but it does offer a more private "at the lake" feel. It is self-labeled as the "Gateway to the Prairie," and trees and grass come to a compromise here, while farther west grasslands dominate the landscape.

Set on a hill above the water, the campsites have an excellent view of Lake Sylvan. Footpaths lead to the lake from the campground. Even though this camping area only has six sites, the park offers an outdoor pool, a playground, and tennis courts.

Campsites, facilities: There are six sites for tents and RVs (full hookups). Picnic tables, fire rings and grills, drinking water, flush toilets, and a dump station are provided. A playground, tennis courts, and an outdoor pool are available. Leashed pets are allowed.

Reservations, fees: Reservations are not accepted. Sites are $10 per night. Pay in the self-registration box at the campground. Open from May to October.

Directions: In Canby, drive south on Highway 75 to Haarfager Avenue. Turn right and follow signs for 0.25 mile to the campground.

Contact: City of Canby, 507/223-7295, www.canby.govoffice.com.

12 STONEHILL REGIONAL PARK CAMPGROUND

Scenic rating: 7

on Del Clark Lake near Canby

If there is a Gone Fishing sign hung on a door in Canby, it is almost a sure bet that whoever put it there is putting a line in Del Clark Lake at Stonehill Regional Park. Regarded regionally as one of the best fishing lakes in the county, Del Clark Lake also has a very accommodating campground.

The camping at Stonehill is more diverse than you might assume at first glance. Drive-in sites and RV hookup areas make car camping easy, but primitive sites away from the parking area are also available. If you choose a primitive campsite you will get more privacy and better shade from the oasis of trees that surrounds the park. The drive-in camping area is a little plain, but the lake atmosphere goes a long way to adding charm throughout the park.

The main draw to the area is fishing in Del Clark. An 80-foot wheelchair-accessible fishing pier extends far out onto the lake. Anglers can catch walleye, bass, northerns, and panfish. Hiking trails follow the lakeshore as well, and are connected to the campground and primitive camping areas.

Campsites, facilities: There are 54 sites for tents and RVs (with electric hookups). Picnic tables, fire rings and grills, drinking water, flush toilets, and showers are provided. Biking and hiking trails, a playground, boat ramp and docking area, and dump station are available. Some facilities are wheelchair accessible. Leashed pets are permitted.

Reservations, fees: Reservations are accepted from May to October at 507/223-7586. Sites are $15 per night for tents and $20 per night for RVs. Open May to October.

Directions: From Canby, take County Road 30 southwest for 1.5 miles. Turn left into the park and follow signs to the campground.

Contact: Stonehill Regional Park Campground, 507/223-7586.

13 LAKE HENDRICKS CAMPGROUND

Scenic rating: 6

on Lake Hendricks

Not many campgrounds get to enjoy the duality of city and lake. Conveniently located on Lake Hendricks and at the edge of town, this campground plugs you into the best of both worlds.

The campsites enjoy a large portion of

lakeshore. Trees have been planted all around the camping area and near the water, providing shade along with the relative quiet of the campground. The shady sites are private with views of the lake, making it hard to believe that the campground is actually in town.

The campground is connected to the Lake Hendricks city park, a county museum, volleyball court, and softball field. Fishing is good on Lake Hendricks, as well, and the campground even has a fish-cleaning station.

Campsites, facilities: There are 27 sites for tents and RVs (full hookups). Picnic tables, fire rings and grills, toilets, showers, and dump station are provided. Biking and hiking trails, boat ramp, playground, fish-cleaning station, and a swimming beach are available. Leashed pets are permitted.

Reservations, fees: Reservations are accepted at 507/275-3192. Sites are $10–16 per night. Open from mid-April to mid-October.

Directions: From Highways 19 and 271, drive north on Highway 271 into Hendricks. Turn left on Cottage Avenue and follow the curve to the north end of street. The campground is on the north end of Cottage Avenue.

Contact: Lake Hendricks Campground, 507/275-3192, www.hendricksmn.com.

14 CAMDEN CAMPGROUND

Scenic rating: 9

in Camden State Park

Camden is the camping capital of southern Minnesota state parks. With 80 sites spread within two campgrounds, Camden enjoys popularity all summer long—and with the great trout fishing, hiking overlooks, and lakeshore access, it's no wonder.

The camping areas are separated into upper and lower campgrounds. The upper campground is larger, with more than 40 sites placed along two loops. The lower campground is a cul-de-sac with a central parking area and two

wheelchair-accessible sites. The forested area of the parkland extends to the campgrounds, making the closeness of the sites less of an inconvenience.

Fishing is my preference at Camden. The nearby Redwood River is home to brown trout and draws fly fishers from miles away. Bass and sunfish can be caught in Brawner Lake, also within the park. Hiking trails winnow through the park, climbing and dipping among the hills and valleys. The Dakota Valley Trail is particularly rewarding, with a heightened lookout point providing an expansive view of the park. Many trails are groomed in the winter for skiing.

Wildlife seems to be particularly abundant here on the high prairie. Hikers may come across minks, whitetail deer, raccoons, and muskrats. In the sky, hawks circle above the openings in the trees and songbirds sing throughout the summer.

It is worth noting that wildflowers bloom here from early spring to mid-autumn. The high prairie is full of butterfly weed, wild asters, blazing stars, bee balm, yarrow flowers, and dozens more native prairie blooms and plants.

Campsites, facilities: There are 80 sites for tents and RVs up to 50–60 feet; 34 sites have electric hookups and seven are pull-through. There are also 12 equestrian sites and one group campsite for up to 50 people. Picnic tables, a picnic shelter, fire rings and grills, flush and vault toilets, drinking water, showers, and dump station are provided. A playground, horseshoe pit, warming house, fishing pier, swimming beach, and boat ramp (electric motors only) are available. Some facilities are wheelchair accessible. Leashed pets are permitted.

Reservations, fees: Reservations are accepted from April 2 to October 31 at 866/857-2757 or online at www.stayatmnparks.com ($8.50 non-refundable reservation fee) and can be made up to one year in advance. Reservations are not required the rest of the year. Sites are $12–24. Open year-round, with limited facilities in winter.

Directions: From Lund, drive southwest on Highway 23 for 3 miles to County Road 68. Turn right into the park entrance and drive 0.2 mile to the park office straight ahead.

Contact: Camden State Park, 507/865-4530, www.dnr.state.mn.us/state_parks.

15 SWENSON PARK CAMPGROUND

🚶‍♀️ 🏊 🛶 🚤 🎣 🦌 🐕 ♿ 🚐

Scenic rating: 7

on Swenson Lake

Swenson Park Campground lies in a harbor of trees in a sea of farmland. Located on Swenson Lake, the campground overlooks the water and a small island just offshore.

The campground consists of 10 RV sites scattered along the eastern shore of Swenson Lake. The shoreline enjoys more trees than the campground, but each site has sufficient shade to keep your RV out of the sun during the day.

A small but pleasant beach is great for swimming and sunbathing. The fishing isn't bad, either; walleyes, northerns, and sunfish are regular catches. A small footpath leads away from the campground along the water but does not circumnavigate the lake.

Campsites, facilities: There are 10 sites for RVs; all sites have electric hookup. Picnic tables, fire rings and grills, toilets, and a dump station are provided. A playground, a boat ramp and dock, and a swimming beach are available. Most sites are wheelchair accessible. Leashed pets are permitted.

Reservations, fees: Reservations are not accepted. Sites are $10 per night, available on a first come, first served basis. Open year-round.

Directions: From Balaton, drive west on Highway 14 for 4.1 miles. Turn left onto Highway 91 and drive south for 5.3 miles to County Park Road. Turn right into Swenson Park and drive 0.3 mile to the campground straight ahead.

Contact: Murray County, 507/836-6163, www.murray-countymn.com, mbambrick@co.murray.mn.us.

16 GARVIN PARK CAMPGROUND

🚶‍♀️ 🏊 🛶 🚤 🎣 🦌 🐕 🚐 ⛺

Scenic rating: 6

north of Garvin

The Garvin Park campground is everything a county park should be: quiet, shady, on the water, and perfect for picnicking. Just north of Garvin, this campground is tucked into a shady bend of the Cottonwood River perfect for a relaxing summer weekend or an overnight winter camping excursion.

The Garvin region is primarily farmland and open fields, but the watershed area around the river has heavy tree cover. The two campgrounds sit on a clearing in the midst of the trees. Campsites are arranged in a ring around a large open grassy area and poke into the tree cover with open views. All sites are near the water, though none have direct access.

A hiking and skiing trail leads near the water from the campground. A large sledding hill is popular here in the winter. The park has several transitional zones between forest and field, making it great for viewing wildlife. Note that the park is also open for bow-hunting seasons for deer and turkey, so you may want to plan your camping trip accordingly.

Campsites, facilities: There are 30 sites for tents and RVs (hookups). Picnic tables, fire rings and grills, showers, toilets, and dump station are provided. A playground and a hiking and skiing trail are available. Leashed pets are permitted.

Reservations, fees: Reservations are not accepted; sites are available on a first come, first served basis. Self-registration is required at the campground. Sites are $9–12 per night. Open year-round.

Directions: From Garvin, drive north for 3.8 miles on Highway 59. Turn right at 150th Street and drive 0.4 mile to the park on your right.

Contact: Garvin Park, 507/532-8214, http://dev.lyonco.org, rickanderson@co.lyon.mn.us.

17 SWIFT LAKE PARK CAMPGROUND

Scenic rating: 7

north of Tracy

Where there is a lake in southern Minnesota's sun country, there is almost sure to be a campground. The trees huddled next to Swift Lake cradle one of the smallest camping areas in the region—a great resting place for road trippers who need a break from the long, treeless farmland highways or for locals who want to head out for a swim.

The beautiful lake, summer breeze, and shady trees really put this campground on the map. The are only 16 sites, and the campground is usually no more than half full in the summer. Complemented by a boat dock, playground, and showers, Swift Lake is a very comfortable place to park for the night.

Recreation is available if you want it, but this park is best used for relaxation. If you are looking to stretch your legs, a paved bike trail passes through the park and near the campground.

Campsites, facilities: There are 16 sites for tents and RVs; eight sites have hookups. Picnic tables, fire rings, toilets, showers, and a dump station are provided. A playground, a boat dock, swimming beach, and bath house are available. Leashed pets are permitted.

Reservations, fees: Reservations are accepted at 507/629-5528. Sites are $8 per night for tents and $15 per night for RVs. Open from May through October.

Directions: From Tracy, drive north on County Road 11 for 1 mile. Turn right at the Swift Lake Park sign on the right sight of the road and drive 0.5 mile to the campground straight ahead.

Note that this campground is only about 100 feet from the town's local airport. There is very little air traffic here, though, and it rarely disturbs campers.

Contact: Swift Lake Park, 507/629-5528, www.tracymn.com.

18 LAKE SHETEK STATE PARK

Scenic rating: 10

in Lake Shetek State Park

BEST (

Occupying a wooded peninsula on Lake Shetek, this campground is for those who like to make use of every minute of their outdoor experience. A recreational mecca for hikers, anglers, skiers, and bird watchers, Lake Shetek State Park is a major southwestern Minnesota destination.

The main campground is a seven-loop behemoth on a chunk of Lake Shetek's eastern shore. The park and all of its campsites are set in a large grove of trees on a peninsula of Lake Shetek. The main campground economizes space by putting sites close together, but the tree cover is substantial enough to make each site feel separate. A small island lies to the west of the campground and provides a beautiful sunrise panorama on early summer mornings.

The cart-in and walk-in sites are on much smaller Park Lake farther east in the park. The sites are buried in the marshy woods near the water, and the low-ground forest is a wonderful wilderness experience, though you may want to plan your trip for the later summer months when the mosquitoes aren't as bad. Nearby Eastlick Marsh is a breeding ground for the little buggers.

Lake Shetek is the largest lake in southwestern Minnesota and forms the headwaters of the

Des Moines River. The walleye fishing here is particularly good. Anglers will also catch crappies, northerns, and panfish all year long. Bird lovers come to the park to see the bird sanctuary on Loon Island, an area on the lake connected to the mainland by a causeway near the campground. Hiking and skiing trails also link the campground to the rest of the park. A bicycle trail, pioneer monument, swimming beach, and canoe and kayak rentals score this park high on the recreational charts.

Campsites, facilities: There are 97 sites for tents and RVs up to 60 feet; 66 sites have electric hookups. There are also eight cart-in sites, six walk-in sites, and one tent-only group camp for up to 50 people. Picnic tables, fire rings and grills, flush and vault toilets, drinking water (via hand pump at walk-in sites), showers, and a dump station are provided. A playground, horseshoe pit, volleyball court, swimming beach, warming house (in winter), fishing pier, and boat ramp are available. Some facilities are wheelchair accessible. Leashed pets are permitted.

Reservations, fees: Reservations are usually accepted from April 2 to October 31 at 866/857-2757 or online at www.stayatmnparks.com ($8.50 non-refundable reservation fee) and can be made up to one year in advance. Reservations are not required the rest of the year. Note: Due to pending construction, reservations will be unavailable after August 1, 2010. Sites are $12–24. Open year-round; however, construction may affect availability.

Directions: From Currie drive north on County Road 38 for 1.6 miles. Turn left on State Park Road for 1.2 miles, following signs to the campground entrance.

Contact: Lake Shetek State Park, 507/763-3256, www.dnr.state.mn.us/state_parks.

🔟 SCHREIERS ON SHETEK CAMPGROUND

Scenic rating: 8

on Lake Shetek, north of Lake Shetek State Park

If you've got it, Schreiers On Shetek can handle it. With accommodations for hundreds of campers, this campground is for the camper who likes all the amenities of home while enjoying the great outdoors. Set on the largest lake in southwestern Minnesota, just north of Lake Shetek State Park, Schreiers has room for you, your family, and your family's families.

Loaded to the gills with big-rig RVs, tents of every shape and color, boats, kayaks, and outboard motors bigger than your college car, this campground is for those who work hard and play harder. Campsites are strung out along the shoreline and organized in a large loop around an open field south of the water. Most of the RV sites are along the water— seasonal campers secure their spots well ahead of time. The shoreline spots have plenty of tree cover and space; the camping loop area is more exposed and has very few trees.

If you don't have a boat, fishing rod, swimsuit, volleyball, or bicycle, you will be out of place here. Schreiers is set up for outdoor recreation, stocked with bike and hiking trails, a swimming beach, boat rentals—even a staffed baby-sitting facility.

Campsites, facilities: There are 120 sites for tents or RVs up to 40–65 feet; 14 sites are tent-only and 30 sites are RV-only (full hookups). All sites have electric hookups. There are also four equestrian sites. Picnic tables, fire rings and grills, showers, drinking water, toilets, and a dump station are provided. A playground, swimming beach, boat ramp, hiking and biking trail, fishing dock and boat mooring area, canoe/kayak/boat rentals, grocery store, and laundry facilities are available. Some facilities are wheelchair accessible. Leashed pets are permitted.

Reservations, fees: Reservations are accepted

at 507/763-3817 ($25 refundable deposit required). Sites are $17 per night for tents and $25 per night for RVs. Credit cards are not accepted. Open year-round.

Directions: From Currie, drive north on County Road 38 for 2 miles. Turn left onto County Road 37 for 0.1 mile, then turn right onto 200th Avenue. Drive north for 1 mile to 181st Street. Turn left for 0.5 mile to the campground entrance.

Contact: Schreiers On Shetek Campground, 507/763-3817, www.schreiersonshetek.com.

20 PLUM CREEK PARK

Scenic rating: 7

near Walnut Grove

Plum Creek County Park is as big as it is beautiful. The park is divided into two sections, and the campground is in the upper portion of the 207-acre park near Lake Laura. Campers come here all year to enjoy the lake, the hills, the hiking, and skiing—but summer is definitely the busy season.

The campground is large, with sites spread throughout four adjacent loops near the southern shore of the lake. Neatly planted trees give most sites a little shade and privacy; however, the 16 sites on the outer edge of the easternmost loop do not have any trees or privacy. The campground is linked to the lake via a hiking trail that leads to the swimming beach and fishing area.

There are plenty of ways to enjoy the lake, including a hiking trail, a swimming beach, and boat ramp. A gazebo built on a hill overlooking the lake is a popular picnic spot. Lake Laura is an artificial lake stocked each year with fish. Anglers can catch walleyes, bass, northerns, and sunfish here from boat or from shore.

Note: Boats can only be used for cruising and fishing. Water-skiing and racing are not allowed.

Campsites, facilities: There are 61 sites for tents and RVs (hookups). Fire rings and grills, toilets, drinking water, and a dump station are provided. A boat ramp, swimming beach, a hiking trail, softball diamonds, a gazebo picnic area, and playground are available. Some facilities are wheelchair accessible. Leashed pets are permitted.

Reservations, fees: Reservations are accepted at 507/859-2005 during Wilder Pageant days only ($5 nonrefundable reservation fee). Sites are first come, first served the rest of the year. Sites are $20–30 per night. Open from May to mid-October.

Directions: From west Highway 14, in Walnut Grove, turn south 1 block and, after crossing the tracks, take a right onto County Road 20. Drive 1 mile west, then turn south onto County Road 78 for 1.5 miles.

Contact: City of Walnut Grove, 507/859-2005, www.walnutgrove.org.

21 SAILORS AND SOLDIERS MEMORIAL PARK

Scenic rating: 6

in Sanborn

One of the most interesting things about southern Minnesota is its abundance of small towns with small campgrounds. Camping in a small town can be just as enjoyable as at a state park or state forest if you can find the right one. The Sailors and Soldiers Memorial Park Campground in Sanborn is as right as rain. Hugging the Cottonwood River, this little park is a real charmer.

Campsites are laced along the river. Lush cottonwood trees grow throughout the park, shading the campsites and giving credence to the aptly named Cottonwood River. The well-maintained park has a clean, crisp feel to it with plenty of open spaces for sunshine, too.

A footpath leads to the river and some well-used shore-fishing spots. A picnic area provides a shady respite, and the updated restroom facilities are clean and modern, providing a higher level of comfort than most city park campgrounds can claim.

Campsites, facilities: There are 24 sites for tents and RVs (hookups). Picnic tables, fire rings and grills, drinking water, showers, toilets, and a dump station are provided. Two picnic shelters, a volleyball court, and playground are available. Some facilities are wheelchair accessible. Leashed pets are permitted.

Reservations, fees: Reservations are accepted at 507/220-5386. Sites are $7 per night for tents and $15 per night for RVs. Open from May to October.

Directions: From Sanborn, drive south on Central Street for less than 1 mile to the park and campground.

Contact: City of Sanborn, 507/648-3510, www.cityofsanbornmn.org.

22 GILFILLAN ESTATE CAMPGROUND
Scenic rating: 6

near Morgan

This sprawling estate was once home to the wealthy Gilfillan family. At the turn of the 20th century, the Gilfillans owned a large spread of farmland here, with a beautifully furnished farmhouse and a wealth of land and farm machinery. Many of the antiques and farm machines that filled the house are now preserved by the Redwood County Historical Society.

The campground here is sheltered by a grove of oak and cottonwood trees just across the road from the estate. The camping area is quite small, and there is little to do here other than tour the estate. Tours are offered by appointment only, so make sure to call ahead and schedule one before camping here.

Campsites, facilities: There are 20 tent sites and 25 RV sites with electric hookups. Picnic tables, fire rings and grills, toilets, showers,

and a dump station are permitted. Leashed pets are permitted.

Reservations, fees: Reservations are accepted at 507/249-3633. Sites are $18 per night. Open June through August.

Directions: From Morgan, drive north on Highway 67 for 4.4 miles to Gilfillan. Turn left into the campground at the Gilfillan Estate sign on the right side of the road.

Contact: Redwood County Historical Society, 507/249-3633.

23 SPRINGFIELD ROTHENBURG CAMPGROUND
Scenic rating: 6

in Springfield

The Rothenburg Campground sits adjacent to Springfield's Riverside Park on the Cottonwood River. The park is very large for such a small town, taking up more than 10 city blocks on the inside of a sharp bend in the river. The riverbank is lined with large cottonwood trees, as you might expect from its name, and the campsites are nestled among them in three loops about a dozen feet from the water. The trees provide a broad, shady canopy; along with the campground being separate from the rest of the park on the west side of it, the trees here give the sites a very quiet, remote feel despite being just across the river from town.

This is an excellent city park with a new pool, a beautiful community center, softball fields, and paved hiking and biking trails that tour the park and lead to the disc golf course. Campers also have access to a boat ramp and fishing areas along the river.

Campsites, facilities: There are 38 sites for tents and RVs (hookups). Picnic tables, fire rings, toilets, showers, and a dump station are provided. Hiking and biking trails, an outdoor pool, playground, disc golf course, and boat ramp are provided. Some facilities are wheelchair accessible. Leashed pets are permitted.

Reservations, fees: Reservations are accepted annually after January 2 at 507/723-3517 or via email to commctr@newulmtel.net. Sites are $11–22 per night. Credit cards are not accepted. Open from late April to early October.

Directions: In Springfield, drive south on Cass Avenue for 0.25 mile across the river and into the park. The campground is on the right, but you must register at the community center on the left directly after crossing the river.

Contact: Springfield Rothenburg Campground, 507/723-3517, http://springfieldmn.org.

24 FORT RIDGELY STATE PARK

Scenic rating: 7

in Fort Ridgely State Park

Infamous for the 1862 Dakota Conflict that happened here, Fort Ridgely and its campground are the stuff of legends. Today, the park's peaceful wooded campsites, meandering hiking trails, and cheerful winter sliding hill belie its dramatic past.

The park has two campgrounds: Creekside and Rustic. Camping at Creekside provides a more modern camping experience, while camping at Rustic ensures greater privacy and quietude. While Creekside's trees offer more shade, the sites are laid out in mostly open space. Rustic is true to its name, with vault toilets, cold running water, and thicker vegetation that give it an off-the-beaten-path feel.

Recreation is an unspoken requirement for camping at Fort Ridgely. The historical fort is open for tours, miles of hiking trails lead through the park, and the Creekside campground is filled with recreation options. A paved trail connects the park to the nearby town of Fairfax and is easily accessed from the campground. In the winter, many of the hiking trails are groomed for cross-country skiing, and the park's massive sliding hill is ever popular on snowy days.

Campsites, facilities: There are 31 sites for tents and RVs up to 60 feet; one site is pull-through and 15 sites have electric hookups. There are also three walk-in sites, 25 equestrian sites (open Apr.–Nov.), and one group campsite for up to 40 people. Picnic tables, fire rings, drinking water (not at walk-in sites), toilets, showers, and a dump station are provided. A playground and picnic shelter, horseshoe pit, and volleyball court are available. Some facilities are wheelchair accessible. Leashed pets are permitted.

Reservations, fees: Reservations are accepted from April 2 to October 31 at 866/857-2757 or online at www.stayatmnparks.com ($8.50 non-refundable reservation fee) and can be made up to one year in advance. Reservations are not required the rest of the year. Sites are $12–24. Open year-round, with limited facilities in winter.

Directions: From Fairfax, drive south on Highway 4 for 6 miles. Follow signs on your right into the park.

Contact: Fort Ridgely State Park, 507/426-7840, www.dnr.state.mn.us/state_parks.

25 SPORTSMANS PARK CAMPGROUND

Scenic rating: 6

north of Sleepy Eye

Just north of Sleepy Eye, on the north shore of Sleepy Eye Lake, is this quaint eight-site campground. The western end of the park is an open grassy area corralled in by trees, lending a quiet, peaceful aura. Although the highway isn't far away, the open fields and handful of trees make camping here a serene, relaxing experience. Sites are lined up near the water among a smattering of trees that give as much shade as they can.

A paved walking and biking path cuts through the park near the lake. Four fishing piers extend into the water, and there is a boat launch used regularly by anglers and water-skiers.

Campsites, facilities: There are eight sites for tents and RVs (electrical hookups). Picnic tables, fire rings and grills, drinking water, toilets, and dump station are provided. A playground, swimming beach, and biking and hiking trail are available. Leashed pets are permitted.

Reservations, fees: Reservations are accepted at 507/794-5724. Sites are $15 per night. Open from May to October.

Directions: From Sleepy Eye, drive north 1.5 miles on Highway 68. Turn left into the campground on the north side of Sleepy Eye Lake.

Contact: Sportsmans Park Campground, 507/794-3731.

26 FLANDRAU CAMPGROUND

Scenic rating: 10

in Flandrau State Park

"Minnesota Nice" may have gotten its start in Flandrau State Park. This accommodating park has something for everyone. Its three campgrounds can furnish you with modern hookups, deliver a basic car camping experience, or give you a rustic, wilderness camping trip. Like hills? The park is lined with wooded bluffs. Enjoy rivers? The Cottonwood River flows right through the park. Are flat hiking and ski trails what you are in the mood for? Flandrau is spilling over with them.

The three campgrounds are lined up on the north side of the Cottonwood River in the flat valley bottom. Sites are nestled among trees and grasses, and there is plenty of shade, along with plenty of room, especially in the rustic camping area.

Hiking trails connect all campgrounds to each other, as well as to a system of trails that wind through the park's bottomlands and bluffs. Hike the wetlands, sandy riverbanks, grassy fields, and thick forest habitats that run throughout the park. Cross-country skiing is very popular here in the winter.

Campsites, facilities: There are 92 sites for tents and RVs up to 66 feet; 34 sites have electrical hookups. There are also three walk-in sites. Picnic tables, fire rings, toilets, showers, and a dump station are provided. Hiking trails, a canoe access, swimming beach, fishing area, skating rink, sliding hill, warming house, and playground are available. Some facilities are wheelchair accessible. Leashed pets are permitted.

Reservations, fees: Reservations are accepted from April 2 to October 31 at 866/857-2757 or online at www.stayatmnparks.com ($8.50 non-refundable reservation fee) and can be made up to one year in advance. Reservations are not required the rest of the year. Sites are $12–24. Open year-round.

Directions: From New Ulm, drive south on Summit Avenue for 3 blocks to the park entrance on your right. Follow signs to the campground.

Contact: Flandrau State Park, 507/233-9800, www.dnr.state.mn.us/state_parks.

27 LAKE HANSKA COUNTY PARK

Scenic rating: 7

on the east shore of Lake Hanska

Lake Hanska is one of the best walleye lakes in southwestern Minnesota. The long, narrow lake has dozens of fishing holes, and most of them are usually occupied during the summer—that shouldn't stop you from coming here and casting your line, though.

The county park campground provides access to the lake and an opportunity for excellent shoreline fishing. There are just 22 sites here in a small loop set in a surprisingly woodsy patch of land on the lake's eastern shore. Though this part of the state is covered with acres and acres of flat farmland, the shores of Lake Hanska are dressed in cottonwood and oak trees. The campground enjoys rich, velvety shade and a sublime swimming beach with white sand so lovely it is almost decadent. The park lies between a state wildlife management area and Minneopa State Park, both beautiful areas that are worth visiting; Minneopa's old mill site and waterfall area are especially fun for the family.

Campsites, facilities: There are 22 sites for tents and RVs. Picnic tables, fire rings, toilets, showers, and a dump station are provided. A hiking and biking trail, cross-country ski trail, fishing dock, and playground are available. Some facilities are wheelchair accessible. Leashed pets are permitted.

Reservations, fees: Reservations are accepted at 507/439-6411. Sites are $9 per night for tents and $18 per night for RVs. Open from May to October.

Directions: From Hanska, drive south on County Road 13 for 1.3 miles. Turn right onto 115th Street and drive for 3 miles to County Road 11. The park is 0.5 mile ahead on the right side of the road just before Countryview Road.

Contact: Lake Hanska County Park, 507/439-6411.

28 EAGLE NEST PARK
🏃 🏊 🎣 🚴 🚐 ⛺

Scenic rating: 6

east of St. James

Southern Minnesota isn't much for trees, but the South Fork of the Watonwan River provides a line of forest that breaks up the farmlands and fields of the region.

This is primarily a tent campground, and folks enjoy the quiet and calm sleeping under the stars. Just 20 sites are hidden among the trees along a gravel road that leads through the campground.

This park is good for river fishing and relaxing. Anglers can catch catfish, northerns, and some bass if they are lucky. The river has plenty of snags and bends as well as shade from overhanging trees that foster fruitful fishing holes.

Campsites, facilities: There are 16 sites for tents only and four sites for tents and RVs. Picnic tables, fire rings and grills, and a dump station are provided. A hiking trail and playground are available. Leashed pets are permitted.

Reservations, fees: Reservations are accepted at 507/375-3393. Sites are $5 per night for tents and $10 per night for RVs. Open from May through September.

Directions: From St. James take Highway 60 east for 6 miles to County Road 118. Turn left and drive 1 mile to the park entrance on the left. Follow signs to the campground.

Contact: Eagle Nest Park, 507/375-3393, www.co.watonwan.mn.us.

29 MINNEOPA CAMPGROUND
🏃 🏊 🎣 🚐 ⛺

Scenic rating: 9

in Minneopa State Park

Oak savanna once dominated the Minnesota River plain, but it is a rare form of habitat these days. Minneopa Campground is located in one of the most beautiful savanna environments left in the state. Just a few hundred feet from the south bank of the Minnesota River, camping here is a lesson in the peace and beauty of the transitional prairie.

The campground is a two-loop design set in the oak savanna near the Minnesota River and Minneopa Creek. The big trees are not abundant enough to form a forest here, but they are large enough to provide plenty of shade to the sites. Prairie grass, wildflowers, and a sweeping view over the western portion of the park make this campground a very pleasant stay. Sunsets over the prairie are unforgettable.

The savanna, river, prairie, nearby waterfalls,

and the historic Seppmann windmill site can keep you as busy as you want to be. Hiking, fishing, and nature watching are the most rewarding activities at Minneopa. A hiking trail leads to the confluence of the creek and the river, then to a set of limestone steps that overlook the falls upstream. Another trail crosses the prairie to the site of the historical windmill the park is home to.

Campsites, facilities: There are 61 sites for tents and RVs up to 60 feet; six sites have electrical hookups. Picnic tables, fire rings and grills, drinking water, toilets, showers, and dump station are provided. A picnic shelter, volleyball court, and horseshoe pit are available. Leashed pets are permitted.

Reservations, fees: Reservations are accepted from April 2 to October 31 at 866/857-2757 or online at www.stayatmnparks.com ($8.50 non-refundable reservation fee) and can be made up to one year in advance. Reservations are not required the rest of the year. Sites are $12–24. Open year-round.

Directions: From Mankato, drive west on Highway 60 for 3.4 miles. Turn right onto Highway 68. Drive north for 1.6 miles to the state park entrance. Turn right into the park and drive for 1 mile to the campground.

Contact: Minneopa State Park, 507/389-5464, www.dnr.state.mn.us/state_parks.

30 SHADY OAKS CAMPGROUND

🚶 🚴 ⛴ 🏊 🛶 🎣 🦌 ♿ 🚐 ⛺

Scenic rating: 7

east of Garden City

Garden City has an alluring name, and an even more alluring river. The Watonwan River loops and twists gracefully across Blue Earth County, trailing a robust green ribbon of cottonwood and hardwood trees through the rich, flat farmland of the region.

Shady Oaks Campground is on the west side of Garden City, cloaked in a grove of shady oak and cottonwood trees in a bend of the river. The sites are close together, spread mostly in a large loop, but also dispersed along the river and closer to the parking area. About half of the sites on the outer side of the loop have footpaths that lead right to the water—these are definitely the most private sites.

This campground has plenty for you to do, whether you are by yourself, camping with your family, or with a group. You can rent canoes, fish from shore, use the arcade and game room, or tour the river and part of town on the paved hiking and biking trails the link the campground to the rest of the city.

Make sure to call ahead or check the campground's website before planning a visit here. The campground is closed for several weekends during the Blue Earth County Fair, which Garden City hosts each year. Groups sometimes rent the entire campground for a weekend, as well.

Campsites, facilities: There are 78 sites for tents and RVs; pull-through sites are available. Picnic tables, fire rings, toilets, showers, and a dump station are provided. Hiking and biking trails, canoe access, playground, game room, boat ramp, and camp store are available. Some facilities are wheelchair accessible. Leashed pets are permitted.

Reservations, fees: Reservations are accepted at 507/546-3986. Sites are $16 per night for tents and $19 per night for RVs. Open from May through October.

Directions: In Garden City, drive east on Fairgrounds Street for 0.25 mile to the campground.

Contact: Shady Oaks Campground, 507/546-3986, www.shadyoakscampground.org.

31 RIVERSIDE PARK AND MUNICIPAL CAMPGROUND

🏃 🚴 ⛵ 🚤 ❄ 🏕 🐎 🚗 △

Scenic rating: 8

in St. Peter's Riverside Park

St. Peter is one of the most beautiful, historic cities of southern Minnesota. It was originally slated to be the capital, but a midnight thievery of the capital charter documents let distant St. Paul usurp the title. St. Peter is still a special place, though, and home to five of Minnesota's former governors. Camping here is camping in style.

The Riverside Park campground is an impeccably clean, modern camping area overseen by the local police department. In fact, you have to register with the police before camping here. Mowed grass, big stately trees, and charming riverbank campsites make camping here preferable. The sites are shaded, well spaced, and connected to trails that tour the park.

This 100-acre spread is on prime riverfront real estate with access to hiking and biking trails, groomed snowmobile routes, a fishing pond, and a view of the historical architecture that has been lovingly preserved by the town.

Campsites, facilities: There are 11 sites for tents and RVs and 10 tent-only sites. Picnic tables, fire rings, toilets, showers, drinking water, and dump station are provided. A biking and hiking trail, groomed snowmobile trail, boat ramp, volleyball court, and playground are available. Leashed pets are permitted.

Reservations, fees: Reservations are not accepted; sites are available first come, first served. Sites are $10 per night for tents and $20 per night for RVs. Campers must register with the police department at 507/931-1550. Open from March through September.

Directions: In St. Peter, drive to 207 S. Front Street to the police station to register and get a map of the campground.

Contact: City of St. Peter Police Department, 507/931-1550, www.ci.st-peter.mn.us/recreation/.

32 LAND OF MEMORIES CAMPGROUND

🏃 🚴 ⛵ 🚤 🏕 🐎 🚗 △

Scenic rating: 7

in Mankato

Mankato is known as one of southern Minnesota's larger cities. Though it has enjoyed a growth spurt over the last decade, you can still find a secluded, private camping experience in Land of Memories on the southwest side of town. Although the name of the campground might be a little cheesy, the park is quite beautiful, situated at the confluence of the Blue Earth and Minnesota Rivers.

The sites are spread throughout the large park and along a gravel road that runs through it. There are various camping landscapes: About half of the sites are in sunny, grassy areas; the other half are in shady, oak- and cottonwood-canopied spots closer to the water. There are fewer than 50 sites in the park, each with a large tent pad area for several tents and up to 50 feet of space between sites.

The park has two large soccer fields and a Frisbee golf course, as well as very well-maintained paved hiking and biking trails that follow the river through the park and into town.

Campsites, facilities: There are 47 sites for tents and RVs. Picnic tables, fire rings, toilets, showers, and a dump station are provided. Hiking and biking trails, a fishing area, canoe access, and a playground are available. Leashed pets are permitted.

Reservations, fees: Reservations are accepted at 507/387-8649. Sites are $11 per night for tents and $13–16 per night for RVs; electrical sites are available. Open from May through October.

Directions: In Mankato, drive southwest on

Highway 169 across the Blue Earth River. Turn right onto Amos Owen Lane and drive 0.25 mile to the campground across the railroad tracks.

Contact: City of Mankato, 507/387-8649, www.mankato-mn.gov/LandOfMemories/Page.aspx.

33 DALY PARK CAMPGROUND

🏃 🚲 🏊 🎣 🚤 🛶 🎯 🐕 🏕️ 🚐 ⛺

Scenic rating: 5

in Mapleton

The Daly Park Campground is one of the friendliest in southern Minnesota, located on the north shore of Lura Lake. A year-round resident caretaker keeps this campground in tip-top condition and welcomes all guests.

Daly Park is wedged into a small peninsula, enjoying lakeshore on both its eastern and western sides. Mixed evenly with trees and open space, camping here is shaded and more private than at many other southern Minnesota county parks. Although there are nearly 90 campsites, they are spread out over four different areas, making each campground feel small and private. Tent sites are located in two camping areas on the eastern side of the park, while RV sites and sites with electrical hookups are on the west side of the park.

I love the layout of this campground. A narrow causeway beach connects a small island about 0.25 mile from the shore of Lura Lake. The lake spreads its arms to the northeast and northwest embracing the park. Full of woods, open space, lush grassy areas, a long sandy beach, and nature trails that connect it all, this is the perfect place to headquarter yourself for a weekend of fishing, swimming, hiking, canoeing, biking, and just hanging out.

Campsites, facilities: There are 71 RV sites and 51 tent sites; 67 RV sites have electrical hookups. Picnic tables, fire rings, drinking water, toilets, showers, and dump station are provided. A swimming beach, canoe/kayak rental, boat docking area, fishing boat rental, boat ramp, bathhouse, a playground, and a tennis court are available. Leashed pets are permitted.

Reservations, fees: Reservations are accepted at 507/524-3000 ($4 reservation fee). Sites are $14 per night. Open from May through October.

Directions: From Mapleton, drive southwest on County Road 7 for 4.5 miles. Follow signs to the campground.

Contact: Daly Park, 507/304-4027, www.co.blue-earth.mn.us/dept/parks.

34 POINT PLEASANT CAMPGROUND

🏊 🎣 🚤 🐕 🏕️ 🚐

Scenic rating: 7

on Madison Lake

Point Pleasant is actually a banquet hall that does some campground work on the side. The place is a popular spot in the Mankato area for wedding receptions, family reunions, and other catered gatherings, but behind the DJ-thumpin' music hall and closer to the lake is an RV park. The sites are clustered way out on Point Pleasant, almost a half mile into the water. The point is covered in oaks, maples, and other hardwoods, and the sites garner a decent amount of shade from them. There is little privacy here, but the tree canopy makes the camping area feel more secluded than it actually is. This isn't an ideal campground for peace and quiet, but it does have a great spot on the lake and excellent fishing.

Campsites, facilities: There are 80 sites for RVs (hookups). Picnic tables, fire rings, toilets, and garbage cans are available. A swimming beach, fishing dock, boat ramp, and playground are available. Leashed pets are permitted.

Reservations, fees: Reservations are accepted at 507/243-3072. Sites are $30 per night. Open year-round.

Directions: From Mankato, drive east on Highway 14 for 8.3 miles. Turn left onto County Road 17 and drive for 2.5 miles to Park Road. Veer right onto Park and take your second right onto Point Avenue in 0.5 mile. The campground is on Sheppard Circle just 0.3 mile ahead at the end of Park Road.
Contact: Point Pleasant Campground, 507/243-3072, www.thepointpleasant.com.

35 BRAY PARK CAMPGROUND

Scenic rating: 8

on Madison Lake near Blue Earth

Bray Park occupies a 100-acre chunk of land on a large peninsula that juts into Madison Lake. Bordered by woodlands to the west and farmland to the east, the park sits in a blend of trees and open space that makes for excellent camping, especially at the tent sites.

The campsites are spread along the lakeshore and in an open-field loop slightly farther from the water. There is plenty of room here for both RVs and tents, but tent camping is the best. Lined up near the deep blue water of Madison Lake, these sites are in the shady trees that line the lakeshore. Each tent site is very private and feels like it could be the only one on the lake.

Hiking trails follow the water and link the campsites to the lake. Swimming is excellent in Madison Lake; its deep blue waters are refreshing and cooling on hot summer days. Fishing from shore is easy from the tent sites, and a boat ramp provides access for anglers and water-skiers. Volleyball and horseshoes are set up in the park's open area.
Campsites, facilities: There are 33 sites for tents and RVs and 10 sites for tents only. Picnic tables, fire rings, toilets, drinking water, showers, and dump station are provided. Hiking trails, an interpretive center, boat ramp, swimming beach, volleyball court, horseshoe

pit, sunbathing deck, fishing dock, and a playground are available. Leashed pets are permitted.
Reservations, fees: Reservations are accepted at 507/243-3885 ($4 reservation fee). Sites are $4 per night for tents and $14 per night for RVs. Open from May through October.
Directions: From Madison Lake, drive southeast on County Road 48 for 2 miles to the campground.
Contact: Bray Park, 507/304-4027, www.co.blue-earth.mn.us/dept/parks.

36 BRENNANS' CAMPGROUND

Scenic rating: 6

on General Shields Lake west of Shieldsville

Shields Lake is often overlooked as a camping destination. It's a modest campground on a modest lake, and most locals don't want you to know that the fishing is a regional phenomenon.

The lake is lined with trees, but their shade doesn't extend far into the nearby camping area. The sites are organized on the lake's north shore in an open field near the water. Seasonal camping is available here, and many people take advantage of it. An RV village of regular summer campers is on the south side of the campground closest to the lake.

A simple playground and a footpath that leads to the water provide some land recreation, but the real sport is on the water. Waterskiing, boating, and especially fishing are very popular on Shields Lake.
Campsites, facilities: There are 45 sites for tents and RVs; partial and full hookups are available. Sites 33–45 are pull-through sites (full hookups). Picnic tables, fire rings and grills, toilets, showers, drinking water, and dump station are provided. Biking and hiking trails, canoe/kayak rental, a playground, fishing boat rental, a boat ramp, dock space, a

swimming beach, and a supply store are available. The entire campground is wheelchair accessible. Leashed pets are permitted.

Reservations, fees: Reservations are accepted at 507/334-8526. Sites are $14–16 per night for tents and $22–24 per night for RVs. Weekly rates are available. Payment is by cash or check only; no credit cards. Open from April to October.

Directions: From I-35W, take Highway 21 N at Faribault. Go north on Highway 21 through Shieldsville (approx. 9 miles), and Brennans' Campground is on General Shields Lake 2 miles past Shieldsville on the left-hand side on Irwin Trail.

Contact: Brennans' Campground, 507/334-8526, www.brennanscampground.com.

37 KAMP DELS CAMPGROUND

Scenic rating: 9

on Sakatah Lake

I know what you're thinking: Why would I pay $97 to sleep outside on the ground?! Believe me, I thought the same thing, but Kamp Dels is well worth every dollar you are willing to spend. They brand themselves as a family vacationing facility, and rightly so. The campground is amid a network of recreational and entertainment choices on Sakatah Lake that can keep any family running on all cylinders all day long.

The camping area dominates the north shore of Sakatah Lake and is almost bigger than the nearby town of Waterville. The 400 campsites are spread along the shoreline, forests, and open fields of the park. This spread of prime lakeshore is enough to justify the site fee, but throw in nightly entertainment (including music and performances), high-speed Internet access, a central lodge, outdoor pool, and tennis courts, and you've got yourself a real bargain.

As you might imagine, hiking trails and biking paths course through the park, connecting the campsites to the nature areas and lakefront paths. A horse stable allows riding in the corral or in the park, and an outdoor water park lets you enjoy all the water you can handle. Fishing from the shore or the pier, as well as from a pontoon or fishing boat (available for rent at the campground), is excellent. Sakatah Lake is rife with walleyes, northerns, bass, perch, and sunfish.

Campsites, facilities: There are 390 sites for tents and RVs and 10 tent-only sites; full hookups and pull-through sites are available. Picnic tables, fire rings and grills, showers, toilets, drinking water, and dump station are provided. A central lodge building with evening entertainment, high-speed Internet access, laundry facilities, outdoor pool and water park, horse riding stable, fishing and pontoon boat rentals, boat ramp, two playgrounds, petting zoo, minigolf, and tennis court are available. Leashed pets are permitted.

Reservations, fees: Reservations are accepted at 507/362-8616. Sites are $97 per night for tents and $181 per night for RVs. Open from April through October.

Directions: From Waterville drive east on County Road 131 for 0.5 mile. The main entrance to the park will be on your left. Follow signs to the campground office.

Contact: Kamp Dels Campground, 507/362-8616, www.kampdels.com.

38 SAKATAH LAKE STATE PARK

Scenic rating: 9

in Sakatah Lake State Park

BEST (

Sakatah means "singing hills," and the rolling hills and bluffs that flow from the southern shore of Sakatah Lake are well named. The heavy, big woods forest blankets the burgeoning earth as it heaves itself from the flat farmland of southern Minnesota.

With the hills, the striking lake, and the dense forest, Sakatah Lake State Park delivers a wilderness experience well worth exploring. Heavy woods characterize the park and the campground. There are four camping loops in the park near the lake, including five bike-in sites on the Sakatah Singing Hills Trail (the sites are about 0.5 mile from the lake on a wooded plateau 75 feet above the water). The nearly 70 sites are very private and enjoy ample shade.

The park holds part of the best stretch of the popular Sakatah Singing Hills paved bicycle trail, which starts in Mankato and stretches for nearly 40 miles to the east. Hiking trails loop through the forests and hills, connecting to both the lake and the Sakatah Singing Hills bike trail. Canoes can be rented at the park office for fishing or for paddling across the lake. Shore fishing or canoe fishing is fruitful; the lake is known for walleye and northern fishing but also holds bass, crappies, and perch.

Campsites, facilities: There are 67 sites for tents and RVs up to 55 feet, including five bike-in sites; 14 sites have electrical hookups. Picnic tables, fire rings and grills, showers, drinking water, toilets, and a dump station are provided. A playground, a picnic area, horseshoe pit, and a fishing pier are provided. Leashed pets are permitted.

Reservations, fees: Reservations are accepted from April 2 to October 31 at 866/857-2757 or online at www.stayatmnparks.com ($8.50 non-refundable reservation fee) and can be made up to one year in advance. Reservations are not required the rest of the year. Sites are $12–24. Open year-round.

Directions: From Faribault, drive west on Highway 60 for 14 miles. The park entrance is on your left. Follow signs to the campground.

Contact: Sakatah Lake State Park, 507/362-4438, www.dnr.state.mn.us/state_parks.

39 KIESLER'S CAMPGROUND AND RV RESORT

Scenic rating: 6

in Waseca

Kiesler's is a high-class RV park and resort on Clear Lake, just a few miles west of Owatonna. With more than 300 sites, several pools and outdoor sports courts, Fourth of July fireworks, and planned weekend events throughout the summer, camping here is more of an entertainment experience than a relaxing weekend on the lake. Luckily for Kiesler's, hundreds of families looking for high-action summer weekends throughout the sunny months keep this place packed. The sites are close together, and about one-third are shaded with a few trees, but the big-rig RVs that come here are usually equipped with air-conditioning and pull out awnings, eliminating the need for much landscape diversity. This campground is designed for volume—you wouldn't want to pitch a tent here after seeing how close together the sites are.

Campsites, facilities: There are 300 sites for RVs up to 60 feet; full and partial hookups and pull-through sites are available. Picnic tables, fire rings, toilets, showers, and a dump station are provided. An outdoor pool, fishing docks and boats, a boat ramp, pontoon rental, playground, laundry facilities, wireless Internet (fee), and a camp store are available. Leashed pets are permitted.

Reservations, fees: Reservations are accepted at 507/835-3179. Sites are $37–56 per night. Open from mid-April to late September.

Directions: From Waseca, drive east on County Road 4 for 0.5 mile to the Kiesler's RV Resort sign on the right side of the road just after Memorial Park. Turn right and drive 0.2 mile straight ahead to the campground office.

Contact: Kiesler's Campground and RV Resort, 507/835-3179, www.kieslers.com.

40 CAMP MAIDEN ROCK
🏃 🚴 🏊 🛶 🎣 🐴 ♿ 🚐 ⛺

Scenic rating: 5

north of Morristown

Camp Maiden Rock is a lovely spot of land on the Cannon River just east of Sakatah Lake. Within driving distance of Sakatah Lake State Park and located right on the Singing Hills State Bike Trail, the campground is a prime location of outdoor recreation in southern Minnesota's beautiful rolling hills, forested river valleys, and grassy, flower-laden fields.

The actual campsites are a little less impressive. Although each site is very large (there is enough room for at least three tents at each site) and comes complete with its own short gravel driveway, they aren't spaced very far apart and have nearly zero tree cover for shade. The river and biking trail are only dozens of feet away, providing convenient access to daytime fun—which is good because you won't want to spend it sitting in the open area next to your tent.

Campsites, facilities: There are 65 sites for tents and RVs (hookups available). Picnic tables, fire rings, toilets, showers, and a dump station are provided. A hiking and biking trail, bicycle rental, outdoor pool, boat ramp, and playground are available. The campground is wheelchair accessible. Leashed pets are permitted.

Reservations, fees: Reservations are accepted at 507/685-2240 ($35 nonrefundable deposit required). Sites are $26 per night for tents and $32–37 per night for RVs. Open from May to early October.

Directions: From Morristown, drive west on Highway 60 for 1 mile. Turn right onto Jackson Avenue and drive for 0.3 mile to the campground on the right side of the road.

Contact: Camp Maiden Rock, 507/685-2240, www.campmaidenrock.com.

41 RIVERVIEW CAMPGROUND

🏊 🎣 🐴 🚐 ⛺

Scenic rating: 6

south of Owatonna

Located on the Straight River, the Riverview Campground serves a slice of the idyllic days when hay rides and swimming holes were the highlight of summer entertainment. This campground is definitely modern, with an arcade, Internet access, and a minigolf course to prove it, but the atmosphere here along the river is one of rural simplicity and peaceful, shady camping. The campground is organized in two loops under shady oak trees lining the river, a bucolic patch of land that looks more like a farm than a campground. Footpaths circumnavigate the campground, connecting the sites to the pool, minigolf course, game room, and playground spread throughout the park.

Campsites, facilities: There are 130 sites for tents and RVs. Picnic tables, fire rings, toilets, showers, and a dump station are provided. A swimming pool, minigolf course, playground, arcade, Internet access, and a camp store are available. Leashed pets are permitted.

Reservations, fees: Reservations are accepted at 507/451-8050. Sites are $25 per night for tents and $35 per night for RVs. Open from May to late October.

Directions: From Owatonna, drive south on County Road 45 for 1.2 miles to 28th Street SW. Turn right and drive 1.4 miles across I-35 to the campground on the right side of the road.

Contact: Riverview Campground, 507/451-8050, www.riverviewcampgroundmn.com.

42 SPLIT ROCK CREEK CAMPGROUND

Scenic rating: 8

in Jasper

Named after the creek, Split Rock Creek State Park is best known for its lake. Nestled among the rolling prairie hills of southwestern Minnesota, Split Rock Lake is the largest lake in Pipestone County.

Rock outcroppings in the highland prairie of the area kept much of the natural prairie unplowed by farmers and undeveloped by settlers. The campground lies on the northeastern shore of Split Rock Lake in a thick clump of oak, maple, and aspen trees surrounded by remnant prairie. The single-loop campground has only 29 sites, which are well shaded and very private. These wooded campsites provide an added sense of seclusion, because much of this park is prairie land, exposed to the wind and sun of the open sky. A hiking trail surrounds the loop, letting you hike to the lake or through the nearby grassland.

The park offers sweeping vistas of the lake and surrounding prairie, best viewed from the Beach Side Trail Center. The best hiking in the park starts here as well. Wildlife loves this area, especially the shoreline areas; keep your eyes peeled for beaver, turtles, and fox squirrels. The lake is home to walleye, bass, perch, northerns, and panfish; fishing is good from the shore or a boat. If you have time, it is worth a short seven-mile drive north to Pipestone National Monument for more hiking and sightseeing.

Campsites, facilities: There are 29 sites for tents and RVs up to 52 feet; 19 sites have electric hookups. There are also six walk-in sites, located less than 30 yards from the parking lot, and one tent-only group campsite for up to 75 people. Picnic tables, fire rings and grills, flush and vault toilets, showers (available seasonally), and a dump station are provided. A playground (swing set only), swimming beach, accessible fishing pier, volleyball equipment, horseshoes, and a warming hut (in winter) are available. Some facilities are wheelchair accessible. Leashed pets are permitted.

Reservations, fees: Reservations are accepted from April 2 to October 31 at 866/857-2757 or online at www.stayatmnparks.com ($8.50 non-refundable reservation fee) and can be made up to one year in advance. Reservations are not required the rest of the year. Sites are $12–24. Open year-round, with limited facilities in winter.

Directions: From Pipestone, drive southwest on Highway 23 for 7 miles. Turn left onto County Road 54 and drive 1 mile south to the park entrance on the left side of the road just after crossing the bridge over Split Rock Creek.

Contact: Split Rock Creek State Park, 507/348-7908, www.dnr.state.mn.us/state_parks.

43 BLUE MOUNDS STATE PARK

Scenic rating: 10

in Blue Mounds State Park

BEST (

Blue Mounds State Park campground is tucked among the rolling hills, quartzite cliffs, and grazing bison of Minnesota's high prairie grasslands. Unlike the farmland that surrounds it, the park is full of craggy rock outcroppings, natural prairie flowers, and prickly pear cacti.

You can have two distinct camping experiences at Blue Mounds State Park. The first experience is at the main campground, a three-loop grouping of 73 sites. Oaks and maples surround the campground and shade the area, but the sites are a little close for comfort. Your second option is the 14 cart-in sites spread throughout the woods along the park's main hiking trail. A primitive wooden shelter sits near the center of the camping area. The trees and hills at the cart-in campground separate each site, giving it full privacy.

The park is a treasure of natural wonders for campers to enjoy. Besides the large cliff, the park has a 1,250-foot rock formation lined up to mark the rising and setting of the sun on the spring and fall equinox. More than 100 bison, as well as coyotes and deer, live in the park.

Campsites, facilities: There are 73 sites for tents and RVs up to 50 feet; 40 sites have electric hookups. There are also 14 cart-in sites and a hike-in group campsite for up to 75 people. Picnic tables, fire rings and grills, drinking water (not at cart-in sites), flush and vault toilets, showers (available seasonally), and a dump station are provided. A playground, a volleyball court, horseshoe pit, swimming beach, snowmobile trails, snowshoeing, and carry-in boat access are available. Some facilities are wheelchair accessible. Leashed pets are permitted.

Reservations, fees: Reservations are accepted from April 2 to October 31 at 866/857-2757 or online at www.stayatmnparks.com ($8.50 non-refundable reservation fee) and can be made up to one year in advance. Reservations are not required the rest of the year. Sites are $12–24. Open year-round, with limited facilities in winter.

Directions: From Luverne, drive north 4 miles on Minnesota Highway 75. Turn east on County Road 20 and go 1 mile to the park entrance.

Contact: Blue Mounds State Park, 507/283-1307, www.dnr.state.mn.us/state_parks.

44 LIME LAKE PARK CAMPGROUND

Scenic rating: 8

on Lime Lake

Notched into the southern shore of Lime Lake near the small town of Avoca, this campground is probably the smallest public campground in the state. With just three campsites, it is a wonder anyone knows about it.

The campsites are tossed among a smattering of trees near the water. There are about a dozen trees in the campground and a few more lining the shore. The campsites take advantage of what shade there is and enjoy the privacy of a small campground. Nights are quiet and the view is unobstructed.

Lime Lake makes for decent fishing. A boat ramp near the campground is a good place to put in. Shore fishing along a footpath that follows several hundred feet of lakeshore is good as well.

Campsites, facilities: There are three sites for RVs only (electric hookups). Picnic tables, fire rings, toilets, drinking water, a boat ramp, and a dump station are provided. Leashed pets are permitted.

Reservations, fees: Reservations are not accepted; sites are available on a first come, first served basis. Sites are $10 per night. Open year-round.

Directions: From Avoca, drive west on 66th Street for 0.6 mile. Turn right at the sign onto the campground driveway for 0.1 mile.

Contact: Lime Lake Park, Murray County, 507/836-6163, www.murray-countymn.com.

45 SEVEN MILE PARK CAMPGROUND

Scenic rating: 6

in Fulda on Seven Mile Lake

Fulda is a small town on a big lake. Fulda and Seven Mile Lake are in the middle of a rural farming community in southwestern Minnesota, and the town has all the charm you would expect. The farmland and fields that blanket this part of the state are gently interrupted at Seven Mile Park with a small grove of oak and maple trees. The park lies on the south side of town, on the outskirts along the narrowest part of the lake.

Water-skiers, anglers, and boaters come here from all around Murray County to use Seven

Mile Lake, and if you want to spend time on the water, Seven Mile Park's campground is a good spot to park your RV or pitch a tent for the night. The campsites are scattered throughout a grassy field with several trees planted at each site for shade and protection from the wind. The park features a swimming beach, boat ramp, and fishing area, and is within driving distance of six state wildlife management areas.

Campsites, facilities: There are 14 sites for tents and RVs and 10 sites for tents only. Picnic tables, fire rings, toilets, showers, and a dump station are provided. A swimming beach, boat ramp, playground, and fishing area are available. Some facilities are wheelchair accessible. Leashed pets are permitted.

Reservations, fees: Reservations are not accepted. Self-registration is required at the campground. Sites are $10 per night. Open year-round.

Directions: In Fulda, drive south on Lafayette Avenue for 0.3 mile. The park is on the left side of the road about one city block after 11th Street.

Contact: Seven Mile Park, 507/836-6163.

46 KILEN WOODS CAMPGROUND

🚶 🏊 🎣 🏕 🚣 🎿 🐕 ♿ 🚙 ⛺

Scenic rating: 9

in Big Stone Lake State Park

Kilen Woods is a peaceful high prairie park with hills, dales, lakes, and prairie grass painting a picture of the Minnesota of the past. The Des Moines River meanders through the park, carving its way through the elevated prairie hills that begin their long sweep west to the Rockies. The mixed forest crowds in around the watershed, creating transitional zones near the open fields that draw wildlife and songbirds from miles around.

There is an abundance of wildflowers at Kilen Woods. The park is a beautiful oasis filled with oak and hardwood trees set among the surrounding farmland, but its open prairies are full of native grasses; bright flowers such as blazing stars, butterfly weeds, and Indian paintbrush are just as alluring.

Two campground loops (A and B) hold more than 30 sites and are connected to walk-in sites by a short hiking trail. The "woods" of Kilen Woods are east of the camping areas, nearer the river. Trees fringe the camping loops, giving some shade and privacy to sites nearby, but for the most part the loops are exposed. The walk-in sites are farther into the woods and offer more privacy.

The hills, forests, river, and prairie of Kilen Woods make it a hot spot for outdoor recreation. The campgrounds are nice and quiet, but the rest of the park can be more active. Anglers, bird watchers, hikers, and—in the wintertime—cross-country skiers, snowmobilers, and sledders use the park for its fun and beauty. The Des Moines River holds walleyes, northerns, and catfish for anglers, a long sliding hill fills with busy sledders during winter, and hiking trails along the water make for top-notch wildlife-watching.

Campsites, facilities: There are 33 sites for tents and RVs up to 50 feet; 11 sites have electrical hookups, and three sites are pull-throughs. There are also four walk-in sites. Picnic tables, fire rings and grills, vault toilets, drinking water, showers, and a dump station are provided. A picnic shelter, volleyball court, horseshoe pit, and a warming house (in winter) are available. Some facilities are wheelchair accessible. Leashed pets are permitted.

Reservations, fees: Reservations are accepted from April 2 to October 31 at 866/857-2757 or online at www.stayatmnparks.com ($8.50 non-refundable reservation fee) and can be made up to one year in advance. Reservations are not required the rest of the year. Sites are $12–24 per night. Open year-round.

Directions: From Lakefield, drive north on Highway 86 for 4 miles. Turn right on County Road 24 for 5 miles to the park. Follow signs to the campground.

Contact: Kilen Woods State Park, 507/662-6258, www.dnr.state.mn.us/state_parks.

47 LOON LAKE CAMPGROUNDS
🚶 🚴 ⛵ 🛶 🚣 ⛵ 🏕 🤽 🚐 ⛺

Scenic rating: 9

near Jackson

Loon Lake has two county campgrounds on its shores: Brown and Robertson. Brown campground lies on an isthmus between the western shore of Loon Lake and the eastern shore of Pearl Lake, offering a loop of 31 sites, half of which are near the water. Trees vary throughout the loop, giving shade to about one-third of the sites. The open area around the campground allows for good views of both lakes, making sunrise and sunset memorable.

On the east shore of Loon Lake lies Robertson campground, with 22 sites packed into a long loop on the southern edge of the park. As at Brown, trees are somewhat scarce in the camping area, creating an open atmosphere between sites. The lakeshore enjoys large oak trees that shade the hiking trail leading along the water.

Fishing is the most common pastime in these parks. Loon Lake and Pearl Lake are good for walleyes, northerns, and sunfish. Some bass can be caught if you know where to find them. A small creek connects the two lakes across Brown County Park near the camping area. Walking paths follow much of the lakeshore and connect the campgrounds to the water.

Campsites, facilities: There are 55 sites for tents and RVs (electrical hookups). Picnic tables, fire rings, toilets, showers, and a dump station are provided. Biking and hiking trails, a playground, and a boat ramp are available. Leashed pets are permitted.

Reservations, fees: Reservations are not accepted. Sites are $7–12 per night for tents and $15 per night for RVs. Open from April 15 to October 15.

Directions: From Jackson drive south on Highway 71 for 6 miles to County Road 4. Turn left for 5.5 miles to Loon Lake. Follow signs to either campground.

Contact: Jackson County, 507/847-2240, www.co.jackson.mn.us/parks.

48 CHECKERS WELCOME CAMPGROUND
🏕 🤽 🚐 ⛺

Scenic rating: 4

in Welcome

Perfect for a quick weekend getaway or as a base for local lake access, the town of Welcome is as friendly as its name would suggest. Tucked into the north end of town, Checkers is a basic country-style campground.

The campsites are organized into two loops in an open area surrounded by farmland to the north and the edge of town to the south. While the campground is not located in a park with outdoor recreation or hiking trails, it still manages to be a comfortable and fun place to stay. A good variety of amenities and proximity to the nearby lakes and town make this an attractive place for overnight stops or as a cheap alternative to a motel.

Campsites, facilities: There are 32 sites for tents and RVs (50-amp hookups available) and three tent-only sites. Some sites are pull-through. Picnic tables, fire rings and grills, drinking water, toilets, showers, and a dump station are provided. A grocery store, laundry facilities, wireless Internet, playground, and a game room are available. Leashed pets are permitted.

Reservations, fees: Reservations are accepted online at www.campingfriend.com. Sites are $16 per night for tents and $24–25 per night for RVs. Open from April to mid-November.

Directions: From Fairmont drive west on I-90 for 9 miles. Take Exit 93 to Welcome. Turn left to go south on 70th Avenue for 0.25 mile to the campground on your right.

Contact: Checkers Welcome Campground, 507-728-8811, www.checkerswelcomecampground.com.

49 FLYING GOOSE CAMPGROUND

Scenic rating: 8

east of Fairmont

The Flying Goose Campground, less than five miles east of Fairmont, is a five-star camping experience. The prices are a little higher here, but the facilities are high quality and make camping here very comfortable.

The campsites cover the entire northeastern shore of Lake Imogene. Light tree cover provides select shade in most sites. Open areas are abundant, giving a breezy, airy feel to the campground. One loop of campsites sits near the park entrance, while lakeshore campsites are strung along the water farther east. Sites are a little crowded, but nothing to squawk about. There is still plenty of privacy, especially in the more wooded areas.

You can rent watercraft at the lodge for recreating in Lake Imogene. Fishing from boat or shore is worthwhile, especially for walleyes. A hiking trail links all the campsites to the lake and follows the shore for more than a mile. When the weather is bad, a game room is open to campers in the lodge.

Campsites, facilities: There are 110 sites for tents and RVs; pull-through sites and full hookups are available. Picnic tables, fire rings and grills, showers, drinking water, toilets, and dump station are provided. A lodge building, swimming beach, hiking trail, canoe/kayak rental, fishing dock, boat docking area, boat ramp, pontoon rental, minigolf course, wireless Internet, laundry facilities, playground, and a store are available. Leashed pets are permitted.

Reservations, fees: Reservations are accepted online at www.flyinggoosecampground.com ($10 deposit required). Sites are $27 per night for tents and $32–42 per night for RVs. There's a two-night minimum on weekends, a three-night minimum on holiday weekends. Open from May through October.

Directions: From Fairmont drive east on Blue Earth Avenue for 4.1 miles. Turn right into the campground.

Contact: Flying Goose Campground, 507/235-3458, www.flyinggoosecampground.com.

50 HICKORY HILLS CAMPGROUND

Scenic rating: 6

north of Twin Lakes

Hickory Hills Campground is on the southern shore of Upper Twin Lake, just north of the city of Twin Lakes. The campground is primarily for RVs, though a handful of tent campers come here as well. Sites are arranged in two loops in a grove of hardwoods adjacent to a large open, grassy field. Plenty of trees give excellent shade and privacy. The sites are in an island of trees surrounded by a large stretch of prairie and the reedy lake, giving you the chance to see wildlife at the transitional zones of the three habitats that meet here.

Although the campground is near the water, the marshy shore doesn't provide an access point for swimming or fishing. The campground does have hiking and biking trails that come near the water. One of the campground's main attractions is its Olympic-sized outdoor swimming pool. Campers have access to it all summer for relaxation, exercise, or play.

Campsites, facilities: There are 18 sites for RVs up to 60 feet (hookups); two sites are pull-throughs. Picnic tables, fire rings, toilets, showers, and a dump station are provided. A hiking and biking trail, outdoor pool, wireless Internet, playground, laundry facilities, lodge and game room, and camp store are available. Leashed pets are permitted.

Reservations, fees: Reservations are accepted at 507/852-4555. Sites are $30–35 per night. Open from mid-April to mid-October.

Directions: From Twin Lakes, drive north on County Road 71 for 1 mile to 154th Street. Turn left and drive 0.5 mile to County Road 80. Continue west for 0.2 mile to 717th Avenue. Turn right and drive 0.5 mile to the campground entrance straight ahead.

Contact: Hickory Hills Campground, 507/852-4555, www.hickoryhillscampground.com.

MISSISSIPPI BLUFF COUNTRY

© JAKE KULJU

BEST CAMPGROUNDS

❰ Canoe-In Campgrounds
St. Croix River Canoe Campsites, **page 165.**

❰ Families
Forestville/Mystery Cave State Park, **page 184.**

❰ Fishing
Camp Lacupolis, **page 179.**
Whitewater State Park, **page 185.**

❰ Lakeshore Campgrounds
Myre Big Island State Park, **page 188.**

❰ Tent Camping
Afton State Park, **page 175.**
Vinegar Ridge Campsites, **page 191.**

❰ Views
Frontenac State Park, **page 178.**
John A. Latsch State Park, **page 186.**
Great River Bluffs State Park, **page 187.**

Minnesota may be known as the land of 10,000

lakes, but just as important to its landscape are the rivers and bluffs that cradle valleys of prairie and forest, giving the land contour. Along with the Mississippi, the southeastern portion of the state holds parts of the St. Croix, Minnesota, Root, Cannon, and Whitewater Rivers, all of which do their part to carve out the scenic rolling bluffs that make this part of the state so beautiful.

The northern reach of this region is home to exposed lava flows on the St. Croix River, 100-foot-deep river potholes in the turbulent Kettle River, and exposed rock cliff faces near Taylors Falls. Following the watershed south, you will encounter an increasing number of bluffs, rolling hills, and a constantly changing landscape of grassland and woodland. Each year trees and grass give ground to one another depending on the amount of rainfall and summer sunlight they receive during the growing season.

The Richard J. Dorer Memorial Hardwood Forest covers a two-million-acre area and houses five of the state's canoe routes, including the popular Cannon River, White River, Root River, and Zumbro River State Canoe Routes. Canoeing and kayaking on the St. Croix, Kettle, Whitewater, and Mississippi Rivers is easily done from campgrounds as well. Several of the state parks have canoe and kayak rentals, access points, and canoe/kayak campgrounds accessible only by river. The Kettle River, in particular, is a challenging and popular kayak route full of rapids and rocky views. The state's largest fish, a 94-pound sturgeon, was caught in a deep 100-foot pothole in this river in 1996.

Early spring and mid-autumn are the best times to visit Mississippi Bluff Country. Spring ephemerals literally burst from the ground each April, sometimes poking their heads through the snow to be seen. The remaining stands of Big Woods forests that have been preserved in the bluff country are prime wildflower habitat and never fail to deliver a wide spectrum of color in the spring. Autumn is even more dynamic, as bluffsides full of maple, oak, basswood, poplar, and aspen change from greens to blazing oranges, reds, and yellows. The bluffs are never as beautiful as they are at the peak of autumn.

Bicyclists will also find this to be one of the more accommodating regions of the state. The Cannon Valley Trail and the Root River Bike Trail offer dozens of miles of paved biking surfaces, and Great River Bluffs State Park has bike-in campsites designed for use only by bicycle campers.

Farther south, near Winona, you can take in sweeping views of the Mississippi River Valley and see for miles into Wisconsin and up and down the watershed. Climb atop Charity Bluff in John A. Latsch State Park for one of the best blufftop views in the state. Other impressive bluffs can be found at Great River Bluffs State Park farther south on Highway 61, where the rare timber rattlesnake still maintains a presence.

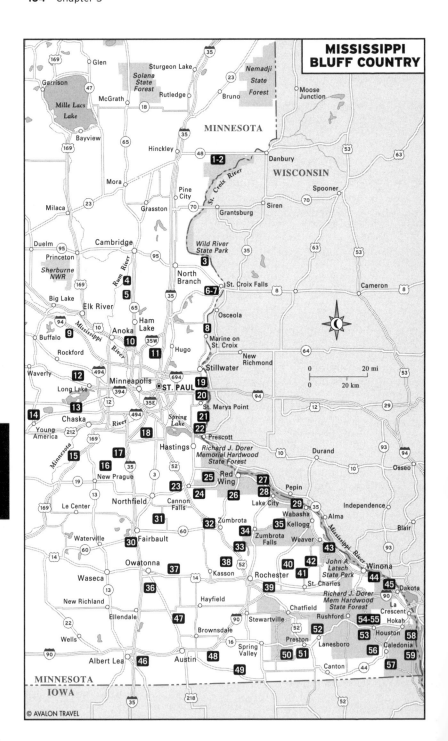

MISSISSIPPI BLUFF COUNTRY

∎ ST. CROIX STATE PARK
👫🏊🎣🛶🎿🐎🏇🚐⛺

Scenic rating: 8

in St. Croix State Park

Perched on a bluff above the St. Croix River, this campground is a river lover's delight. Popular with river kayakers and canoeists, the St. Croix State Park campground is also near the Kettle River, a state wild and scenic river.

Three campgrounds are set on a nicely wooded bluff above the St. Croix. There are more than 200 campsites spread over a large area on the bluff, and the heavy tree cover keeps the sites well spaced and uncrowded. The campgrounds overlook a small island in the middle of the river and have direct access to a gravel road that leads to a water access point.

The Kettle River is particularly good for fishing and canoeing as it is full of manageable rapids and is home to the ancient sturgeon. The largest fish ever caught and recorded in Minnesota was a 94-pound sturgeon hooked in the Kettle River in 1996.

Campsites, facilities: There are 211 sites divided into three adjacent campgrounds: Riverview, Paint Rock Springs, and Old Logging Trail. There are also two backpacking sites that require a 5-mile hike (must bring your own water), and four walk-in sites approximately 100 feet from the parking area. There are 42 electric sites in the Riverview campground, which can accommodate larger RVs and trailers; RV length is restricted to 60 feet. Picnic tables, fire grills and rings, drinking water, showers, toilets, river access, a volleyball court and horseshoe pit, playground, swimming beach, warming house, and a dump station are provided. Leashed pets are permitted.

Reservations, fees: Reservations are accepted from April 2 to October 31 at 866/857-2757 or online at www.stayatmnparks.com ($8.50 non-refundable reservation fee) and can be made up to one year in advance. Reservations are not required the rest of the year. Sites are $12–24 per night. Open year-round, with limited facilities in winter.

Directions: From Hinckley, drive east on Highway 48 for 15 miles. Turn right onto County Road 22 and continue for 5 miles. A large state park sign on the right will direct you into the park. Drive past the Trail Center and turn left at the Park Headquarters to the campground.

Contact: St. Croix State Park, 320/384-6591, www.dnr.state.mn.us.

∎ ST. CROIX RIVER CANOE CAMPSITES
🛶🛶🏇⛺

Scenic rating: 9

on the St. Croix River in St. Croix State Park

BEST (

Some of St. Croix State Park's best campsites are the ones you can only get to by paddling to them. These 10 riverside sites are along some of the most scenic shoreline in the park, tucked into the banks of two of Minnesota's most attractive rivers. The sounds of nearby rapids and falls will lull you to sleep at night.

The sites sit directly on the river bank and are marked by small wooden state park signs. Each landing area has an undeveloped canoe access point, a tent pad amidst the trees, a fire ring, and a pit toilet; some sites have picnic tables. Keep your eyes peeled when looking for these sites while on the river and make sure to have an accurate map with you. Drinking water is not provided, so pack your own in or bring a water filtration system.

In the early spring when water is high, these campsites may be closed, so make sure to call the park ahead of time for updates. St. Croix State Park is very popular with canoeists and kayakers. Even though these sites are fairly remote and only accessible by water, you will likely hear and see other paddlers as they pass by during the day. If you don't mind camping in chilly weather, the Kettle and St. Croix Rivers have captivating autumn colors; there is also less river traffic when the weather gets colder.

Campsites, facilities: There are 10 tent-only sites located along stretches of the Kettle and St. Croix Rivers. Fire rings and grills, rustic pit toilets, and water access are provided. There is no drinking water. Leashed pets are permitted.

Reservations, fees: Reservations are not accepted. There is no fee. Open year-round, whenever the river is accessible by canoe.

Directions: From Hinckley, drive east on Highway 48 for 15 miles. Turn right onto County Road 22 and drive for 5 miles. A large state park sign on the right will direct you into the park. Drive past the Trail Center and turn left at the Park Headquarters to the water access.

Contact: St. Croix State Park, 320/384-6591, www.dnr.state.mn.us/state_parks.

⒊ WILD RIVER STATE PARK
🧍🏊🛶🚣❄️🐕♿🚐⛺

Scenic rating: 8

on the St. Croix River in Wild River State Park

Wild River State Park covers nearly 20 miles of the St. Croix River as its slices through the thick forests of north-central Minnesota. The park is used regularly throughout the year as a hiking, fishing, and cross-country ski area.

The campground has five loops laced along the top of a bluff high above the river. The Trillium Trail links the campground loops together and leads steeply down the bluffside to the River Trail on the southern end of the camping area. Heavy tree cover blankets the entire bluff, including the campground, offering you plenty of privacy but eliminating your view of the river just a few hundred feet away.

Campsites, facilities: There are 96 sites for tents and RVs up to 60 feet; 17 sites have electricity, and two are pull-throughs. There are also eight backpacking sites, eight canoe-in sites, and a separate horse campground with 20 sites. Picnic

tables, drinking water, flush toilets (rustic toilets for the backpacking and canoeing sites), showers, a picnic area, water access, warming house, and a dump station are provided. There are also hiking and skiing trails. There is one wheelchair-accessible site with electric hookup. Leashed pets are permitted.

Reservations, fees: Reservations are accepted from April 2 to October 31 at 866/857-2757 or online at www.stayatmnparks.com ($8.50 non-refundable reservation fee) and can be made up to one year in advance. Reservations are not required the rest of the year. Sites are $12–24 per night. Open year-round.

Directions: From North Branch, drive east on Highway 95 for 9.8 miles. Turn left onto Park Trail and continue for 2.9 miles. Turn left onto County Road 71 and drive 1.2 miles to the park entrance. The entrance will be on your right.

Contact: Wild River State Park, 651/583-2125, www.dnr.state.mn.us/state_parks.

⒋ COUNTRY CAMPING RUM RIVER CAMPGROUND
🧍🏊🛶🚣🐕🐎🚐⛺

Scenic rating: 7

near Isanti

The Country Camping Rum River Campground may be a mouthful to say, but it is full of simple pleasures. The campground is near Isanti and isn't exactly a wilderness experience. RVs take up the majority of the campsites, but the emphasis here is on what goes on during the day. River tubing, canoeing, hiking trails, a sand volleyball court, and peaceful fishing on the Rum make this spot a great place for a summer vacation.

The sites are laid along two loops in a large clearing along the otherwise densely forested Rum River's west bank. The sites on the east side of the two loops enjoy some tree cover, but the majority of sites are close together with no shade or privacy.

River tubing is a kind of cult activity in southeastern Minnesota that makes some people jump with joy and others shudder in revulsion. If you like tubing, this Rum River campground is one of the better experiences. A free shuttle will carry you back to the campground after a day on the river. The campground provides tubes and you can even bring a cooler full of food and beverages with you.

Campsites, facilities: There are 35 sites for tents and 65 sites for RVs. Some sites are pull-through and have electricity (50-amp). Drinking water, restrooms with toilets and showers, picnic tables, fire rings, and grills are provided. A dump station, picnic shelter, playground, wireless Internet, heated pool, coin laundry, game room, a boat ramp, canoe rental, and a grocery store are available. Leashed pets permitted.

Reservations, fees: Reservations are accepted at 763/444-9626 or online at www.country-camping.com. Sites are $23–33 per night. There is a pet fee of $2.50 per night. There is a two-night minimum stay on weekends and a three-night minimum stay on holiday weekends (deposit required for both). The campground encourages weekly stays and has special rates for extended stays. Open May 1 to October 1.

Directions: From Isanti drive west on County Road 5 for 1.5 miles to County Road 10. Turn left and drive 0.5 mile. Veer left onto County Road 68. The campground entrance is 1 mile ahead on your left at 277th Avenue. Turn left and then take an immediate right onto Palm Street to the campground office 0.25 mile straight ahead.

Contact: Country Camping Tent & RV Park, 763/444-9626, www.country-camping.com.

5 AVATAN

Scenic rating: 6

in East Bethel

Avatan is a premier family campground—if you don't mind being in the buff. Not everyone's cup of tea, Avatan is Minnesota's largest nudist campground. It is very tastefully designed, with plenty of privacy for each campsite. Large groves of shady trees separate the sites, and a large common area for recreation, both indoors and out, lets you be as public as you want to be. There is plenty to do here: A game room, outdoor sports, a beach, and annual events, including the big annual Fourth of July pig roast, keep everyone busy.

Note: Although the campground is open to the public, you must call for specific directions.

Campsites, facilities: There are 120 sites for tents and RVs (full hookups, no pull-throughs) and three cabins. Drinking water, fire rings, picnic tables, toilets, and showers are provided. A heated pool, recreation room, swimming beach, wireless Internet, evening entertainment, and laundry facilities are also provided. Facilities are wheelchair accessible. Leashed pets are permitted.

Reservations, fees: Reservations are accepted online at www.avatan.com. Sites are $27 per night for tents and $55 per night for RVs. Cabins are $60–95 per night; children stay for free. There is a 10 percent discount for groups of seven or more. Open May 1 to October 15.

Directions: Call 763/434-4922 for directions from East Bethel.

Contact: Avatan, 763/434-4922, www.avatan.com.

6 WILDWOOD RV PARK & CAMPGROUND

Scenic rating: 6

on the St. Croix River near Taylors Falls

Taylors Falls is the hub of tourism on the St. Croix, and Wildwood RV Park & Campground is at the center of it all. Just a few miles out of town on the river, this campground is best for active families. Wildwood is just a stone's throw from Interstate State Park, but its campground has more modern amenities, including minigolf, free wireless Internet, and a heated pool; hiking trails, horseshoes, and volleyball are also available. The campground itself looks more like a parking lot, with RV sites stacked next to each other in an open clearing with nary a tree in sight. There is only the shade from the RV in the next slot and privacy is nonexistent.

Wildwood draws a crowd each summer, so don't come here looking for peace and quiet. There is a distinct RV camping culture with many people spending the day in town or at the state park and coming back to Wildwood to spend the afternoons and evenings outside.

Campsites, facilities: There are 201 sites for tents or RVs; 36 sites are tent-only and 30 sites are only for RVs. Picnic tables, fire rings and grills, drinking water, toilets, showers, and a dump station are provided. A game room, heated pool, minigolf course, nature trail, shuttle service to canoe rental, and basketball court are available. Leashed pets are permitted.

Reservations, fees: Reservations are accepted online at www.wildmountain.com. Sites are $29.58 per night for tents, $35.69 per night for RVs, and $40.85 per night for full hookups. There is fee of $4.70 per night for more than two adult campers and a pet fee of $5.64 per night. Open from May to October.

Directions: From the Twin Cities, drive north on I-35 for 28.2 miles. Exit onto Highway 8 toward Taylors Falls. Follow Highway 8 for 21.2 miles. Wildwood will be on your left after the Highway 8/95 intersection.

Contact: Wildwood RV Park & Campground, 651/465-6315, www.wildwoodcamping.com.

⑦ INTERSTATE STATE PARK

Scenic rating: 8

in Interstate State Park

Interstate State Park is one of the most interesting and captivating parks in the state.

Lava flows, glacial potholes, and five miles of river bluff hiking trails make this a great park for nature lovers with curious minds. The interpretive trail has piles of information about the geology of the region, especially concerning the mysterious potholes that cover this area, some of them dozens of feet deep. In winter, snowshoeing is allowed in the park.

Unfortunately, the campground is less captivating. Tall white pine trees canopy the camping area, and many of the sites are near the river, but Highway 8 passes overhead just a few hundred feet away, putting the sound of traffic right in your tent. The camping loop accommodates nearly 40 sites, which makes camping here a little crowded, especially given the sites' proximity to the highway. Bring earplugs if you want a good night's rest.

Campsites, facilities: There are 37 sites for tents and RVs up to 45 feet; there are 22 sites with electricity (20- and 30-amp) available April–November. There are also four group campsites for up to 25 people each. Sites 4–22 are nearest the river and provide the best view; sites 23, 24, 25, 26, 27, 28, 29, and 30 are nonreservable. Picnic tables, fire rings and grills, drinking water, showers, flush and vault toilets, and a dump station are provided. Hiking trails, a fishing area, boat ramp, and canoe access and rentals are available. Some facilities are wheelchair accessible. Leashed pets are permitted.

Reservations, fees: Reservations are accepted for some sites from April 2 to October 31 at 866/857-2757 or online at www.stayatmn-parks.com ($8.50 nonrefundable reservation fee) and can be made up to one year in advance. Reservations are not required the rest of the year. Sites are $12–24 per night. Open year-round, with limited facilities in winter.

Directions: From Taylors Falls, drive south on Highway 95 for 1 mile. The park entrance is on your left. Turn left after the park office to the campground.

Contact: Interstate State Park, 651/465-5711, www.dnr.state.mn.us/state_parks.

8 WILLIAM O'BRIEN STATE PARK

Scenic rating: 8

in William O'Brien State Park

If bluffs had foothills, this is where you would find William O'Brien State Park. This woodsy campground has tucked itself into the land just as the riverbanks begin to rise into undulating prairie and forested hills.

Hiking is the best way to experience the park, with 12 miles of trails winding throughout the gentle hills, rising from the lowland forests to open prairies of tallgrass and wildflowers on the soft hilltops. While the elevation gain is barely noticeable, you will be able to tell the difference when you get a view of the area from the higher points in the park. If you'd rather hang around the campground, fishing and swimming are both excellent. Campsites are set in a wide loop of thick, shady trees that dampen the sounds of nearby campers and give a good amount of privacy, even though more than 100 campsites are spread throughout the area.

Campsites, facilities: There are 124 sites for tents and RVs up to 60 feet (some 30-amp sites available). There are also four group camping sites and four camper cabins. Drinking water, fire rings, showers, flush and vault toilets, and a dump station are provided. A swimming beach, fishing pier, hiking and biking trails, picnic tables, and volleyball court are available. There are seven wheelchair-accessible sites. Leashed pets are permitted.

Reservations, fees: Reservations are accepted from April 2 to October 31 at 866/857-2757 or online at www.stayatmnparks.com ($8.50 non-refundable reservation fee) and can be made up to one year in advance. Reservations are not required the rest of the year. Sites are $12–24 per night. The camper cabins are $45–50 per night. Open year-round, with limited facilities in winter.

Directions: From Stillwater, drive north on Highway 95 for 12 miles. Turn left into the park just past Marine-on-St. Croix.

Contact: William O'Brien State Park, 651/433-0500, www.dnr.state.mn.us/state_parks.

9 CROW-HASSAN PARK RESERVE HORSE CAMPSITES

Scenic rating: 8

in Crow-Hassan Park Reserve near St. Michael

Crow-Hassan Park Reserve is a blanket of 2,600 acres, much of it natural and restored prairie, along the Crow River near St. Michael. Four group campsites for horse camping are spread out along the Crow River in the swatch of woodland that covers the riverbanks. The camping areas are quite large—big enough for horse trailers, vehicles, and camping equipment. Each campground is directly linked to the trail system that spreads across the park. Early summer is by far the best time to visit Crow-Hassan, as countless wildflowers are in bloom, painting the vast grassland in dozens of seasonal hues.

Campsites, facilities: There are four sites for group equestrian camping. Toilets, hand pumps for drinking water, picnic tables and shelters, fire rings and grills, and hitching posts are provided. Leashed pets are permitted.

Reservations, fees: Sites are $11 per night. Parking is free. A Three Rivers Park District permit for horseback riding is required.

Directions: From St. Michael, drive east on Central Avenue for 1.4 miles. Veer right onto 40th Street NE for 0.6 mile, then turn right at Territorial Road. Drive for 1.4 miles to Sylvan Lake Road and take a right. Drive for 0.8 mile to Park Drive and turn left. Follow Park Drive for 0.6 mile, then turn right onto Park Preserve Road. The parking and information area will be 0.3 mile ahead on your right.

Contact: Crow-Hassan Park Reserve, 763/694-7860, www.threeriverrsparks.org/parks/crow-hassan-park.aspx.

10 BUNKER HILLS CAMPGROUND

Scenic rating: 5

in Bunker Hills Regional Park

A local favorite for privacy and affordability, the Bunker Hills campground delivers a very buried-in-the-woods feel to campers who are near the Twin Cities and don't have time to drive all the way up north. Each campground has a private gravel driveway and is surrounded by dense stands of trees that provide shade and seclusion.

The area is also used as a day-use facility, so a park atmosphere can take over during the summer months, especially since Bunker Hills has an outdoor pool and water park. Camping in mid-autumn is usually best here, as there are rolling hills full of brightly colored trees.

Campsites, facilities: There are 20 rustic tent sites and 24 RV sites. Picnic tables, fire rings, an outdoor pool, bike trail, and hiking trail are provided. A restroom and shower building and a sanitation station for RVs are available. Evening entertainment is regularly scheduled during the summer. Leashed pets are permitted.

Reservations, fees: Sites are $17 per night for tents and $25 per night for RVs, along with a $5 vehicle permit fee. Reservations are accepted online at www.maxsolutionsonline.com/anoka/ for a $3 fee. Open May 1 through October 25.

Directions: From Blaine, take Highway 65 north for 0.5 mile to 109th Avenue. Turn left and drive for 1.5 miles to Northdale Boulevard NW. Take Northdale for 0.8 mile and turn right onto Foley Boulevard. Drive for 1.6 miles and cross 125th Avenue onto County Road A. Drive for 0.6 mile pas the golf course to County Road B, turn right for 0.5 mile to the park entrance on your left.

Contact: Bunker Hills Campground, 763/862-4970, www.anokacountyparks.com/camping/bunker_hills.htm.

11 RICE CREEK CAMPGROUND

Scenic rating: 7

in Rice Creek Chain of Lakes Park Preserve

Rice Creek is in the Chain of Lakes area of Anoka County and the Rice Creek Campground is the jewel in the crown of the Anoka County Park system. The park is only 25 minutes from the Twin Cities but has more than 5,000 acres of wooded land and lakes.

The sites are spread throughout a tangle-town of loops on a peninsula of land between George Watch and Centerville Lakes. Oak, aspen, maple, and pine trees cover the camping area and help to bolster the privacy between the sites. Some sites are still rather close together, especially those in the center of the camping loops, but the trees go a long way in creating a serene and woodsy atmosphere. The park is usually full of campers in the summer, so don't expect much peace and quiet, but it's worth it for access to one of the region's largest county parks and grouping of recreational lakes.

Campsites, facilities: There are 40 sites for tents and 38 sites for RVs. Drinking water, picnic tables, fire rings, a restroom and shower building, and a dump station are provided. Hiking and biking trails, a swimming beach, cross-country ski trail, canoe rental, boat ramp, and playground are available. Evening entertainment is regularly scheduled during the summer. Leashed pets are permitted.

Reservations, fees: Reservations are accepted online at www.maxsolutionsonline.com/anoka ($3 reservation fee). Sites are $17 per night for tents and $25 per night for RVs. There is a $5 vehicle permit fee. Open May 1 through October 11.

Directions: From Centerville drive north on County Road 14 for 1 mile. Turn left onto E Street into the park. The campground is ahead on your right in 0.7 mile.

Contact: Rice Creek Campground, 763/757-3920, www.anokacountyparks.com.

12 BAKER PARK RESERVE

Scenic rating: 6

in Baker Park Reserve

Baker Park Reserve consists of 2,700 acres of land that hug the southern and eastern shores of Lake Independence, just west of Minneapolis. The campground is on the southeast corner of the lake in a unique setup with five loops contained within one large loop. The arrangement allows for a swath of trees to grow between and within the smaller loops, making them distinctly separate even though they are adjacent to one another.

A beautiful swimming beach draws the crowds during the summer, but Baker uniquely offers winter camping at one of their camping loops. (You must make reservations at least two weeks ahead of time to use the winter campground.) Hiking and biking trails, including cross-country ski trails, round out the recreational options.

Campsites, facilities: There are 204 sites for tents or RVs and six group campsites. Drinking water, picnic tables, fire rings, flush toilets, showers, a boat launch, and dump station are provided. Showers, a play area, hiking and biking trails, golf course, ski trails, and chalet are available. Some facilities are wheelchair accessible. Leashed pets are permitted.

Reservations, fees: Reservations are accepted at 763/559-6700 ($7.50 reservation fee). Sites are $17 per night for tents and $25 per night for RVs. Open year-round.

Directions: From Maple Plain, take County Road 19 east for 0.5 mile to Baker Park Road. Turn left and drive for 0.5 to Perkinsville Road. Turn right and drive for 0.8 mile to the third right on Perkinsville Road. Follow the gravel road for 0.6 mile to the park entrance.

Contact: Baker Park Reserve, 763/694-7670 or 763/559-6700, www.ci.orono.mn.us/baker_park_reserve.htm.

13 LAKE AUBURN CAMPGROUND

Scenic rating: 6

in Carver Park Reserve

This single-loop campground on the western shore of Lake Auburn is in a miraculously peaceful park reserve within just a few miles of the metro area. It is hard to believe you could be in downtown in less than 15 minutes when you are walking around Lake Auburn, bird-watching on the interpretive nature trails, or taking a nap under the shady oaks and maples.

The park is devoted to the preservation of wildlife and natural habitat. The Lowry Nature Center, Grimm Farm Historic Site (open during scheduled programs), and King Waterbird Sanctuary are three popular sites in the park reserve that serve thousands of visitors each year, offering education and tours and exposing folks to the wilderness in their own backyard. You will almost certainly see trumpeter swans, whitetail deer, mink, and owls.

Campsites, facilities: There are 55 sites for tents or RVs and two hike-in sites. Vault toilets, hand-pumped drinking water, picnic tables, and a fire ring are provided. A swimming beach, boat ramp, playground, and dump station (fee) are available. Some facilities are wheelchair accessible. Leashed pets are permitted.

Reservations, fees: Reservations are accepted at 763/559-6700 ($7.50 reservation fee). Sites are $11 per night. Open year-round; camping is available only on weekends between Labor Day and Memorial Day.

Directions: From Minneapolis drive west on I-394 for 9.2 miles. Take Exit 1A and merge onto I-494 South. Drive south for 3.2 miles and turn right onto Highway 7 W. Drive for 13.8 miles to Victoria Drive. Turn left into the park.

Contact: Carver Campground, 952/443-2911, www.threeriversparks.org/parks/carver-park.aspx.

14 BAYLOR REGIONAL PARK
🏃🏊🏕♿🚐⛺

Scenic rating: 5

in Baylor Regional Park

Baylor Regional Park is situated on the western shore of Eagle Lake. The park sticks a tongue-shaped peninsula into the small lake with a fishing pier at the end. The campground is well-manicured, giving it a city park feel. Campsites are stacked in two loops about 0.25 mile from the lake. Each site has a tree that offers some shade and shelter, providing moderate privacy moderate between sites. The campground sits adjacent to a large marsh that extends from the lake, making mosquitoes much more than just a nuisance, especially in June.

An 18-hole disc golf course is a recent addition to this park that makes for a fun afternoon. The park also houses an observatory operated by the Minnesota Astronomical Association. Hiking trails circumnavigate the park and pass through the campground, linking guests to the lake, the golf course, and the park office.

Campsites, facilities: There are 15 primitive sites for tents and 35 sites for RVs. Drinking water, showers, picnic tables, toilets, and fire rings are provided. A ball field, tennis courts, sand volleyball court, disc golf course, a swimming beach and beach house, and a dump station are available. Some facilities are wheelchair accessible. Leashed pets are permitted.

Reservations, fees: Reservations are accepted online at http://reservations.co.carver.mn.us ($6 reservation fee per site). Sites are $15 per night for tents and $21 per night for RVs. A $5 vehicle permit fee is required. Open May to mid-October.

Directions: From Norwood Young America, drive north on County Road 33 for 2.5 miles. The park entrance will be on your right.

Contact: Baylor Regional Park, 952/466-5250, www.co.carver.mn.us/departments/PW/parks/baylor.asp.

15 MINNESOTA VALLEY STATE PARK
🏃🚴🏊❄🐴🚐⛺

Scenic rating: 7

in Minnesota Valley State Park

Minnesota Valley State Park is plopped on top of a big, juicy swamp. The wildlife and wetland habitat here are stunningly abundant, but the mosquitoes are horrific in early summer, and midsummer, and late summer—all summer, actually! There are only 25 sites here, which is nice for privacy. They are well spaced and all have their own short driveways in an island of trees amid the swamp.

The Minnesota River makes several courageous loops and twists here, creating a small chain of tiny lakes, sloughs, and oxbows that are rife with migratory birds, wetland fowl, whitetail deer, minks, muskrats, raccoons, and dozens of other animals. A nearby heron rookery ensures you will see plenty of great blues and possibly other rarer varieties of heron.

Campsites, facilities: There are 25 sites for tents or RVs up to 60 feet, eight walk-in sites, six horse campsites, and one group campsite for up to 45 people. Picnic tables, fire rings and grills, vault toilets, and a dump station are provided. A picnic area, hiking and ski trails, and a warming house are available. Leashed pets are permitted.

Reservations, fees: Reservations are accepted from April 2 to October 31 at 866/857-2757 or online at www.stayatmnparks.com ($8.50 non-refundable reservation fee) and can be made up to one year in advance. The group campsite can be reserved at 952/492-6400. Reservations are not required the rest of the year. Sites are $12–24 per night. Open year-round.

Directions: From Shakopee, drive south on Highway 169 for 9.5 miles to Acorn Way. Turn right and drive 300 feet to Valley View Drive. Turn left and drive 2.3 miles to County Road 57/Park Boulevard. The campground is 1.2 miles ahead on the right side of the road after passing the historical Brimms home site.

Contact: Minnesota Valley State Park, 952/492-6400, www.dnr.state.mn.us.

16 FISH LAKE ACRES CAMPGROUND

🏃‍♂️🏊‍♂️🚣‍♂️🛥️🐎🚴‍♂️🚗🏕️

Scenic rating: 6

on Fish Lake

Beautiful and largely undeveloped, Fish Lake is a gem of a spot south of the metro just west of Lakeville. The campground is a long, narrow loop wrapped around the southwestern shore of the lake. Wedged between a set of farm fields and the water, sites are buffeted from the sounds of traffic, although the county roads don't generate much traffic as it is.

Fish Lake is in a mostly open, rural area. Each campsite has large trees for shade and enough privacy to make you feel like you're in a state park. The level sites have dozens of feet of distance between them, which gives Fish Lake Acres a park-like feel. Sites on the eastern side of the loop have views of the lake and the entire campground is connected to the water via a hiking trail.

Campsites, facilities: There are 50 sites for tents only and 93 sites for tents or RVs (some with full-hookups). Picnic tables, fire rings, drinking water, toilets, showers, and a boat ramp are provided. A hiking trail, swimming beach, fish cleaning station, playground, and boat rental station are available. Leashed pets are permitted.

Reservations, fees: Reservations are accepted at 952/492-3393 or online at www.frontiernet. net/~busacker/RateRegistrationForm.htm. Sites are $21–25 per night. There is a fee of $1 per night for pets. Open from May to mid-October.

Directions: From Prior Lake, drive southeast on Country Road 13 for 2.3 miles to Fairlawn Avenue. Turn left and drive for 3.2 miles. Turn left onto Malibu Avenue and drive for 0.5 mile to 210th Street E. The campground is 0.5 mile ahead on your left.

Contact: Fish Lake Acres, 952/492-3393, www.frontiernet.net/~busacker/.

17 RED PINE HIKE-IN FAMILY CAMPGROUND

🏃‍♂️🚴‍♂️❄️🐎♿🏕️

Scenic rating: 7

in Cleary Lake Regional Park

Cleary Lake Regional Park is one of the most popular parks in the south metro, largely due to its excellent hiking, biking, and night-lit skiing trails. After work and on the weekends during the spring, summer, and fall, the day-use areas of the park are crawling with joggers, bikers, and nature lovers. South of the lake, deep in the pines, sits the quaint Red Pine Campground. There are only five walk-in sites with little more than a pit toilet and a picnic table. While people are buzzing around the trails, you can be sleeping under the stars in a cathedral of red pines. The walk-in sites are only a few hundred yards from the parking area and provide excellent privacy and quiet.

Campsites, facilities: There are five primitive walk-in sites for tents only. Picnic tables, fire rings, pit toilets, and hand-pumped drinking water are provided. Hiking and skiing trails are available. Some facilities are wheelchair accessible. Leashed pets are permitted.

Reservations, fees: Reservations are accepted at 763/559-6700 ($7.50 reservation fee). Sites are $11 per night. Open year-round.

Directions: From Prior Lake, drive east on County Road 21 for 2.5 miles to Texas Avenue. Turn right and drive for 0.6 mile to Park Road. Turn right and follow Park Road for 0.6 mile past the golf course to the park office.

Contact: Cleary Lake Regional Park, Three Rivers Park District, 763/559-9000, www.threeriversparks.org.

18 LEBANON HILLS CAMPGROUND
🚶🏊⛺🛶🏕️🚴♿🚐⛺

Scenic rating: 7

in Lebanon Hills Regional Park near Apple Valley

Lebanon Hills does not disappoint. The 2,000 acres of woods and lakes in the Minnesota River Valley make a prime place for summer camping. Adjacent to the Minnesota Zoological Gardens, Lebanon Hills has two large camping loops south of Gerhardt Lake. The thick forests that engulf these lakes are rare in the metro area and the campground feels like a little clearing in a giant forest, which it more or less is.

Hiking trails are splayed throughout the woods and around the lakes, and the campground is connected by trail to a nice, private swimming beach. Gerhardt Lake is also a decent fishing destination for panfish, some small bass, and northern pike.

Campsites, facilities: There are 58 sites for tents and RVs (full hookups). Picnic tables, fire rings, drinking water, toilets, showers, and laundry facilities are provided. Hiking trails, a swimming beach, playground, fishing area, and a dump station are available. Some facilities are wheelchair accessible. Leashed pets are permitted.

Reservations, fees: Reservations are accepted at 651/688-1376 ($7 reservation fee). Sites are $16–$29 per night. Open from May to mid-October.

Directions: From St. Paul, drive south on I-35 E for 13 miles. Exit onto Cliff Road and turn left. In 0.8 mile turn right onto Johnny Cake Ridge Road. The park entrance is on the left in 1.1 miles.

Contact: Lebanon Hills Regional Park, 651/688-1376, www.co.dakota.mn.us/LeisureRecreation/CountyParks/Locations/LebanonHills/Campground.htm.

19 LAKE ELMO PARK RESERVE
🚶🚴🏊⛺🚐🏕️♿🚐⛺

Scenic rating: 7

in Lake Elmo Park Reserve

The Lake Elmo campground has the advantage of being in one of the metro area's largest and most pristine regional parks. Several lakes are clustered in the reserve, and islands of pines and hardwood trees dot the rolling hills and prairie lands of the park. Unfortunately, the campsites don't afford much privacy. Sites are spaced far enough apart and each has a short gravel drive, but little (and in some cases no) tree cover makes camping not quite as relaxing as the rest of the park might suggest. Hiking here is superb, though, and will take you around Eagle Point Lake, through swaths of wildflowers, and into stands of beautiful pines.

Campsites, facilities: There are 80 electric sites for tents or RVs, 20 equestrian sites, and three group campsites for up to 100 people each. Picnic tables, fire rings, drinking water, flush toilets, showers, and firewood are provided. A playground, swimming pond, boat launch and fishing pier, hiking, biking, horseback riding, and ski trails, picnic shelters, and dump station are available. Some facilities are wheelchair accessible.

Reservations, fees: Reservations are accepted at 651/430-8370 or online at www.co.washington.mn.us ($7 reservation fee). Sites are $22–25 per night. Group sites are $45–55 per night. A $5 vehicle permit is required. Open from May to November, with limited water available in October.

Directions: From the intersection of I-94 and I-694 near Oakdale, drive east on I-94 for 0.5 mile. Exit onto Keats Avenue N and turn left. In 2 miles you will enter the park after crossing County Road 70. Drive north for another 0.3 mile to the campground on your right.

Contact: Lake Elmo Park Reserve, Washington County Parks, 651/430-8370, www.co.washington.mn.us/info_for_residents/parks_division/parks_and_trails/lake_elmo_park_reserve/#campground.

20 ST. PAUL EAST RV PARK

Scenic rating: 4

east of St. Paul near Woodbury

Located about 0.25-mile from I-94 in a treeless patch of suburban Woodbury, St. Paul East RV Park is nothing to write home about but will do the job in a pinch. The park feels more like a temporary trailer park but does its best to accommodate its campers. A swimming pool and playground offer some friendly recreation, but don't come here looking for the great outdoors.

Campsites, facilities: There are 66 sites for tents and RVs up to 70 feet; some sites are pull-through and some have full hookups. Picnic tables, fire rings, showers, toilets, and a dump station are provided. A heated pool, playground, horseshoes, volleyball court, free Internet, and coin laundry are available. Some facilities are wheelchair accessible. Leashed pets are permitted.

Reservations, fees: Reservations are accepted online at www.stpauleastrvpark.com. Sites are $25–$41 per night. Open from mid-April to October, weather permitting.

Directions: From St. Paul, drive east on I-94 for 9 miles to Exit 251. Turn right onto County Road 19. In 3.1 miles turn left at Lake Road, then take the first right onto Richmond Parkway in 0.3 mile. The RV park is on the right in 0.2 mile.

Contact: St. Paul East RV Park, 651/436-6436, www.stpauleastrvpark.com.

21 AFTON STATE PARK

Scenic rating: 7

in Afton State Park

BEST (

Located just 15 minutes from St. Paul, Afton is the closest spot from the Twin Cities to pitch your tent in a backpacking site. The backpacking campsites are spread throughout a large savanna blanketed with an alternating patchwork of grass and oak trees. Small wildflowers bloom in the transitional zones between field and forest. Each site has its own pathway and is separated from view—and usually from earshot—of the other hike-in sites.

The park is best known as a popular skiing destination during the winter. Groomed trails and a warming house accommodate hundreds of skiers every year. Afton also has a riverside trail and a fun geocaching program. You can check out GPS units for free and follow Afton's geocaching course.

Campsites, facilities: There are 28 backpacking sites for tents only and two group sites for up to 40 people each. Picnic tables, fire pits, wood, and vault toilets are provided. Drinking water is available from a solar pump. Hiking trails, a swimming area, boat access, warming house, and volleyball court are available. Some facilities are wheelchair accessible. Leashed pets are permitted.

Reservations, fees: Reservations are accepted from April 2 to October 31 at 866/857-2757 or online at www.stayatmnparks.com ($8.50 non-refundable reservation fee) and can be made up to one year in advance. Reservations are not required the rest of the year. Sites are $12–24 per night. The group campsites are $50 per night. Open year-round.

Directions: From St. Paul, drive east on I-94 for 9 miles. Exit right onto Highway 95 and drive for 7 miles to Country Road 20. Turn left and drive for 3 miles to the park entrance.

Contact: Afton State Park, 651/436-5391, www.dnr.state.mn.us/state_parks.

22 ST. CROIX BLUFFS REGIONAL PARK

Scenic rating: 7

on the St. Croix River

More than 500 acres and almost a mile of riverside property along the St. Croix River provide the perfect spot for this bluffside campground. Spread into two large loops, a little more than 70 sites are sprinkled throughout the trees at the top of a bluff overlooking the river. The view is best during autumn when the leaves are changing and beginning to fall, offering great views of both riverbanks and the blazing seasonal colors that streak the countryside.

The campsites are winnowed through heavy tree cover, both deciduous and evergreen. Campers often go to nearby state parks that are along the river, leaving St. Croix Bluffs ripe for the picking for campers who know of this semi-secret spot.

There is more to this place than just the view. A boat launch and fishing pier provide access to great angling on a large, undeveloped stretch of the river. A lengthy hiking trail also tours the blufftop. Look for ruffed grouse, raccoons, and whitetail deer in the woods.

Campsites, facilities: There are 73 sites for tents and RVs; some sites are pull-through and some have full hookups. There is also a group camping area for up to 50 people. Picnic tables, fire rings, drinking water, flush toilets, showers, and firewood are provided. A play area, volleyball court, picnic shelters, ski trails, boat launch and fishing pier, hiking trails, and a dump station are available. Some facilities are wheelchair accessible.

Reservations, fees: Reservations are accepted at 651/430-8370 or online at www.co.washington.mn.us ($7 reservation fee). Sites are $15–22 per night. The group site is $45–55 per night. A $5 vehicle permit is required. Open from May to mid-October, with limited facilities after October 1.

Directions: From Hastings, drive north on Highway 61 for 3.6 miles. Turn right at Highway 95. In 1 mile, turn right onto County Road 78. Drive for 2.8 miles to St. Croix Trail. Turn left and drive for 1 mile to 102nd Street. Turn right and drive 0.8 mile through the park to the campground.

Contact: St. Croix Bluffs Regional Park, 651/430-8240, www.co.washington.mn.us.

23 LAKE BYLLESBY CAMPGROUND

Scenic rating: 7

on Lake Byllesby

This campground is squeezed onto a peninsula that leads to Echo Point on Lake Byllesby. The novelty of camping on a narrow peninsula is fun, but the close quarters can tarnish the experience somewhat. There is little privacy, although the recreational facilities here do a lot to make up for it. A hiking trail follows the entire stretch of shoreline in the park and an excellent swimming beach makes coming here on summer days a lot of fun. Many campers enjoy afternoons of water-skiing, which the lake is particularly popular for.

Campsites, facilities: There are 22 sites for tents and 35 sites for RVs. Picnic tables, fire rings, toilets, and showers are provided. A swimming beach, camp store, hiking trail, playground, boat ramp, and a dump station are available. Some facilities are wheelchair accessible. Leashed pets are permitted.

Reservations, fees: Reservations are accepted at 507/263-4447 ($7 reservation fee). Sites are $15–25 per night. Open from May to mid-October.

Directions: From Cannon Falls, drive west on County Road 17 for 0.5 mile. Continue west on 295th Street for another 1.0 miles to Harry Avenue. Turn left and drive 0.5 mile to Gerlach Way. Take a right and drive 0.5 mile to Echo Point Road. Turn left and drive 0.1 mile to the campground on the left side of the road.

Contact: Lake Byllesby Regional Park, 507/263-4447, www.co.dakota.mn.us/LeisureRecreation/CountyParks/Locations/Lake-Byllesby/LakeByllesbyCampground.htm.

24 CANNON FALLS CAMPGROUND

Scenic rating: 4

near Cannon Falls

Although this campground bears the name of the town, it is actually about a mile east of Cannon Falls. Carved into a large patch of hardwood forest, this simple campground consists of one single circular loop and a large open field for RV camping.

The campground has somewhat of a theme park feel to it. Regularly scheduled activities and entertainment during the summer, along with wagon rides, tractor and train rides, and sports fields are great for kids and families looking for a carnival atmosphere in a summer campground.

Campsites, facilities: There are 198 sites for RVs; some sites have 50-amp service. Picnic tables, fire rings, toilets, coin showers, and a dump station are provided. A heated pool, playground, camp store, coin laundry, train and tractor rides, sports fields, and a camp store are available. Some facilities are wheelchair accessible. Leashed pets are permitted.

Reservations, fees: Reservations are accepted at 507/263-3145 ($5 handling fee for credit cards). Sites are $30–36 per night with a two-night minimum stay on weekends and a three-night minimum stay on holiday weekends. Open from late April to early October.

Directions: From Cannon Falls, drive east on Highway 19 for 1.5 miles. Turn right onto Oak Lane. The campground is one block ahead on your right.

Contact: Cannon Falls Campground, 507/263-3145, www.cannonfallscampground.com.

25 HIDDEN VALLEY CAMPGROUND

Scenic rating: 6

on the Cannon River

Deep in the Richard J. Dorer Memorial Forest along the lazy Cannon River, Hidden Valley isn't just a clichéd name for a campground. This valley really is hard to find—you'll be cruising your car over three gravel roads before you get here.

The grassy, shaded sites here are for tents and RVs, but Hidden Valley is primarily an RV destination. Families often come here to spend a weekend tubing on the river; you can even check the river's level on the website before planning a trip. The Cannon Valley Trail passes through the campground as well, a paved bike and hiking trail that follows the Cannon River for nearly 20 miles.

Campsites, facilities: There are 200 sites for tents and RVs (most sites are pull-through, full hookups). Picnic tables, fire rings, flush toilets, showers, wireless Internet, and a dump station are provided. Biking and hiking trails, canoe and kayak rental, tube rental, and a playground are available. Some facilities are wheelchair accessible. Leashed pets are permitted.

Reservations, fees: Reservations are not accepted. Sites are $35 (with tax) per night. Payment accepted by cash or check only. Open from May to mid-October.

Directions: From Red Wing, drive west on Highway 61 for 11 miles to County Road 7. Turn left and drive for 2.8 miles. Turn right onto Mill Road. In 0.3 mile turn right onto 144th Avenue Way. The campground is 0.5 mile ahead on the right.

Contact: Hidden Valley Campground, 651/258-4550, www.hvcamping.com.

26 HOK-SI-LA CAMPGROUND
🏃‍♂️ 🏊 ⛴ 🐕 🎣 ⛺

Scenic rating: 9

on Lake Pepin, north of Lake City

Sometimes a city park is more than a park. Sometimes it is the center of a healthy, thriving little town. Lake City's 252-acre Hok-Si-La municipal park and campground is just that. The park lies on a heavily wooded peninsula that juts into Lake Pepin just off of Highway 61.

Camping here at the height of summer is about as close to an island paradise as you can get in Minnesota. Sailboats slice through the sparkling waters of the lake, lush bluffs rise steeply from the shores of the lake on all sides, and the sunrise and sunset change the entire spectrum of color in the sky for hours each day.

The campsites are spread throughout a small clearing in the trees, delivering a spectacular view of Lake Pepin. The sandy beach on the end of the peninsula is connected via a hiking trail to the campground, as are the dock, boat access, and playground.

Campsites, facilities: There are 34 sites for tents and eight group sites. Picnic tables, showers, toilets, hiking trails, and a boat access are provided. A swimming beach, playground, and camp store are available. Leashed pets are permitted.

Reservations, fees: Reservations are accepted up to one year in advance at 651/345-3855 with the first night's fee required as a deposit. Sites are $15–30 per night for two people; $5 per person per night for each additional person. Group sites are $15–90. Open from April through October, weather permitting.

Directions: From Lake City drive north on Highway 61 for 2 miles. Turn right into the campground across the railroad tracks.

Contact: City of Lake City, Hok-Si-La Municipal Park and Campground, 651/345-3855, http://lakecitymn.govoffice2.com.

27 FRONTENAC STATE PARK
🏃‍♂️ 🏊 ❄ 🐕 🎣 🚐 ⛺

Scenic rating: 9

on the Mississippi River

BEST (

Perched high atop the bluffs surrounding Lake Pepin, Frontenac State Park is one of Minnesota's finest camping experiences. The lake and surrounding bluffs have long been a destination for relaxation, healing, and lakeside luxury. Lake Pepin almost looks like a jungle paradise in the height of summer when the steep bluffsides are shedding morning mists through the atmospheric sunlight.

Frontenac State Park is also home to a rich ancient history. Archaeological digs in the 1970s revealed that the Hopewellian culture resided here as early as 400 BC. Both habitation sites and burial grounds have been discovered within the park. It is no wonder that the Hopewellians and later the Dakota and Fox Indians frequented this area. The high bluff is covered with wildlife, dense forests, and sweeping views of the lake and river valley. During the spring and fall, hundreds of bird species flock to the lake and surrounding bluffs during migratory seasons.

The campsites are spread throughout four loops on a high bluff above Lake Pepin along the Mississippi River. Heavy stands of oak, maple, basswood, and aspen blanket the camping area, sheltering the 59 sites from wind, rain, and sun and providing privacy and quiet, while a breathtaking view of the lake is just steps away.

Campsites, facilities: There are 59 sites for tents and RVs up to 53 feet and six cart-in sites 0.3 mile from the parking area. Picnic tables, toilets, showers, and a dump station are provided. Hiking trails, a playground, swimming beach, boat access, sledding hill, and warming house are available. Leashed pets are permitted.

Reservations, fees: Reservations are accepted from April 2 to October 31 at 866/857-2757 or online at www.stayatmnparks.com ($8.50 non-refundable reservation fee) and can be made up to one year in advance. Reservations are not required the rest of the year. Sites are $12–24 per night. Open year-round.

Directions: From Red Wing, drive southeast on Highway 61 for 10 miles. Turn left onto County Road 2. The park entrance is one mile ahead.

Contact: Frontenac State Park, 651/345-3401, www.dnr.state.mn.us/state_parks.

28 CAMP LACUPOLIS

Scenic rating: 5

north of Wabasha

BEST (

Sometimes the perfect campsite isn't one that has secluded, private campsites sheltered by old growth oak trees in proximity to world-class hiking trails atop pristine bluffs with panoramic views of picturesque river valleys. Sometimes the perfect campsite just has good fishing. That's Camp Lacupolis, an RV-only campground.

Anglers wedge themselves between the railroad tracks and the river not for the peace and quiet, but for the phenomenal riverside fishing. The camp is designed as a small fishing village, with cabins and a small campground for just eight RVs. Lacupolis rents boats, sells bait, and gives campers direct access to a choice fishing locale on the Mississippi. You can dock your boat here, spend a day cruising the river, or just drop a line from shore.

Campsites, facilities: There are eight sites for RVs. Toilets, showers, and a dump station are provided. A boat ramp, fishing pier, dock space, and fishing boat rental are available. Pets are allowed only allowed in RVs.

Reservations, fees: Reservations are accepted at 651/565-4318. Sites are $25 per night. There is a $10 fee per night for pets. Open from late May to late September.

Directions: From Wabasha, drive north on Highway 61 for 3.9 miles. Turn right and cross the railroad tracks into the campground.

Contact: Camp Lacupolis, 651/565-4318, www.camplacupolis.com.

29 HAY CREEK VALLEY CAMPGROUND

Scenic rating: 6

south of Red Wing

The Hay Creek Valley Campground smacks of good times and the good old days. Nestled along Hay Creek along the Cannon Valley Trail, the park office is an old saloon and the campground is on a rolling bluff full of sunshine and wildflowers. The old saloon serves as a restaurant, serving daily specials for campers who want an extra touch of comfort.

Campsites are peppered throughout a thick knot of trees that provide shade more shade and privacy than your average RV campground. Hiking and biking are a cinch, as the campground is adjacent to the Richard J. Dorer Memorial Hardwood Forest, which has dozens of miles of trails throughout. In the winter, two dozen of the campgrounds sites are kept open for skiers and winter enthusiasts.

Campsites, facilities: There are 150 campsites for tents or RVs; 14 sites are open during the winter. Picnic tables, fire rings, toilets, showers, and a dump station are provided. A playground, biking and hiking trail, skiing trail, outdoor pool, camp store and restaurant, and laundry facilities are available. Some facilities are wheelchair accessible. Leashed pets are permitted.

Reservations, fees: Reservations are accepted at 651/388-3998. Sites are $32 per night. Open year-round.

Directions: From Red Wing, drive south on County Road 58 for 6 miles. The campground is on the right-hand side of the highway at Hay Creek Trail.

Contact: Hay Creek Valley Campground, 651/388-3998, www.haycreekvalley.com.

30 CAMP FARIBO

Scenic rating: 5

south of Faribault

Camp Faribo sits wedged between I-35E and a county road, yet this crowded location doesn't stop this place from being packed during the summer. People fill the outdoor pool and the more than 70 campsites during summer, especially when there are town celebrations and summer events in nearby Faribault.

The campground is primarily an RV facility. Some trees separate the sites, but privacy is limited to the interior of your RV. Noise from the freeway is also common, as I-35 is only about 400 feet away. Still, the campground does its best to give itself a "summer camp" feel by renting bicycles, having an outdoor pool, and selling all manner of food at the camp store.

Campsites, facilities: There are 71 sites for tents and RVs; most sites have full hookups. Picnic tables, fire rings, toilets, coin showers, and a dump station are provided. An outdoor pool, playground, laundry facilities, camp store, bicycle trail, and bike and kayak rentals are available. Some facilities are wheelchair accessible. Leashed pets are permitted.

Reservations, fees: Reservations are accepted at 507/332-8453. Sites are $27.50–35 per night. Open from April to late October.

Directions: From Faribault, drive south on Bagley Avenue for 1.25 miles. Turn left into the campground.

Contact: Camp Faribo, 507/332-8453, http://campfaribo.com.

31 NERSTRAND-BIG WOODS

Scenic rating: 8

in Nerstrand-Big Woods State Park

Think of a thick forest—the black forest, Little Red Riding Hood's forest, or the forest of your dreams—and you've got Nerstrand-Big Woods State Park. A gargantuan cluster of dense woods south of Northfield, this state park is living history of how much of southern Minnesota used to be forest before settlement.

The Big Woods type of forest is full of large, broadleaf trees and delicate wildflowers that fill the forest floor during the early spring—the best time to camp if you're a nature lover. Some of the rarest flowers in the Midwest bloom here every year.

Like everything else in this park, the campground is buried in the trees. Privacy is superb, each site being enveloped by forest and having a short gravel driveway. Hiking trails lead to four walk-in sites that are deeper in the woods and offer even more privacy.

Hiking is the main activity here, with 11 miles of trails to choose from, but skiing during the winter is also popular. The park provides a warming house for skiers. A common area also has a volleyball court if you need respite from the tree cover.

Campsites, facilities: There are 51 sites for tents and RVs up to 60 feet; 27 sites have 30-amp electricity, one site is pull-through, and two sites are wheelchair accessible. There are also four walk-in sites within 200 yards of the parking area and three group camp sites for up to 16, 24, and 32 people each. Picnic tables, fire rings, drinking water, flush toilets, showers, and a dump station are provided. A playground, hiking and skiing trails, volleyball court, and warming house are available. Some facilities are wheelchair accessible. Leashed pets are permitted.

Reservations, fees: Reservations are accepted from April 2 to October 31 at 866/857-2757 or online at www.stayatmnparks.com ($8.50 non-refundable reservation fee) and can be made up to one year in advance. Reservations are not required the rest of the year. Sites are $12–24 per night. Open year-round, with limited facilities in winter.

Directions: From Northfield, drive south on Highway 246 for 11.3 miles. Turn right at

170th Street. The park entrance is 0.5 mile straight ahead.

Contact: Nerstrand-Big Woods State Park, 507/333-4840, www.dnr.state.mn.us/state_parks.

32 SHADES OF SHERWOOD

Scenic rating: 5

on the Zumbro River east of Wanamingo

This is one of the most unique campgrounds in Minnesota. Some people might find the King Arthur's Court–themed campground corny, but that doesn't stop hundreds of people from camping here every year.

There are seven camping areas are spread throughout the park; most are hidden among the trees. So while other campers are playing putt-putt on the minigolf course and trumpets are announcing King Arthur's arrival, you can lounge in the shade of your campsite and hear nary a thing. But if you and your family want to get involved in the festivities, just head to the campground's common area for a schedule of the royal court.

Campsites, facilities: There are 355 sites for tents and RVs (some hookups available). Picnic tables, fire rings, restrooms with showers and laundry facilities, and a dump station are provided. A camp store, heated pool, minigolf course, river tubing service, game room, hiking and biking trails, and wagon rides are available. Some facilities are wheelchair accessible. Leashed pets are permitted.

Reservations, fees: Reservations are accepted at 507/732-5100 (with a reservation fee of one night's deposit). Sites are $29–47 per night. Open from late April to early October.

Directions: From Wanamingo, drive north on Highway 57 for 0.5 mile. Turn right onto 440th Street. In 1.4 miles turn left onto 135th Avenue. Turn right in 0.3 mile onto Sherwood Trail. The campground is 1 mile ahead on the right.

Contact: Shades of Sherwood, 507/732-5100, www.shadesofsherwood.com.

33 LAKE LOUISE STATE PARK

Scenic rating: 8

in Lake Louise State Park

Lake Louise is a small lake in southern Minnesota that enjoys a dense huddle of forest amid the vast fields and farmlands of the region. The state park has a small, 20-site campground on the northwest shore of the lake hidden in the trees. A hiking trail tours the woods and the lake's northern shore. A footbridge spans an inlet of the lake and connects the campground to the eastern shore.

Lake Louise is close to the popular Mystery Cave, managed by the state park of the same name. You will often find this campground much less crowded than the Forestville/Mystery Cave State Park campground just two miles to the northeast.

Campsites, facilities: There are 20 sites for tents and RVs up to 60 feet. Picnic tables, fire rings, showers, vault toilets, and a dump station are provided. A swimming beach, biking and hiking trail, cross-country skiing trail, and snowshoe area are available. Leashed pets are permitted.

Reservations, fees: Reservations are accepted from April 2 to October 31 at 866/857-2757 or online at www.stayatmnparks.com ($8.50 non-refundable reservation fee) and can be made up to one year in advance. Reservations are not required the rest of the year. Sites are $12–24 per night. Open year-round.

Directions: From LeRoy, drive northwest on County Road 56 for 0.5 mile. Turn right onto 770th Avenue. In 1.6 miles turn left onto 766th Avenue into the park.

Contact: Lake Louise State Park, 507/352-5111, www.dnr.state.mn.us/state_parks.

34 BLUFF VALLEY CAMPGROUND
🏃 🚴 🏊 🛶 🎣 🏕 🐕 🛶 ♿ 🚐 ⛺

Scenic rating: 6

on the Zumbro River north of Rochester.

The Zumbro River makes so many cuts and curves canoeists sometimes feel that it turns back on itself, running loops through the Zumbro bottomlands. Bluff Valley is tucked into one of the sharpest bends in the river just before it reaches the nearby town of Zumbro Falls.

The campground is in an open clearing on the north side of the river. A series of five small adjacent rectangles is set up for efficient RV parking. This place packs them in like sardines, but the dense forest of the river bottomland and the compartmentalized design of the park make the nearly 300 campsites feel like far fewer.

A paved biking trail and several hiking trails explore the river and the surrounding woodlands, and fishing along the riverbend is excellent. The park rents canoes and kayaks as well, giving you access to the lazy and relaxing current of the Zumbro River.

Campsites, facilities: There are 275 sites for tents and RVs (full hookups). Pull-through sites are available. Picnic tables, fire rings, flush toilets, showers, and a dump station are provided. A playground, hiking and biking trails, fishing area, canoe and kayak rental, outdoor pool, swimming beach, and camp store are available. Some facilities are wheelchair accessible. Leashed pets are permitted.

Reservations, fees: Reservations are accepted at 507/753-2955. Sites are $42–49 per night for two people. Additional adults are $2 per night per person; $1 per night per youth (age 3–16). There is a two-night minimum stay, and a three- to four-night minimum stay on holiday weekends. Credit cards or cash only. Open from mid-April to late September.

Directions: From Rochester, drive north on Highway 63 for 19 miles. Turn left onto County Road 68 in Zumbro Falls. In 1.7 miles, turn left onto T 105. Take the first right 0.8 mile ahead, then turn left in about 200 feet onto the park road. The campground will be on the left in 1 mile.

Contact: Bluff Valley Campground, 507/753-2955, www.BluffValley.com.

35 KRUGER CAMPGROUND
🏃 🛶 🏊 🏕 ♿ 🚐 ⛺

Scenic rating: 7

on the Zumbro River west of Wabasha

Kruger Campground is a quiet, rustic camping area along the Zumbro River State Canoe Route, in the Richard J. Dorer Memorial Forest. It is one of the lesser-known camping areas in the RJD Forest, and you will usually be one of just a handful of campers here, even on weekends.

The primitive sites are set in a tiny loop just north of the county road in a dense patch of forest, with only a hand pump for water. A hiking trail passes through a downright astounding grove of white pines that create an exceedingly peaceful sanctuary. A canoe access point lets you dip your Alumacraft in for a spin on the winding Zumbro River.

Campsites, facilities: There are 19 sites for tents and RVs. Picnic tables, fire rings, garbage, a hand pump for water, and vault toilets are provided. A boat ramp, hiking trail, and canoe route are available. One campsite is wheelchair accessible. Leashed pets are permitted.

Reservations, fees: Reservations are not accepted. Sites are first come, first served, and are $12 per night. Open year-round.

Directions: From Wabasha, drive southeast on Highway 60 for 5 miles. Turn left at County Road 81. In 0.6 mile turn left into the campground.

Contact: Kruger Campground and Management Unit, 651/345-3401, www.dnr.state.mn.us/state_forests/facilities/cmp00041/index.html.

36 HOPE OAK KNOLL CAMPGROUND

Scenic rating: 3

south of Owatonna

What this campground lacks in beauty, it makes up for in convenience. Located less than 0.25 mile off of I-35, Hope Oak Knoll is only about 10 miles from Rice Lake State Park to the northeast, about the same distance from the town of Owatonna and within driving distance of two state wildlife management areas.

The campground isn't much more than a few loops in a grove of oak trees, but it does its best to be comfortable. The oak grove is large and shady and every campsite has plenty of trees and shade. The freeway is noisy at almost all times of day and night, especially during the busiest weekends of summer.

This is a good spot to park your RV for a week or two and explore the area parks and towns. The campground has a low rate per site, which is a deal in this part of the state.

Campsites, facilities: There are 90 sites for tents and RVs; some sites are pull-through. Picnic tables, fire rings, toilets, showers, and a dump station are provided. A playground, laundry facilities, and camp store are available. Leashed pets are permitted.

Reservations, fees: Reservations are accepted at 507/451-2998. Sites are $20 per night. Open from April 15 to October 15.

Directions: From Owatonna, drive south on I-35 for 9.5 miles. Exit at County Road 4 and turn left. Drive east for 0.8 mile to County Road 3. Turn left and drive for 0.3 mile to the campground.

Contact: Hope Oak Knoll Campground, 507/451-2998, www.hikercentral.com/camp-grounds/106543.html.

37 RICE LAKE STATE PARK

Scenic rating: 7

on Rice Lake in Rice Lake State Park

Rice Lake State Park's campground is the yin and yang of state park campgrounds. The loop is set half in the dense woods near the lake and half in a large, open grassland meadow in the middle of the trees. The impression is that of a big donut being dunked into a dark cup of coffee.

There are only 42 sites here, on a charming, well-designed campground loop. Each site has a short gravel driveway and plenty of space for several tents. Trees separate each site from the other, even in the grassy section of the loop. A hiking trail leads to the lake and to a trail system that runs throughout the park.

Rice Lake is a very shallow lake full of marsh grasses, reeds, and waterfowl habitat. During the big migrations each year, thousands of birds flock here to feed. The park's main trail also tours several types of habitat that occur in the park, from lake to prairie to woodland to wetland.

Campsites, facilities: There are 42 sites for tents and RVs up to 55 feet. There are also five walk-in sites and four cart-in sites within 100 yards of the parking area, and five canoe sites. Picnic tables, fire rings, toilets, showers, and a dump station are provided. A boat and canoe access, hiking and cross-country ski trails, and a playground are available. There is one wheelchair-accessible campsite. Leashed pets are permitted.

Reservations, fees: Reservations are accepted from April 2 to October 31 at 866/857-2757 or online at www.stayatmnparks.com ($8.50 non-refundable reservation fee) and can be made up to one year in advance. Reservations are not required the rest of the year. Sites are $12–24 per night. Open year-round.

Directions: From Owatonna, drive east on County Road 19 for 8.7 miles. Turn right at the state park sign at County Road 40. The campground is 0.3 mile ahead.

Contact: Rice Lake State Park, 507/455-5871, www.dnr.state.mn.us/state_parks.

38 OXBOW PARK CAMPGROUND
🚶 🐕 🚗 ♿ 🚐 ⛰️

Scenic rating: 6

on the Zumbro River north of Byron

Located on the Zumbro River, Oxbow Park houses a zoo and garden area in addition to the campground. The camping area is situated at the apex of the river's bend, so camping here means having running water on three sides of you, filling the days with the serene sounds of slow moving water.

The campsites are few and far between, nestled among groves of oak, maple, and cottonwoods that line the river's bank. Directly across the river the terrain steeply rises, giving the campground the comforting feel of a small, sheltered valley.

Campsites, facilities: There are 29 sites for tents and RVs. Picnic tables, fire rings, drinking water, restrooms, and showers are provided. A playground, zoo, nature center, and hiking trails are available. There are three wheelchair-accessible sites. Leashed pets are permitted.

Reservations, fees: Reservations are not accepted; sites are first come, first served. Sites are $15–18 per night. Open from May to October.

Directions: From Byron, drive north on Country Road 5 for 3 miles. Turn right onto Valleyhigh Road NW and take the first left in about 100 feet onto Country Road 105. The park is 1 mile ahead on the right.

Contact: Oxbow Park, 507/775-2451, www.co.olmsted.mn.us/parks/camping_at_oxbow.asp.

39 CHESTER WOODS
🚶 🚴 🏊 ⛵ 🎣 ❄️ 🏕️ 🐎 ♿ 🚐 ⛰️

Scenic rating: 5

on the Bear Creek Reservoir

This camping loop is laced through an absolute tangle of trees on the north end of the Bear Creek Reservoir. If you don't mind that the lake isn't a natural one, this park is lovely. The campsites have plenty of privacy amongst the trees and the park is chock full of hiking trails, a swimming beach, and a big playground. You can also rent canoes and kayaks from the park office and dip your paddle in the reservoir or fish for large-mouth bass in the stocked lake.

Campsites, facilities: There are 52 sites for tents or RVs; 37 sites have electrical hookups. Picnic tables, fire rings, toilets, showers, drinking water, and a dump station are available. A playground, swimming beach, canoe rental, hiking, biking, horseback riding, and ski trails, and boat ramp are available. Two sites are wheelchair accessible. Leashed pets are permitted.

Reservations, fees: Reservations are accepted at 507/285-7050. Sites are $15–18 per night. A $5 vehicle permit is required. Open mid-May to late October.

Directions: From Rochester, drive east on Highway 14 for 7 miles. Turn left into the park and follow signs to the camping area.

Contact: Chester Woods Park, 507/285-7050, www.co.olmsted.mn.us/departments/pw/index.asp.

40 FORESTVILLE/MYSTERY CAVE STATE PARK
🚶 🚴 ❄️ 🐎 🚐 ⛰️

Scenic rating: 7

in Forestville/Mystery Cave State Park

BEST (

When you get to Forestville, you will find it is one of the most aptly named places in the state. The trees grow so thick here and are so notable in southern Minnesota's big farm fields, prairies, and grasslands that it could be named nothing but Forestville.

The campground is in one of the park's few clearings, cutting a small swath in the dense forest. The sites are still tucked into trees that encroach on the meadow, providing quiet and shade. The more than 70 sites are spread out in three loops, making this woodsy campground very private and peaceful.

The park is a testament to the value of the state park system in Minnesota. Mystery Cave is maintained by the park, with naturalists giving tours throughout the summer of the stalactites, underground pools, and dark caverns that run for miles underground. There is a historical village, also maintained by the park, where settlers tried to make a go of it in the thick woods of the 1800s. Hiking, cross-country skiing, and spelunking can all be enjoyed here for most of the year.

Campsites, facilities: There are 73 sites for tents and RVs up to 50 feet; 23 sites have hookups. Picnic tables, fire rings, toilets, showers, and a dump station are provided. Firewood, hiking and skiing trails, a paved bike trail, sliding hill, and warming house are available. Leashed pets are permitted.

Reservations, fees: Reservations are accepted from April 2 to October 31 at 866/857-2757 or online at www.stayatmnparks.com ($8.50 non-refundable reservation fee) and can be made up to one year in advance. Reservations are not required the rest of the year. Sites are $12–24 per night. A $5 state park vehicle permit is required. Open year-round, with limited facilities in winter. Note that the cave is only open mid-April through October.

Directions: From Preston, drive north on Lafayette Freeway for 1 mile to County Road 16. Turn left and drive for 8 miles. Turn left onto Township Road 349. In 1 mile, take the second left onto Township Road 347. Drive for 2.5 miles to County Road 118 and turn right. The park office is 1.3 miles ahead.

Contact: Forestville/Mystery Cave State Park, 507/352-5111, www.dnr.state.mn.us/state_parks.

41 WHITEWATER STATE PARK

🏃 🏊 🛶 ❄ 🐕 ♿ 🚐 ⛰️

Scenic rating: 9

in Whitewater State Park

BEST (

Whitewater State Park was somehow missed by the glaciers of the last ice age. As a result, the landscape is full of folded, wooded hills, lush valleys, trout streams, and high rocky cliffs that rise above the river valley.

The campground consists a five-loop cluster of more than 100 sites set a bend of the Whitewater River. The campground has a quiet, cool valley bottom feel, and tree cover is heavy, providing sites with shade and privacy. Forest turf trails winnow through the trees between the campsites, connecting the campground to the river and trail system that runs throughout the park. People particularly love this place because of its noticeable lack of mosquitoes during the summer.

Anglers will be happy here, with brook, rainbow, and brown trout aplenty to choose from. One of the parks' most notable features is Inspiration Point, set atop a rocky bluff that rises more than 200 feet from the valley bottom. There are hundreds of steps to climb up to get to the narrow top of the bluff, but the view is unforgettable and rather rare in Minnesota, a state that was mostly laid flat by glaciers thousands of years ago.

Campsites, facilities: There are 104 sites for tents and RVs up to 50 feet, five pull-through sites, and two walk-in sites. Picnic tables, fire rings, toilets, showers, and a dump station are provided. A fishing pier, hiking and cross-country ski trails, a swimming beach, volleyball court, and warming house are available. There are two wheelchair-accessible sites. Leashed pets are permitted.

Reservations, fees: Reservations are accepted from April 2 to October 31 at 866/857-2757 or online at www.stayatmnparks.com ($8.50 non-refundable reservation fee) and can be made up to one year in advance. Reservations are not required the rest of the year. Sites are $12–24 per night. Open year-round.

Directions: From Elba, drive south on Highway 74 for 3 miles. Turn right and drive a few hundred feet to the park office.

Contact: Whitewater State Park, 507/932-3007, www.dnr.state.mn.us/state_parks.

42 LAZY 'D' CAMPGROUND

Scenic rating: 5

south of Elba adjacent to Whitewater State Park

Right on the popular Whitewater River, Lazy 'D' takes full advantage of the waterway. The campground offers river tubing and canoe and kayak rental, as well as a free shuttle that will return you to the campground after spending the afternoon floating downstream. The park is right on the northern edge of Whitewater State Park, giving you quick access to all the perks of the park, including Inspiration Peak and great trout fishing.

The campsites are in two loops separated by the river and several stands of maple, oak, and cottonwood trees. The sites are well-spaced and have several trees in and between them, making the riverside sites especially nice. A footpath follows both sides of the river within the park.

The campground is only about a hundred feet from County Road 74, but there is usually minimal traffic on the road. The heavy woods of the region keeps the area peaceful, quiet, and shady despite the fact that the campground accommodates more than 100 sites.

Campsites, facilities: There are 115 sites for tents and RVs. Picnic tables, fire rings, toilets, coin showers, and a dump station are provided. Canoe rental, river tubing, shuttle service, swimming pool, playground, game room, horse trail rides, wagon rides, and a camp store are available. Some facilities are wheelchair accessible. Leashed pets are permitted.

Reservations, fees: Reservations are accepted

at 507/932-3098 (a one-night deposit is required). Sites are $24–37 per night for tents and $27–42 per night for RVs. There is a two-night minimum on weekends and a three-night minimum on holiday weekends. Open from mid-May to mid-October.

Directions: From Plainview, drive south on County Road 4 for 8 miles. Then turn left onto County Road 2, which will turn into County Road 39, and go 5 miles. The campground will be on the left side.

Contact: Lazy 'D' Campground, 507/932-3098, www.lazydcampground.com.

43 JOHN A. LATSCH STATE PARK

Scenic rating: 9

in John A. Latsch State Park

BEST (

This campground's most attractive feature is its proximity to the park's hiking trail, which climbs more than 300 feet to the top of Charity Bluff, overlooking the Mississippi River. From the bluff, hikers can see for miles up and down the river valley and well into Wisconsin. You'll definitely need sturdy legs and a bottle of water to make it to the top. I would also recommend bringing a lunch, as it takes at least an hour to climb to the top, even though the trail is barely more than 0.5 mile long.

The campground is basically a clearing cut into the forest adjacent to the small parking loop at the park's entrance. There is no office here, just a self-registration box, a few picnic tables, and a vault toilet. Most folks use this park as a day-use area for the hiking trail, so camping here is often a solitary experience. If you are brave enough to climb the bluff at night, the view of the night sky is unparalleled anywhere in the county.

Campsites, facilities: There are seven walk-in sites. Picnic tables, fire rings and grills, a hand pump for drinking water, a vault toilet, and garbage cans are provided. Hiking trails, wild berries, and a snowshoeing area are available. Leashed pets are permitted.

Reservations, fees: Reservations are not accepted. Sites are $12–24 per night. Self-registration is required at the campground. Open year-round.

Directions: From Winona, drive northwest on Highway 61 for about 12 miles. The park is to the left directly off the highway.

Contact: John A. Latsch State Park, 507/643-6849, www.dnr.state.mn.us/state_parks.

44 PLA-MOR CAMPGROUND AND MARINA

🚶 🏊 ⛵ 🚤 🚣 ♿ 🚐 ⛺

Scenic rating: 6

south of Winona

A marina on the Mississippi River, Pla-Mor is just a hop, skip, and a jump away from Winona and provides direct access to the Mississippi River. The marina is full of colorful sailboats and watercraft, and the river traffic near Winona is always entertaining. The Mississippi is wide and bright here, especially on sunny summer days.

The campsites aren't as impressive as the location might suggest. The open-field setup is mostly made for packing the RVs in. That being said, there are more trees and space between the sites here than there are in most RV campgrounds.

Fishing and boating is excellent and is the main attraction by far. The campground and marina rents speed boats, water-skiing equipment, fishing boats, and pontoons.

Campsites, facilities: There are 107 RV sites and 45 tent sites. Pull-throughs and hookups are available. Picnic tables, fire rings, toilets, showers, and a dump station are provided. A playground, swimming pool, boat and equipment rental, boat ramp, hiking trail, wireless Internet, a camp store, and laundry facilities are available. Some facilities are wheelchair accessible.

Reservations, fees: Reservations are accepted online at www.camppla-mor.com ($10–20

deposit required). Sites are $24–26 per night for tents and $31–39 per night for RVs. There is a two-night minimum summer weekends and a three-night minimum holiday weekends. Open from mid-April to mid-October.

Directions: From Winona, drive southeast on Highway 61 for 6 miles. Turn left into the marina and park office.

Contact: Pla-Mor Campground and Marina, 507/454-2851, www.camppla-mor.com.

45 GREAT RIVER BLUFFS STATE PARK

🚶 ❄ 🐕 ♿ 🚐 ⛺

Scenic rating: 9

south of Winona

BEST (

The towering bluffs above the Mississippi River Valley are as good as they get at Great River Bluffs State Park. Views of the valley and the Wisconsin side of the border seem to stretch endlessly toward the horizon.

There is hardly a patch of flat land large enough here to pitch a tent, but the park has managed to make a nice camping area carved into the bluffside. Sites are scattered in the trees and prairies on the bluffside away from the river valley. Trails connect the campground to the large bluffs and the heavy woods that surround them. The trail to King's Bluff is particularly popular, leading through prairie wildflowers and pine stands to break open into a beautiful view of the north side of Queen's Bluff and the surrounding valley.

With patience, you may see the rare timber rattler and painted turtle. Other wildlife opportunities include whitetail deer, mink, raccoon, hawk, and eagles.

Campsites, facilities: There are 31 sites for tents and RVs up to 60 feet. There are also 5 bike-in sites accessible from Highway 61 and two primitive group sites for tents only. Picnic tables, drinking water, fire rings and grills, vault and flush toilets, and showers are provided. Hiking, skate-ski, cross-country ski, and snowshoe trails are available. A sliding hill and picnic area are also available. There are two wheelchair-accessible sites adjacent to the shower building. Leashed pets are permitted.

Reservations, fees: Reservations are accepted from April 2 to October 31 at 866/857-2757 or online at www.stayatmnparks.com ($8.50 non-refundable reservation fee) and can be made up to one year in advance. Reservations are not required the rest of the year. Sites are $12–24 per night. Open year-round, with limited facilities in winter.

Directions: From Winona, drive southeast on Highway 61 for 11 miles. Turn right onto County Road 3 and drive for 3.3 miles to Kipp Drive. In 2.0 miles, turn right onto Campground Road, which leads past the park office to the camping area.

Note: Large RVs may experience difficulty driving into and through the campground.

Contact: Great River Bluffs State Park, 507/643-6849, www.dnr.state.mn.us/state_parks.

46 MYRE BIG ISLAND STATE PARK

🧍 🚲 🛶 🎣 🛥 🏊 ❄️ 🐕 🚐 ⛺

Scenic rating: 8

on Albert Lea Lake in Myre Big Island State Park

BEST (

Everyone's first question when they think about camping here is: Can we camp on the island? The answer is: Yes. About a third of the park's campsites are located on the heavily wooded Big Island the park derives its name from.

The heavy tree cover and the novelty of island camping are a perfect combination for a great outdoors experience. The campsites on the island are coveted little dens of privacy. The White Fox campground, north of the island in the prairie and savanna, is a larger two-loop campground. The mainland campground is somewhat underappreciated, but no less lovely with wildflowers, breezy prairie grasses, and

sparse oak savanna that create a relaxing atmosphere no forest could ever replicate. The two loops are just west of a narrow inlet that feeds Albert Lea Lake; a stand of trees lies between the campsites and the water.

This park is a perfect example of the constant transition between prairie and forest that occurs in Minnesota. The borders areas between tree and grass, water and marsh, marsh and prairie are excellent for viewing wildlife, especially near the water at dawn and dusk.

Campsites, facilities: There are 93 sites for tents and RVs up to 60 feet. There are also four backpacking sites within two miles of the parking area. Picnic tables, toilets, showers, and a dump station are provided. A swimming beach, boat access, fishing area, and hiking, biking, skiing, and snowshoeing trails are available. Leashed pets are permitted.

Reservations, fees: Reservations are accepted from April 2 to October 31 at 866/857-2757 or online at www.stayatmnparks.com ($8.50 non-refundable reservation fee) and can be made up to one year in advance. Reservations are not required the rest of the year. Sites are $12–24 per night. Open year-round.

Directions: From Albert Lea, drive east on Highway 65 for 1.5 miles. Turn right at Prospect Avenue and drive for 0.3 mile to County Road 91. Turn left and drive for 1.2 miles. Turn right at 780th Avenue and drive through the park for 1.2 miles. A sign for the campground will be on the left. Turn left and drive 0.3 mile to the camping area.

Contact: Myre Big Island State Park, 507/379-3403, www.dnr.state.mn.us/state_parks.

47 BROOKSIDE CAMPGROUND

🧍 🚲 🛶 🎣 🐕 🚶 ♿ 🚐 ⛺

Scenic rating: 6

near Blooming Prairie

Situated on the Cedar River near the town of Blooming Prairie, you'll see why this town got its name. From early spring to mid-autumn wildflowers cover the grasslands with their scents and colors.

As with many prairie rivers, a ribbon of trees follows the water. Brookside Campground is burrowed into the woods along a gentle bend of the river in a large two-loop configuration. The campground is a full service facility, making you feel like you are living in a small village in the middle of the prairie, with amenities located in the wooded grove along the riverbank.

Campsites, facilities: There are 90 campsites for tents and RVs. Picnic tables, fire rings, showers, toilets, and a dump station are provided. A swimming beach, water access, a playground, hiking and biking trails, outdoor pool, high speed Internet, and camp store are available. Some facilities are wheelchair accessible. Leashed pets are permitted.

Reservations, fees: Reservations are accepted at 507/583-2979. Sites are $25 per night for tents and $25 per night for RVs. Open from May to October.

Directions: From Blooming Prairie, drive south on Highway 218 for 4 miles. Turn left at 320th Street. In 1 mile, turn left at the Brookside Campground sign. The campground is 0.1 mile ahead.

Contact: Brookside Campground, 507/583-2979, www.campbrookside.com.

sites are in an open field with little shade or privacy. There are approximately 20 loops to accommodate the 320 sites that are jammed into the park. The gravel roads can get dusty in the summer when there is a lot of traffic, but the prospect of taking your child to Yogi Bear's Jellystone Park could be a once-in-a-lifetime opportunity. If you're lucky, that is.

Campsites, facilities: There are 320 sites for tents and RVs; 15 sites are for tents only. Pull-through sites are available. Picnic tables, fire rings, showers, toilets, a dump station, and high-speed wireless Internet are available. Hiking and biking trails, a playground, outdoor pool, camp store, and restaurant are available. Some facilities are wheelchair accessible. Leashed pets are permitted.

Reservations, fees: Reservations are accepted at 507/584-6611. Sites are $30 per night with no hookups, and up to $45 per night with full hookups. There is a $15 reservation fee that can be refunded if cancelled two weeks prior to reservation date. Open from April 15 to October 15.

Directions: From Austin, drive east on I-90 for 8.6 miles to Exit 187. Turn right onto 630th Avenue and drive 0.1 mile to the campground on the right side of the road.

Contact: Yogi Bear's Jellystone Park Camp-Resort, 507/584-6611, www.beavertrails.com.

48 BEAVER TRAILS CAMPGROUND

🚶 🚴 ⛱ 🎣 🏕 ♿ 🚐 ⛺

Scenic rating: 4

east of Austin off I-90

A Yogi Bear's Jellystone Campground, Beaver Trails is what you'd call a tourist trap. If you want one part amusement park, one part campground, Beaver Trails is the place to bring your family. The facility has its own exit off of I-90—and is sizable enough to really deserve it.

Primarily an RV campground, Beaver Trails'

49 PONDEROSA CAMPGROUND

⛱ 🚣 🚐 🎣 ♿ 🚐 ⛺

Scenic rating: 6

on Zumbro Lake, just north of Oronoco

Ponderosa is an RV campground situated on a peninsula on Zumbro Lake. There are some tent sites, but almost everyone that camps here has an RV. Anglers come for the bass, crappies, and northerns in the lake, and the campground provides a boat ramp and fishing dock. Water-skiing is also very popular.

All the attention here is focused on the

lake. Half of the campers come to fish and the other half come to water-ski and swim. The campsites are in a mostly cleared area near the water. Privacy is minimal, but there is usually at least one tree per site.

Campsites, facilities: There are 80 sites for tents or RVs. Picnic tables, fire rings, toilets, showers, and a dump station are provided. A boat ramp, swimming beach, camp store, and dock space are available. Some facilities are wheelchair accessible. Leashed pets are permitted.

Reservations, fees: Reservations are accepted at 507/843-3611. Sites are $28 per night for tents and $35 per night for RVs. Open from mid-April to mid-October.

Directions: From Oronoco, drive east on White Bridge Road NW for 1 miles. Turn left onto Power Dam Road NW. In 1.7 the road merges into County Road 21. Drive north for another 1.7 miles to County Road 90. Turn right and drive 0.8 mile to the campground.

Contact: Ponderosa Campground, 507/843-3611.

50 MAPLE SPRINGS CAMPGROUND
🏃🚣🏠🐕🚐⛰️

Scenic rating: 6

on the Forestville Creek near Forestville

Maple Springs is close to all the action, but not quite in it. Located just off of dusty County Road 118, near Forestville/Mystery Cave State Park, Maple, this campground provides access to the park via a hiking trail that leads to Forestville Creek where canoeing, fishing, hiking, and biking opportunities abound. (Basically, if you can't stay in the state park, this is your backup plan.)

Campsites, facilities: There are 63 sites for tents and RVs up to 60 feet. Picnic tables, toilets, water pumps, and a dump station are provided. Hiking trails, a horse area, volleyball court, and a fishing area are available. Leashed pets are permitted.

Reservations, fees: Reservations are accepted at 507/352-2056. Sites are $18 per night for tents and $25 per night for RVs. Open from mid-April to late October.

Directions: From Preston, drive west on County Highway 12 for 4 miles. Turn left onto County Road 118. The campground is 1.6 miles ahead on the left.

Contact: Maple Springs Campground, 507/352-2056, www.maplespringscampground.com.

51 CARLEY STATE PARK
🏃🚣❄️🏠🐕🚶♿🚐⛰️

Scenic rating: 8

in Carley State Park

Charmer of charmers, Carley State Park is an absolute beauty along the Whitewater River in southeastern Minnesota. The park draws trout anglers, nature lovers, and hikers who enjoy the undulating hills and ridges on offer. The winding Whitewater River cuts deeply into the park's high ridges, at times creating a swift moving current and at other times a lazy stream-like quality. My favorite part is the lookout deck on top of the highest ridge near the park office. The view of the surrounding countryside and river valley is spectacular, evoking a sense of what the unsettled state must have once looked like hundreds of years ago.

The campground is a small 20-site loop near the picnic grounds and river. The sites are well-spaced between the trees. Few people camp here, as most visitors are headed for the nearby and far more popular Whitewater State Park.

Campsites, facilities: There are 20 sites for tents or RVs up to 30 feet and three tent-only group sites for up to 15, 20, and 25 people. Picnic tables, fire rings, vault toilets, and drinking water (hand pump in winter) are provided. Hiking trails, fishing area, picnic area, a playground, and ski trails are available. Some facilities are wheelchair accessible. Leashed pets are permitted.

Reservations, fees: Reservations are accepted from April 2 to October 31 at 866/857-2757 or online at www.stayatmnparks.com ($8.50 non-refundable reservation fee) and can be made up to one year in advance. Reservations are not required the rest of the year. Sites are $12–24 per night. A $5 state park permit is required. Open Memorial Day through Labor Day.

Directions: From Plainview, drive south on County Road 4 for 4 miles. Turn right into the park and drive 200 feet to the park office.

Contact: Carley State Park, 507/932-3007, www.dnr.state.mn.us/state_parks.

52 EAGLE CLIFF CAMPGROUND

🥾🚴🏊🎣🛶🛥🐕🏕👨‍🦽🚐🏕

Scenic rating: 6

on the Root River near Lanesboro

Although Eagle Cliff Campground is just on the outskirts of Lanesboro, the single loop campground does a nice job of creating a relaxing outdoor getaway. The park is across the Root River from town and lies along the Root River State Trail, a paved trail for biking and hiking that follows the river for miles upstream and down. A large buffer of trees grows on the riverbank, blocking wind, creating shade and giving the a nice, campground the enclosed feeling.

The park sits in the middle of the two-million-acre Richard J. Dorer Memorial Hardwood Forest, which is rife with hiking trails, trout streams, horse trails, quaint small towns, and oodles of wildlife. This campground makes a great base camp for outdoorspeople who like access to the wilderness without having to sleep in it.

Campsites, facilities: There are 221 sites for tents and RVs. Pull-through sites are available. Picnic tables, fire rings, showers, toilets, and a dump station are provided. A playground, boat ramp and river access, canoe and kayak rental,

biking and hiking trails, bicycle rental, a swimming beach, camp store, and laundry facilities are available. Some facilities are wheelchair accessible. Leashed pets are permitted.

Reservations, fees: Reservations are accepted at 507/467-2598. Sites are $22 per night for tents and $29 per night for RVs. Open from April to December.

Directions: From Lanesboro, drive east on Ashburn Street E for less than 1 mile. The campground is on the right side of the road across the Root River State Trail.

Contact: Eagle Cliff Campground, 507/467-2598.

53 VINEGAR RIDGE CAMPSITES

🥾🚴🎣🛶❄🐕👨‍🦽🏕

Scenic rating: 6

in the Richard J. Dorer Memorial Hardwood Forest

BEST (

The Vinegar Ridge Campsites are off of a small township road that is off of a small county road, that is just outside of the small town of Rushford. You guessed it: The campground is small, too. There are only eight tent sites in woods that follow the twisting and turning Root River through southern Minnesota. The Root River State Trail is about 0.25 mile from the campground following the river south.

The campground has a quiet, buried-in-the-woods feel to it that you usually associate with northern Minnesota. Down here in the bottomlands of the Root River, in the deep shade of the Richard J. Dorer Memorial Hardwood Forest, time melts away and nature becomes your main perspective. You will see plenty of wildlife here, including whitetail deer, minks, hawks, herons, and raccoons. Carry your canoe in and drift and fish in the Root or just kick back and fish from shore.

Campsites, facilities: There are eight sites for tents only. Picnic tables, vault toilets, garbage cans, and drinking water are provided.

A biking, hiking, and snowmobile trail; canoe access; and fishing area are available. Some facilities are wheelchair accessible. Leashed pets are permitted.

Reservations, fees: Reservations are not accepted. Sites are $12 per night. Open year-round.

Directions: From Rushford, drive east on County Road 26 for 1.5 miles. Turn right and drive southeast on Township Road 270 for 4 miles. The campground is on the right marked by a wooden sign.

Contact: Minnesota Department of Natural Resources, 507/724-2107, www.dnr.state. mn.us/state_forests.

54 CUSHON'S PEAK CAMPGROUND

Scenic rating: 5

on the Root River west of Houston

This campground hugs the edge of a forested area along the Root River near the town of Houston. The campground is best known for the two bluegrass festivals it holds each year in May and August. Camping during these times is impossible without reservations made well in advance. The rest of the year, the two small campground loops are very quiet and peaceful. The western side of the campground enjoys more trees and privacy, with several clusters growing between the sites. The paved Root River Bike Trail is nearby.

Campsites, facilities: There are 44 sites for tents and RVs. Picnic tables, fire rings, toilets, showers, and a dump station are provided. A bike and hiking trail, river tubing, and a fishing area are available. Some facilities are wheelchair accessible. Leashed pets are permitted.

Reservations, fees: Reservations are accepted at 507/896-7325. Sites are $17 per night for tent sites and $24 per night for RVs. Open from May to September.

Directions: From Houston, drive west on Highway 16 for 2.5 miles. Turn right into the campground.

Contact: Cushon's Peak Campground, 507/896-7325, www.camppeak.com.

55 TRAILHEAD PARK CAMPGROUND

Scenic rating: 5

in Houston

Just outside of the small town of Houston, the nature center's campground is surprisingly secluded. There are 10 walk-in sites that aren't exactly buried in the woods, but they do give a feeling of separateness from the nearby town and the well-manicured grounds of the rest of the park.

The nature center is primarily a day-use area and operates several programs for youth, including nature walks, conservation classes, and various environmental educational programs.

Campsites, facilities: There are 10 walk-in tent sites. Picnic tables, fire rings, showers, and toilets are provided. A nature trail; visitors center; a shuttle service (donation requested) for bikes, canoes, and kayaks; and summer programs are available.

Reservations, fees: Reservations are not accepted. Sites are $10 per night for up to six campers, $2 per person per night for any additional campers. Self-registration is required at the campground (registration envelopes are in the bathrooms). Open year-round.

Directions: From Houston, drive north on County Road 76 for 0.1 mile to W. Plum Street. Turn left and drive for a few hundred feet to the campground on the right.

Contact: Houston Nature Center, 507/896-HOOT (507/896-4668), www.houstonmn. com/HNC.html.

56 BEAVER CREEK VALLEY STATE PARK

🏃 ⛵ 🐕 🎣 ♿ 🚐 ⛺

Scenic rating: 7

in Beaver Creek Valley State Park

The campground in Beaver Creek Valley State Park is strung the west bank of Beaver Creek as it flows south through the park. The park is enveloped by a dense forest that fills the valley surrounding the creek. The entire watershed is a thick forest of maple, oak, cottonwood, and basswood filled with wildlife and wildflowers. Spring ephemerals color the drab early spring, and in autumn the valley is ablaze with the hues of changing leaves.

The campsites are well-spaced and close to the creek; you will fall asleep to the sound of babbling water each night. A trail follows the creek, running through the campground and connecting you to the rest of the park both upstream and down. Across the river from the campsites is a natural spring that feeds much of east Beaver Creek as it flows south and out of the park. Coming here to see the natural spring alone is well worth your trip.

Campsites, facilities: There are 42 sites for tents and RVs up to 55 feet. There are also six walk-in sites within 200 yards of the parking area. Picnic tables, showers, toilets, fire rings, and a dump station are provided. A playground, fishing area, volleyball court, and hiking trails are available. There is one wheelchair-accessible site. Leashed pets are permitted.

Reservations, fees: Reservations are accepted from April 2 to October 31 at 866/857-2757 or online at www.stayatmnparks.com ($8.50 non-refundable reservation fee) and can be made up to one year in advance. Reservations are not required the rest of the year. Sites are $12–24 per night. Open year-round.

Directions: From Caledonia, drive west on Highway 76 for 0.7 mile. Continue straight on County Road 1 for 3.2 miles directly into the park.

Contact: Beaver Creek Valley State Park, 507/724-2107, www.dnr.state.mn.us/state_parks.

57 DUNROMIN' PARK CAMPGROUND

🏃 🚴 🏊 🐕 🎣 ♿ 🚐 ⛺

Scenic rating: 5

south of Caledonia

RVers love DunRomin' because a seasonal camping rate includes winter storage. So, if you drive by in January and see RVs clustered in the woodsy campground, chances are there isn't a cadre of hearty winter campers here—just people saving money by storing their rig for the winter.

DunRomin' sits at the end of a small gravel Township road in a swatch of trees between surrounding farm fields. The campground accommodates tent and RV campers, but is much more popular with visitors in RVs. Almost every site has tree cover and a small driveway that allows a good amount of privacy as well as shade on sunny days. The park has plenty for families to do—bike rental, hiking trail, a mini golf course, and heated pool are the most popular amenities. Despite all of the accoutrements, the campground maintains a peaceful, country-style feel to it that campers appreciate.

Campsites, facilities: There are 104 sites for tents and RVs. Pull-through sites are available. Picnic tables, fire rings, toilets, showers, and a dump station are provided. A heated pool, minigolf course, laundry facilities, bicycle rental, hiking trail, a playground, laundry facilities, and a camp store are available. Some facilities are wheelchair accessible. Leashed pets are permitted.

Reservations, fees: Reservations are accepted at 507/724-2514 or online at www.dunrominpark.com. Sites are $20–25 per night for tents and $22–35 per night for RVs. There is a two-night minimum stay summer weekends and a three-night minimum stay holiday weekends. Campers must register at the park office upon arrival. Open from May to October.

Directions: From Caledonia, drive south on Highway 76 for 5.1 miles. Turn left onto Dun-Romin' Drive. The campground is 0.3 mile straight ahead.

Contact: DunRomin' Park Campground, 507/724-2514, www.dunrominpark.com.

58 WILDCAT LANDING PARK CAMPGROUND

🏊 🚣 🚐 🐕 ♿ 🚙 ⛺

Scenic rating: 7

south of Brownsville

Less than five minutes south of Brownsville, Wildcat Landing is a shoreline park on the Mississippi River. Whether you are an avid angler, a sunbather, or someone who just likes to watch the river traffic go by, Wildcat Landing is a great spot to enjoy the summer weekends. The campsites are divided into two loops—one each on the north and south ends of the park. Sandy beaches, docks for mooring boats, fishing areas, and plenty of shoreline make this an attractive camping destination.

Campsites, facilities: There are 68 sites for tents and RVs. Picnic tables, fire rings and grills, toilets, showers, and a dump station are provided. A sandy swimming beach, fishing area, firewood, boat ramp, and a camp store are available. Some facilities are wheelchair accessible. Leashed pets are permitted.

Reservations, fees: Reservations are accepted at 507/482-6250. Sites are $20 per night for tents and $25 per night for RVs. Open from May through September.

Directions: From Brownsville, drive south on Highway 26 for 0.5 mile to Leone Lane. Turn left and drive for 0.3 mile into the park and camping area.

Contact: Wildcat Landing Park Campground, 507/482-6250.

59 RENO NORTH RECREATIONAL AREA

🥾 ❄ 🐕 ⛺

Scenic rating: 7

north of Reno

The Reno North campsites sit on top of the bluff-line the follows the Mississippi River south out of the state. Located just south of Brownsville on a tiny Township Road up on the hill, there are only two primitive sites. Most people, locals included, don't even know this place exists.

The sites lie in a heavily wooded blufftop forest. In autumn, you can catch glimpses of the river valley, but plan on spending most of your time under heavy tree cover. Hiking trails lead into the Richard J. Dorer Memorial Hardwood Forest. Cross-country skiing is also available in the winter. Drinking water is not provided here, so make sure to pack in your own.

Campsites, facilities: There are two primitive sites for tents. Picnic tables, fire rings, and a vault toilet are provided. Drinking water is not provided. Hiking and horseback riding trails are available. Leashed pets are permitted.

Reservations, fees: Reservations are not accepted. Sites are $12 per night. Self-registration is required at the campground. Open year-round.

Directions: From Reno, drive northwest on T-105 gravel road for 4 miles to the campground parking lot.

Contact: Minnesota Department of Natural Resources, 507/724-2107, www.dnr.state.mn.us/state_forests/facilities/cmp00076/index.html.

RESOURCES

© JOHN MCLAIRD/WWW.123RF.COM

PARKS AND WILDLIFE REFUGES

State Parks
www.dnr.state.mn.us/state_parks/index.
html

Afton State Park
6959 Peller Avenue South
Hastings, MN 55033
651/436-5391
www.dnr.state.mn.us/state_parks/afton/index.
html

Banning State Park
P.O. Box 643
Sandstone, MN 55072
320/245-2668
www.dnr.state.mn.us/state_parks/banning/
index.html

Carley State Park
c/o Whitewater State Park
Route 1, Box 256
Altura, MN 55910
507/932-3007
www.dnr.state.mn.us/state_parks/carley/
index.html

Charles A. Lindbergh State Park
1615 Lindbergh Drive South
Little Falls, MN 56345
320/616-2525
www.dnr.state.mn.us/state_parks/charles_a_
lindbergh/index.html

Crow Wing State Park
3124 State Park Road
Brainerd, MN 56401
218/825-3075
www.dnr.state.mn.us/state_parks/crow_wing/
index.html

Father Hennepin State Park
41294 Father Hennepin Park Road
Isle, MN 56342
320/676-8763

www.dnr.state.mn.us/state_parks/father_hen-
nepin/index.html

Flandrau State Park
1300 Summit Avenue
New Ulm, MN 56073-3664
507/233-9800
www.dnr.state.mn.us/state_parks/flandrau/
index.html

Forestville State Park
21071 County 118
Preston, MN 55965
507/352-5111
www.dnr.state.mn.us/state_parks/forestville_
mystery_cave/index.html

Fort Snelling State Park
101 Snelling Lake Road
St. Paul, MN 55111
612/725-2389
www.dnr.state.mn.us/state_parks/fort_snel-
ling/index.html

Frontenac State Park
29223 County 28 Boulevard
Frontenac, MN 55026
651/345-3401
www.dnr.state.mn.us/state_parks/frontenac/
index.html

Great River Bluffs State Park
43605 Kipp Drive
Winona, MN 55987-9427
507/643-6849
www.dnr.state.mn.us/state_parks/great_river_
bluffs/index.html

Interstate State Park
P.O. Box 254
Taylors Falls, MN 55084
651/465-5711
www.dnr.state.mn.us/state_parks/interstate/
index.html

Jay Cooke State Park
780 Highway 210

Carlton, MN 55718
218/384-4610
www.dnr.state.mn.us/state_parks/jay_cooke/
index.html

Lake Maria State Park
11411 Clementa Avenue Northwest
Monticello, MN 55362
763/878-2325
www.dnr.state.mn.us/state_parks/lake_maria/
index.html

Mille Lacs Kathio State Park
15066 Kathio State Park Road
Onamia, MN 56359-2207
320/532-3523
www.dnr.state.mn.us/state_parks/mille_lacs_
kathio/index.html

Minneopa State Park
54497 Gadwall Road
Mankato, MN 56001
507/389-5464
www.dnr.state.mn.us/state_parks/minneopa/
index.html

Minnesota Valley State Park
19825 Park Boulevard
Jordan, MN 55352
952/492-6400
www.dnr.state.mn.us/state_parks/minneso-
ta_valley/index.html

Moose Lake State Park
4252 County Road 137
Moose Lake, MN 55767
218/485-5420
www.dnr.state.mn.us/state_parks/moose_
lake/index.html

Myre-Big Island State Park
19499 780th Avenue
Albert Lea, MN 56007
507/379-3403
www.dnr.state.mn.us/state_parks/myre_big_
island/index.html

Nerstrand Big Woods State Park
9700 170 Street East
Nerstrand, MN 55053
507/333-4840
www.dnr.state.mn.us/state_parks/nerstrand_
big_woods/index.html

Rice Lake State Park
8485 Rose Street
Owatonna, MN 55060
507/455-5871
www.dnr.state.mn.us/state_parks/rice_lake/
index.html

Sakatah Lake State Park
50499 Sakatah Lake State Park Road
Waterville, MN 56096
507/362-4438
www.dnr.state.mn.us/state_parks/sakatah_
lake/index.html

Sibley State Park
800 Sibley Park Road Northeast
New London, MN 56273-9664
320/354-2055
www.dnr.state.mn.us/state_parks/sibley/
index.html

St. Croix State Park
30065 St. Croix Park Road
Hinckley, MN 55037
320/384-6591
www.dnr.state.mn.us/state_parks/st_croix/
index.html

Whitewater State Park
Route 1, Box 256
Altura, MN 55910
507/932-3007
www.dnr.state.mn.us/state_parks/carley/
index.html

Wild River State Park
39797 Park Trail
Center City, MN 55012
651/583-2125
www.dnr.state.mn.us/state_parks/wild_river/
index.html

William O'Brien State Park
16821 O'Brien Trail North
Marine-on-St. Croix, MN 55047
651/433-0500
www.dnr.state.mn.us/state_parks/william_
obrien/index.html

County Parks
State parks don't have all the best camping!
These county parks provide beautiful natural settings full of wildlife, wildflowers, and wilderness.

Carver County Parks
11360 Highway 212 West, Suite 2
Cologne, MN 55322
952/466-5250
www.co.carver.mn.us/departments/pw/parks/
index.asp

Dakota County Parks
651/437-3191
www.co.dakota.mn.us/LeisureRecreation/
CountyParks/Locations/default.htm

Ramsey County Parks
5287 Otter Lake Road
White Bear Township, MN 55110
651/407-5350
www.co.ramsey.mn.us/parks/index.asp

Three Rivers Park District
3000 Xenium Lane North
Plymouth, MN 55441-1299
763/559-9000
www.threeriversparkdistrict.org/parks/

Washington County Parks
11660 Myeron Road North
Stillwater, MN 55082
651/430-4300
www.co.washington.mn.us/info_for_
residents/parks_division/

Wright County Parks
1901 Highway 25 North
Buffalo, MN 55313

763/682-7693
www.co.wright.mn.us/department/parks/

City Parks
Minneapolis Park and Recreation Board
2117 West River Road
Minneapolis, MN 55411
612/230-6400
www.minneapolisparks.org/home.asp

St. Paul Parks & Recreation
50 West Kellogg Boulevard, Suite 840
Saint Paul, MN 55102
651/266-6400
www.ci.stpaul.mn.us/index.asp?NID=243

National Wildlife Refuges
www.fws.gov/refuges/

Minnesota Valley National Wildlife Refuge
3815 American Boulevard East
Bloomington, MN 55425
952/854-5900
http://midwest.fws.gov/minnesotavalley

Rice Lake National Wildlife Refuge
36298 State Highway 65
McGregor, MN 55760
218/768-2402
www.fws.gov/midwest/ricelake

INTERNET RESOURCES

Flora and Fauna
Minnesota Wildflower Information
www.dnr.state.mn.us/wildflowers/index.
html

Zumbro Valley Audubon Society
www.zumbrovalleyaudubon.org

Hiking and Outdoors Clubs
Meet new people and enjoy the outdoors with
friends.

Minnesota Hiking and Backpacking Club
www.hikingandbackpacking.com/minneso-
taclubs.html

**Minnesota North Star Chapter
Sierra Club**
http://northstar.sierraclub.org

Minnesota Rovers Outdoors Club
www.mnrovers.org

Minnesota Speleological Survey
www.mss-caving.org

Minnesota State Park Hiking Club
www.dnr.state.mn.us/state_parks/clubs.html

Outdoors Club
www.outdoorsclub.org

Hiking Trails and Gear Reviews
Backcountry.com
www.backcountry.com

GORP
www.gorp.away.com

REI
www.rei.com

Trails.com
www.trails.com

Index

Index 201

www.moon.com

DESTINATIONS | ACTIVITIES | BLOGS | MAPS | BOOKS

MOON.COM is ready to help plan your next trip! Filled with fresh trip ideas and strategies, author interviews, informative travel blogs, a detailed map library, and descriptions of all the Moon guidebooks, Moon.com is all you need to get out and explore the world—or even places in your own backyard. While at Moon.com, sign up for our monthly e-newsletter for updates on new releases, travel tips, and expert advice from our on-the-go Moon authors. As always, when you travel with Moon, expect an experience that is uncommon and truly unique.

MOON IS ON FACEBOOK—BECOME A FAN!
JOIN THE MOON PHOTO GROUP ON FLICKR

 OUTDOORS

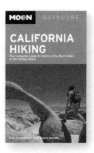

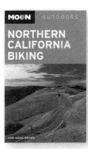

"Well written, thoroughly researched, and packed full of useful information and advice, these guides really do get you into the outdoors."

—GORP.COM

ALSO AVAILABLE AS FOGHORN OUTDOORS ACTIVITY GUIDES:

250 Great Hikes in
  California's National Parks
California Golf
California Waterfalls
California Wildlife
Camper's Companion
Easy Biking in Northern
  California
Easy Hiking in Northern
  California

Easy Hiking in Southern
  California
Georgia & Alabama Camping
Maine Hiking
Massachusetts Hiking
New England Cabins
  & Cottages
New England Camping
New Hampshire Hiking

Southern California
  Cabins & Cottages
Tom Stienstra's Bay Area
  Recreation
Vermont Hiking
Washington Boating
  & Water Sports

MOON MINNESOTA CAMPING

Avalon Travel
a member of the Perseus Books Group
1700 Fourth Street
Berkeley, CA 94710, USA
www.moon.com

Editor and Series Manager: Sabrina Young
Copy Editor: Deana Shields
Graphics Coordinator: Tabitha Lahr
Production Coordinator: Tabitha Lahr
Cover Designer: Tabitha Lahr
Interior Designer: Darren Alessi
Map Editor: Brice Ticen
Cartographers: Kat Bennett, Albert Angulo
Indexer: Sabrina Young
Illustrations: Bob Race

ISBN-13: 978-1-59880-531-4
ISSN: 2151-9560

Printing History
1st Edition – June 2010
5 4 3 2 1

Text © 2010 by Jake Kulju.
Maps © 2010 by Avalon Travel.
All rights reserved.

Some photos and illustrations are used by permission and are the property of the original copyright owners.

Front cover photo: Canoe Along Lakeshore © Layne Kennedy/CORBIS
Title page photo: A canoe rests on the edge of a BWCAW entry point. © Kerstin Hansen; Page 3, Northwoods © John McLaird/www.123rf.com; Page 4, Flood Bay along the north shore of Lake Superior © John McLaird/www.123rf.com; Page 5, Northwoods © John McLaird/www.123rf.com
Back cover photo: © Al Valeiro / Getty Images

Printed in Canada by Friesens

Moon Outdoors and the Moon logo are the property of Avalon Travel. All other marks and logos depicted are the property of the original owners. All rights reserved. No part of this book may be translated or reproduced in any form, except brief extracts by a reviewer for the purpose of a review, without written permission of the copyright owner.

Although every effort was made to ensure that the information was correct at the time of going to press, the author and publisher do not assume and hereby disclaim any liability to any party for any loss or damage caused by errors, omissions, or any potential travel disruption due to labor or financial difficulty, whether such errors or omissions result from negligence, accident, or any other cause.

Keeping Current

We are committed to making this book the most accurate and enjoyable camping guide to the state. You can rest assured that every campground in this book has been carefully reviewed in an effort to keep this book as up-to-date as possible. However, by the time you read this book, some of the fees listed herein may have changed and campgrounds may have closed unexpectedly.

If you have a favorite gem you'd like to see included in the next edition, or see anything that needs updating, clarification, or correction, please drop us a line. Send your comments via email to feedback@moon.com, or use the address above.